Continuous Digital

An agile alternative to projects

Allan Kelly

Continuous Digital

An agile alternative to projects

Allan Kelly

ISBN 978-1-912832-14-9

Contents

Free Book

Xanpan is available for free

Xanpan: Team Centric Agile Software Development is available for free to all subscribers to Allan Kelly's newsletter[1]

[1]https://www.allankellyassociates.co.uk/xanpan_offer/

What others are saying...

'This book is terrific! It accurately diagnoses a problem with our model of software delivery and charts a new course. Well researched and well argued it shows the future.'

Kristian Kristensen, VP of Engineering, Ecommerce at The New York Times

'Over the past few years Allan has done a huge amount to bring #NoProjects into mainstream IT conversations. This book is a deep dive into #NoProjects, and I highly recommend it.'

Steve Smith

'The great thing about Continuous Digital is the plain sense that it all makes, so you realize this is exactly the way you want to work in the future. The bad thing about the book is that it doesn't include a Tardis to go back and start working in this way when you set out on your last 'project'. So bury that pain and just look forward, with this book to navigate by."

Steve Parks, CEO, Convivio

'What Allan has created here is nothing short of groundbreaking. This book is an insightful vision of the future of work that is emerging within organizations around the world. Be it #NoProjects or Continuous Digital, the movement towards funding and working along continuous value streams rather than finite projects is reaping benefits.

Beyond the vision, what Allan has written will provide you with a clear and practical grounding in how to get started across your organization. Whether you lead a team, a division or a company, you will learn something new about creating value.'

Evan Leybourn, author of *Directing the Agile Organization*

'Careful! Not only does this book offer you plenty of food for thought, it is practical enough to be your handbook for transforming a business into a digital one. Without resorting to boring management-speak, Allan explains how to take an organization to the next level by putting customers first, focussing on value and building effective feedback loops to emphasize learning.'

Sergey Timanin, Infrastructure Team Lead at Clarivate Analytics

'Those with an engineering background can sometimes feel it in the air when limits are reached too easily in a process. Then you start to get some intuitions, then you try to tackle some points. But if you have the chance to read this book, you can have the great feeling to be in an accelerator.

Allan Kelly is not only able to identify the recurrent issue that other people don't want to see. He is also able to structure and use the exact word on concepts that will make you more confident in your daily management process.

In this cookbook, many solutions are proposed for your organization and it's up to you to do the right thing in your context. I warmly recommend you to read this book today as the golden age of pure project agility is about to end.'

Gwendal Tanguy, Director of Product Development, Swissquote Bank

Project Myopia

Project Myopia: A #NoProjects book

Project Myopia: the belief that the project model is the only way of managing business change and development; not seeing digital development as a continuous commitment to growing the business; believing it will end and working for the end. #NoProjects

Project Myopia was the beginning of *Continuous Digital*. But Continuous Digital outgrew Project Myopia and the two seperated.

Preface

Practical men, who believe themselves to be quite exempt from any intellectual influence, are usually the slaves of some defunct economist. John Maynard Keynes

Keynes was speaking long before Digital and long before there was a software industry, but his words still ring true. In the world of digital business too many people cling to the old model and assumptions of the pre-digital age, an age when *information technology* was simply a means of making a business more efficient.

As this still-young century continues, it has become clear that the business world is increasingly a digital world. The software companies of the last century are but the prototypes of the modern digital business.

Digitization forces companies to rethink the way they organize to do software development, technology operations and business alignment. Digitalization also means new management paradigms need to be embraced and some old ones let go.

Continuous is an alternative management model for digital businesses – a management model, a new way for managers to think about technology. This book sets out that model.

Many practical men and women are today slaves to the project model of software development. The project model condemns many digital initiatives, programmers and companies to failure. Continuous offers an alternative.

The project model has always been a problematic fit for software development, but things have become more difficult in the last few years. The Continuous model supersedes the project model. Projects by definition end, but successful business doesn't end and successful software doesn't end. Agile and continuous delivery provide the tools for successful digital business.

The business is technology, and technology is the business.

When the business is based on technology, 'finishing' the technology destroys the businesses. The mindset encouraged by the project model – that software can be created as an independent activity and 'finished' – is anathema to digital businesses, where building technology is business building.

The rise of agile software development has made the problems with the project model more apparent. The arrival of Continuous Delivery[2] (CD) broke many of the principles on which the project model was based. Digital business demands a new way of thinking.

Digital

Few businesses have not felt the effects of increased digitization in the last decade. Modern business is digital. Fewer still are the number of high-growth businesses that are not dependent on software technology. If you want to be a high-growth business in the twenty-first century, you almost certainly need to build on top of a digital platform.

The digitization of business represents a force so powerful that few businesses are unaffected. Unleashing this force in your business creates massive opportunities: not unleashing the force creates massive threats. To some this will sound counterintuitive. Flexibility, according to this line of thinking, comes from being able to assemble a team when needed. Agile thinking postulates the opposite: flexibility comes by having a well-practiced team that is available when needed.

Information technology is no longer a side-show, something that happens off to the side of the real business. In the age of digital business, technology *is* the business, and the business is digital. Having a separate IT function is a luxury few growing companies can afford.

In the digital company technology development isn't something that happens elsewhere, bounded within a 'project' that will one day be 'finished'. The business has technology running all the way through it, like traditional English seaside rock. If this is not true in your company, then ask yourself and all those around you, if you foresee the business growing in the next decade?

Next ask yourself and your colleagues: "If a competitor wanted to disrupt our business, how would they do it?". The answer is – Digital.

It follows that not only are businesses digital, but business lines within businesses are digital. If a business line is to succeed and grow, the business line must be tied to an information technology capability, and that capability must be ongoing. Structuring technology change as a series of stand-alone 'projects' no longer makes sense. Projects end, but who wants their business line to end? Who wants their company to end?

---

[2]*Continuous Delivery: Reliable Software Releases through Build, Test, and Deployment Automation*, Humble and Farley, 2010

Agile and continuous delivery

Before agile many companies and teams considered a three-month release cycle as aggressive; an annual release was more common. Agile started to ask teams to make fortnightly releases, or at the very least be able to release every two weeks. Being *releasable* was more important than actual releasing, because staying at a releasable level forced teams to keep a high technical standard and thus gave options to business customers.

The best digital teams have now accelerated far beyond every two weeks. The Guardian newspaper in London commonly releases several thousand times a week and Amazon.com releases on average every 11 seconds.

A release every two weeks still looks like an impossible challenge to an average team – typically one working inside some large corporation. But for the best teams a two-week gap between releases looks like an eternity.

Regular releases well and truly break the link between project end date and software release. The parameters of date, scope and quality at the heart of the project model are managed completely differently.

Agile had already relaxed the idea of fixed – or at least predetermined – scope, such as requirements or work requests. In a continuous delivery environment teams build all sorts of feedback loops. When done well these feedback loops cause work to be added – that is, teams discover more valuable work – and other predetermined low-value work can be discarded.

Unlike some endeavors, the relationship between quality and time/cost is reversed in software development. Higher-quality (code) is delivered faster and at a lower cost than low-quality code that requires fixes and is hard to change.

Project managers are trained to see a tradeoff between higher quality and speed of delivery: *reducing quality reduces time*. But in software development the relationship is inverse – higher quality requires less time. Those schooled in the project model have been making things worse by advocating lower quality to reduce time.

The best agile teams were always multi-skilled and cross-functional. Rapid continuous delivery is simply not possible when organizational boundaries force teams to wait on others. As a consequence the idea of project teams working with specialist parts of the organization needs to change.

Such teams need to practice together, work together, adjust behavior and fine-tune their work. It no longer makes sense to create special, temporary teams for projects. Teams need far more continuity. Each piece of work is a rehearsal for the next piece of work.

To some this will sound counterintuitive. Flexibility comes not from being able to assemble a team when needed, but by having a well-practiced team available when needed.

The project model always had limitations when applied to software development. The project model set out an approach that did not accurately reflect what actually happened in software development. As a result traditional project managers spent much of their time patching the model to keep it relevant.

When one has an inaccurate model of the world it is hard to make good decisions and reliable predictions. Iterative agile presented an alternative model of the world within which it became easier to make reliable decisions.

Continuous Delivery makes the project model an even more inaccurate model of technology development. Once managers and teams have a mental model that correctly describes the work they do they can reason more effectively, become more effective and deliver greater value.

Products, not projects

One frequent riposte is the claim that there are two types of company: *project-oriented companies* and *product-oriented companies.* Project companies do something, finish it and move on, while product companies continue to build their products.

Imagine for a moment you are the Product Manager for Microsoft Office. One day you walk into Satya Nadella's office and say "Good news, project Microsoft Office is done, we can lay off the team and save some money." Think what that would mean.

Microsoft's second biggest cash-cow is dead.

Microsoft is a product company: Office, Windows, X-Box and much more. Unfortunately many product companies have succumbed to the project model: they do one project on their product, then another project on their product, then another, until the end of time. Product companies applying the project model delude themselves and make their work more complicated.

Software product companies can be considered the prototypes of modern digital businesses. Like modern digital businesses, their success depended on their ability to build software technology. But being Digital is much more than being a software business as of old. Being Digital isn't confined to *the product*: being Digital cuts across everything.

There is much digital companies can take from the product model and mindset, but they need to go further.

Once upon a time...

Most organizations are structured along pre-digital lines – functional divisions and cross-cutting projects. Such thinking, including the project model itself, dates from the 1960s. Software people call this model 'waterfall' and date it to a 1970 paper[3]. Let's remember 1970 for a moment; I was still in nappies, but...

In 1970 the IBM 360 Model 195 was the cutting-edge mainframe of its time. This machine had 10 MIPS of CPU power, 4Mb of RAM and cost $250,000 a month to rent (about $1.75m in 2018 terms). Commercial programming was in Cobol against an IMS hierarchical database running on OS/360. It used green screen monitors and teleprinters for output.

By 2016 one could buy a Raspberry Pi computer for about $35. This has 4,744 MIPS, 1Gb of RAM (which is 1,024Mb, so 256 times more than the IBM), and runs an OpenSource Linux OS that can be programmed in languages such as Python, Scala, Ruby, C and even Cobol if you so wish. The results can be displayed graphically on your TV screen. Plus a Raspberry Pi can be connected to an Internet of several billions nodes. In 1970 there were less than a dozen Internet nodes.

When technology has changed so completely, is it not right to question the management practices and models that grew up at a time when CPU cycles were expensive?

In 1970 planning was cheap in relation to expensive CPU cycles. In 2018, with CPU cycles too cheap to measure, planning is extremely expensive.

And now for something completely different...

This book sets out to describe an alternative to the project model for developing software. Why do we need an alternative?

Because digital competition changes the way businesses need to operate.

Because the tools digital makes available allow different structures and new thinking.

Because the project model complicates reasoning about software development, and is holding back further improvements in software development in many organizations today.

Because digital companies need to rethink the traditional ways of managing and find new, effective, models to reason about their world. Management models developed in the 1950s and 1960s are not necessarily the best for leveraging modern technology.

---

[3]*Managing the Development of Large Software Systems*, Winston Royce, Proceedings of IEEE WESCON 26, 1970

Paradoxically, in the age of hyper-speed and rapid change the project model is too short-sighted. In the digital age acting fast, in ultra-short timescales, requires thinking and structuring for the longer term.

Adopting a Continuous model rather than a project model does not mean abandoning everything in the project model. As with so many models – agile in particular – it is necessary to look beyond the label and consider exactly what practices and processes the label refers to. Some of these practices and processes may be entirely appropriate in other models.

For example, some regard planning, objective-setting and governance as inherently part of the project model, but they are not. As this book will describe, planning, objectives and governance can be a meaningful part of the Continuous model.

Yet there is still much in the project model that needs rethinking for digital businesses to advance. Creating projects, assembling teams, waiting for the team to become productive and then dismantling the whole thing before starting again takes too long. Structures with longevity and devolved authority eliminate the start-up and shutdown phases that take so much time.

I will do my best in these pages to outline an alternative model, a model that I call *Continuous*. This model is a work in progress. There are examples of companies that work without projects, but that does not mean that your company can simply copy these as they stand.

The Continuous model is still evolving. It may never reach a point at which there is a fixed model – in fact I don't want to reach such a point. I want practitioners, managers and my readers to think!

I do not have a guaranteed risk-free solution. I have pieces of a solution that you need to examine for yourself and apply in your context. For this I recommend thinking, reflection and discussion.

Being an early adopter of this model may not be risk-free, but the benefits are substantial. Remember the old maxim: *profit is the return for risk*. Early adopters may risk more, but they will benefit more.

I An alternative

It's in the doing of the work that we discover the work that we must do. Doing exposes reality. Woody Zuill

1. Omnipresent software

Software is eating the world. Marc Andreessen, 2011

Here at the beginning of the twenty-first century every company is a software company.

If that sounds a little overblown, let's agree: every *growth* company is a software company. Companies depend on software to deliver products and services that would not be possible with it. Companies that want unique products and services increasingly find that this means unique software. Anyone can have identical software – ctrl-C, ctrl-V – but identical software leads to identical offerings, identical products, identical services.

For decades high-growth companies have been predominantly technology-based, and increasingly all technology has become software-based; or perhaps, increasingly software has become an essential part of every new technology. Think of it as coupling your business to Moore's Law: microprocessor power doubles while price halves every 18 to 24 months.

> 'Firms that use more IT tend to have higher levels of productivity and faster productivity growth than their industry competitors.' Brynjolfsson & McAfee[1]

Last year – 2016 – I met a programmer in Sweden who works for a steel company. You don't get much more old-school than a steel manufacturer, and 30 years ago the only software such a company might use would be for the payroll. But today software is essential for scheduling production, routing molten steel around the works and improving performance.

Look at the way software has upended the world of media. TV programmes are broadcast digitally to powerful computers: today's TV sets. But then, who watches broadcast television? iPlayer, Netflix and Amazon mean we can watch what we want, when we want, thanks to software. Or consider newspapers: software running on tablets, phones and desktops has consigned profitable print-only newspaper companies to history.

Once a product becomes digital, everything changes. Ask the music industry. First expensive hardware allowed music to be digitized, then software reduced the price, then software created new ways of purchasing digital music. At first the industry resisted, but that didn't

---

[1] *The Second Machine Age*, Brynjolfsson & McAfee, 2014

stop the likes of Napster. It was only when Apple arrived with the iStore and iTunes that the industry started to see how it could survive.

As old industries such as newspaper publishing change and even die, the same technologies allow new ones to come into being. Look at print-on-demand services such as Lulu.com, which allow anyone to publish their own book without capital investment, or LeanPub.com, which is a totally electronic publisher.

Or take cars. A well-established industry is in the process of being disrupted before our very eyes. Who is making the most interesting cars today? Maybe it is Tesla, a company founded on software. A Tesla needs hardware, but could hardware substitute for software? It's not just the maps and the music: the drive train requires advanced software to optimize battery performance.

The engines of most modern cars require significant software to work. I read somewhere that 25% of the value of a new car is software. I can't find that quote any more, but I found sources saying that traditionally 10% of car's value was electronics but today it is nearer 50%. When I've mentioned these figures to people who know they say they are on the low side.

The fact that Apple and Google are developing cars demonstrates that something is changing. Being able to build a physical car is no longer enough – in fact you can outsource that bit to Magna. Ford, Fiat, Toyota and other car manufacturers have been turning out very similar cars – similar to their previous cars, and even similar to each others' – for years. After the early 1980s 'quality revolution' little changed in the world of cars: successive Golfs, Camrys and Mondeos were hard to tell apart.

Then software arrived... Cars now have maps and navigation systems. Cars can park themselves, and soon they will drive themselves. For a car to be worth buying it must contain software technology: without it a car is a utility item that cannot demand a high price.

Now that the cars of tomorrow will compete on software capabilities it is logical for companies that have an advantage in the creation of software – Apple, Google and others – to enter the market.

Software is indeed eating the world.

Note the consequence of business dependence on software:

Software *is* the business

When delivering the fundamental product or service of the company becomes highly dependent on software, the software is no longer optional: software can no longer be done by 'IT' in a back room – the business and the software technology are one.

Increasingly this gets called *Digital*.

Digital includes not just online sales and electronic delivery. Digital business includes 'big data' and analytics, the Cloud, phone apps – indeed cellphones and smartphones altogether, GPS positioning[2], artificial intelligence and the things that they make possible: drones, the gig economy and more.

Digital hides the underlying truth that is software. All these technologies are only possible with software. Digital business is dependent on software, which means that the business is dependent on those who create software.

Digital implies software development, but while 'software development' is a bit of a mouthful, 'digital' is short and sweet. This is not to say that the digital business is only a software development business; there is a lot more to digital as well, but the need to have access to, or to be able to create, software is fundamental to the business.

Software technology is now as important as marketing or accounting.

Unfortunately in 2016 it is still acceptable for even senior executives to say "I don't really understand software" and "Programmers are expensive geeks who I don't understand." Could you imagine these same executives saying:

> "I don't really understand accounting – whether to expense or capitalize..."

> "Why do those accounting nerds demand double-entry? Surely if we just did it once we could save money?"

> "I don't really understand marketing – I only know that half the money is wasted."

> "I just want marketing that works."

It is not so much that every company is a software development business, as that every company is software-dependent business. The more a business becomes digital, the more it takes on the characteristics, attributes and business models of what we used to call 'software houses'.

So let's talk about projects...

[2] In *Pinpoint*, 2016, Greg Milner suggests that the significance of global positioning systems has been overshadowed by the rise of the parallel Internet, and that the impact of positioning systems is potentially bigger than the Internet.

The project model of working dominates software development. (Let's leave the different definitions of 'project' until later.)

The project model is inherently short-sighted. Call it *Project Myopia*: projects end.

Do you want your business to end?

"When will this business be done?"

"When will your company finish?"

Questions like these are only asked about businesses that are in trouble. We don't want businesses to end. We want businesses to continue: to continue employing people, to continue supplying their products to grateful customers, to continue paying dividends to shareholders.

If the company *is* software and we want the company to continue, why do we think the software will ever be 'done'? Again, imagine the head of Microsoft Office development meeting with the Microsoft CEO, Satya Nadella, and saying "Great news, we finally finished Office after 26 years. We can lay off the team and get started on the next thing." Microsoft's profits would collapse.

Software businesses such as Microsoft are the prototype of future businesses. Software businesses have been exposed to the threats and opportunities created by software for longer. Those who work in these companies have long had access to early versions of the tools that are now becoming commonplace. This doesn't mean that these companies have always got it right – only that others can learn from such businesses.

The idea that software is never 'done' may terrify some readers – how does one know how much to spend? Some will rail against this idea – after all, we can control 'scope', we can push back on requests, and we don't need to upgrade with every new technology or OS change, and we...

Personally I don't think scope can be controlled. However, if you have an example where it can, then OK, I concede. But...

Changes are opportunities. Rather than viewing requests to change software as a bad thing that should be resisted in the name of 'done-ness' and cost control, we should see change as a positive that provides our businesses with growth opportunities.

How many times has Microsoft sold you Word?

How many times has Oracle sold your company their eponymous database?

Software companies have long succeeded in using the cycle of software upgrades to extract money from customers. It's true that the business models of software companies are changing too. In a world in which all companies start to look like software businesses, it becomes harder and harder to find any which are purely software businesses.

It is not just in extracting more payment from customers that software can deliver value to business. Take my Swedish friend: continuing to improve their software allows the steel mill to continually extract more cost saving from their plant.

In many companies – perhaps most – there is no single long-lasting 'optimal' point of production, or optimal processes. Many businesses never approach the optimal point because they don't know what it is. More likely they operate at some local optimum, which may be fine for a while, but when faced with a new competitor, a new technology or even just a change of personnel they are forced to find a new and hopefully better local optimum.

When a business is based on software, moving to a new optimum requires changing the software – or rather, changing the software allows a move to a new optimum.

Since it is not only a single business that is software-based, but all the other businesses with which it works, there are continuing opportunities to optimize one business by responding to or even initiating changes in others.

Take parcel delivery, for example. This was once a physical business: collect parcels, move them, deliver them. Then FedEx, UPS and others arrived, they allowed you to track a parcel online. But technology goes deeper: such companies could not run their businesses the way they do *without* software. This change has sparked changes in other businesses, not just competitors such as Royal Mail or US Mail, but in businesses that can now send parcels reliably across the globe in hours.

Is UPS' parcel software ever done? For such companies software is not a project to be completed. Software is their lifeblood. Finish the software and you finish the business.

I can already hear readers who work for delivery companies shouting "But we have software projects! And they work!"

I'm not disputing that many companies organize their software development using the project model, although I admit that I don't know the internals of FexEx or UPS. My point is that running such a model hinders such businesses, and that breaking free of the project model offers opportunities for companies to improve. The project model complicates the management of software development and induces myopia.

The problem is that the project model is ill-suited to software development. When software was a sideshow – an optional extra – companies could get away with patching a broken model. Now that software *is* the business, using an ill-fitting model adds complexity, hinders improvement, and in some cases may well break the company.

Because the project model promises 'an end' – and because people like closure – executives and managers suffer from myopia. They fail to comprehend the implications of the fight against a never-ending process, and so pass up opportunities for growth and market leadership.

Software technology has allowed businesses – whether they be delivery companies, steel mills, banks, airlines or whatever – to grow ('scale' in the jargon) beyond the wildest dreams of company managers 100 years ago. But if they are to continue to exist, let alone grow, over the next 100 years, then they need to think differently.

One of the ways they need to think differently is to accept software development – 'digital' – into the core of the business as an ongoing activity, rather than something that happens over to the side and that will be done 'one day'.

2. Software as an Asset (SaaA)

Total factor productivity growth increased more between the 1990s and 2000s in IT-using industries, while it fell slightly in those sectors of the economy that did not use IT extensively. Brynjolfsson & McAfee[1]

Could JustEat operate as a large call centre? Why, when customers can already call their local takeaway service, would a central call centre benefit customers?

What advantage would Amazon have as a mail-order catalog? Would they have been able to break into a market already served by successful national mail-order businesses?

Software products are assets: they bring value to the owners of those assets. Perhaps the asset is a product that can be sold repeatedly to multiple customers, such as Microsoft Office. Perhaps the asset operates as a service that customers pay for, such as Salesforce.com. Sometimes services are paid for indirectly. Google provides GMail as a free service while generating revenue from adverts sold around it. GMail is a huge asset.

Increasingly software assets provide a platform upon which the digital business operates: think of JustEat's food-delivery brokerage site, or FedEx's parcel-delivery system. Without the platform the business couldn't exist, or at least could not exist as it does. JustEat and Amazon would lose the customer experience that makes them what they are: for Amazon, FedEx and JustEat their software platform is a huge asset.

Once software was seen as a way for companies to reduce costs. Software still helps companies reduce costs – and improve customer experience – but a company that still thinks purely in terms of cost savings clearly lacks a digital strategy. Not that one necessarily needs a digital strategy: Mrs Miggins' Pie Shop mightn't have a digital strategy, but then Mrs Miggins' Pie Shop doesn't aim to be a growth business, or face international competitors (yet).

Business digitization is about far more than cost-cutting. Perhaps the hallmark of a digital business is that it uses a digital platform to deliver the business service or product. One struggles to see how a business can claim to be *digital* if technology is merely a cost-reduction plan.

---

[1] *The Second Machine Age*, Brynjolfsson & McAfee, 2014

A digital business depends on software assets to make the business what it is. It may be operating one of the models described above, or something more innovative, but in each case the business needs a platform and that platform is based on software.

Before the dawn of digital business, information technology was something that happened on the side. IT might reduce cost, it might improve customer service, it might give a competitive edge, but 'the business' was something else. As such IT could be implemented as a 'project' that just happened to impact the business.

Digital companies don't have the option of treating technology as something that happens on the side. Software technology is core to the business and it doesn't end. Digital businesses sell services and products that are only possible because of digital technology: the development of these unique assets *is the business*.

For software product companies this has been true for a long time. The software-as-a-service business model formed a bridge between the world of ISVs such as Microsoft and Oracle and digital businesses such as Uber and Airbnb.

One could think of pre-millennial software vendors as the prototype of today's digital businesses. Many of the business patterns for software creators I described in Business Patterns [2] now have wider applicability.

These digital platforms, products and services are themselves assets for the company concerned. Uber's software platform is far more important to the company than any building it might own. The physical assets of Airbnb – buildings, desks, foosball tables, expresso makers – are insignificant compared to its software assets.

Assets decay

Like many other assets, software assets decay if they are not maintained. They decay differently than other assets, but they decay just the same. Unfortunately many people fail to appreciate this.

Suppose a Silicon Valley start-up buys a foosball football table for $500. It is a company asset: it sits in the kitchen and people play on it. Its return on investment comes from happier employees, and happier employees should make for more productive employees. The table requires little maintenance, and when wear and tear take their toll it is thrown away and another one purchased.

---

[2]Business Patterns for Software Developers, Allan Kelly, 2012, John Wiley & Sons

The foosball table may never even be listed on the company balance sheet, but if the same company spends $10,000 on an espresso machine they *will* list it as a company asset. A high-end espresso machine requires maintenance, regular cleaning and fresh supplies of coffee beans. Fail to supply these and it quickly becomes valueless, and $10,000 is wiped off the company's value.

So which does a software platform more closely resemble?

- A foosball table, a cheap one-off purchase that is thrown away at the end of its useful life, and possibly replaced.
- An expensive coffee machine that requires ongoing expenditure, but can be expected to last for many years.

A hotel chain would certainly list any buildings it owns on its balance sheet, and would invest to keep the buildings in good condition[3]. Airbnb doesn't own any hotels but could not operate without a software platform. Surely the Airbnb software is just as much of an asset as a 500-room Hilton hotel and should be managed as one?

Fighting decay

Bridges are huge assets to countries and populations. Until recently the Forth Bridge in Scotland famously required continuous repainting. In the time it took to paint from one end of the bridge to the other, the 'new' paint at the start was weathered and required repainting. As soon as the painters finished painting the bridge at one end, it was time to start again at the other end.

If like me you are lucky enough to own your own home, you will know that from time to time there are jobs that need to be done. Baths start to leak, carpets wear out, paint dulls, brickwork needs repointing and so on.

Now consider roads. They may not need resurfacing very often, but they do need to be policed. All roads need some level of service support, even if they rarely need major works. This however is changing. 'Smart motorway' technology, providing active management of motorways, allows the same roads carry more cars than before. A major road is an asset;

---

[3]Hotel chains actually own very few, if any, of the hotels that carry their name. The hotel industry is a complex web of brands, franchises and franchisees, management companies, leases and lessors, and asset owners. The buildings themselves most definitely appear somewhere on a balance sheet as an asset, but the actual owner may be quite different than the name on the outside.

the asset is worth more if it is combined with services. However, constant service is needs to maximize benefit.

One way to increase capacity on a road is to build an extra lane. An extra lane would most certainly be considered an asset. Another way to increase road capacity is use active traffic management – a combination of software technology and human activity. In effect a software asset replaces a physical asset.

Adding services to an asset increases the value of the asset.

Some people like to think that software is different. After all, software doesn't weather, it doesn't rust, it has no moving parts to wear out, and if the hardware that supports it does wear out you can just install it on another machine.

But software does decay. Like every other asset, software needs to be maintained.

Software decay

Software might be the ultimate static entity – no moving parts to wear, no metal to rust or humans to tire, just repeated identical functioning. Despite that, software decays.

In a world of constant change, failure to change is itself the source of decay. Software is too static; it needs humans to help it change. In fact, since the creation and deployment of software in itself sets in motion a series of changes, the software initiates its own decay.

Software decays because the world around it changes. Laws change, currencies appear and disappear, user expectations change: an iPhone-toting 20-something digital native might well find it hard to use a green-screen terminal, let alone a Teletype.

Even if software doesn't break, changes in the people who use it and the surroundings in which it is used can mean that the software is not generating as much business benefit as it might. When new software is introduced or modified it sets off a series of changes that are impossible to predict. As people and teams become accustomed to using a new piece of technology, their understanding and behavior changes. Over time these changes create new opportunities for the software to deliver more value, for example by supporting new working practices.

Cameras built into phones are used not just to take pictures of happy memories, but for taking visual notes, or for amusing children. Digital phone cameras don't just replace analog cameras – they create a whole new set of uses. Think of QR codes, or the lady I saw on Eurostar using her iPhone to photograph pictures on her Windows PC.

Nor does software exist in isolation – no software is an island, especially in the age of the Internet of Things. Changes to another piece of software may well create beneficial business opportunities that require changes to an existing and stable package.

If you are lucky your organization will be able to seize these new opportunities. If you are unlucky, your competitors will take the advantages first. How many taxi companies in the world are threatened because Uber found a way to exploit smartphones?

> *Digital businesses find it far easier to globalize rapidly. Without a digital platform, how could a San Francisco taxi company offer rides in London and Bangalore, let alone in both cities, within six years of opening?*

Because software runs on technology that is subject to Moore's Law[4], new opportunities are becoming possible every day.

Because of Moore's Law the things that software technology is capable of, and how that technology is used, are constantly advancing. Your organization can choose to take advantages of changes induced by experience and Moore's Law, or carry on as it is and let others take advantage of those changes.

---

[4]The number of transistors on integrated circuit doubles approximately every two years. Thus the power of CPUs approximately doubles while the price halves in the same period.

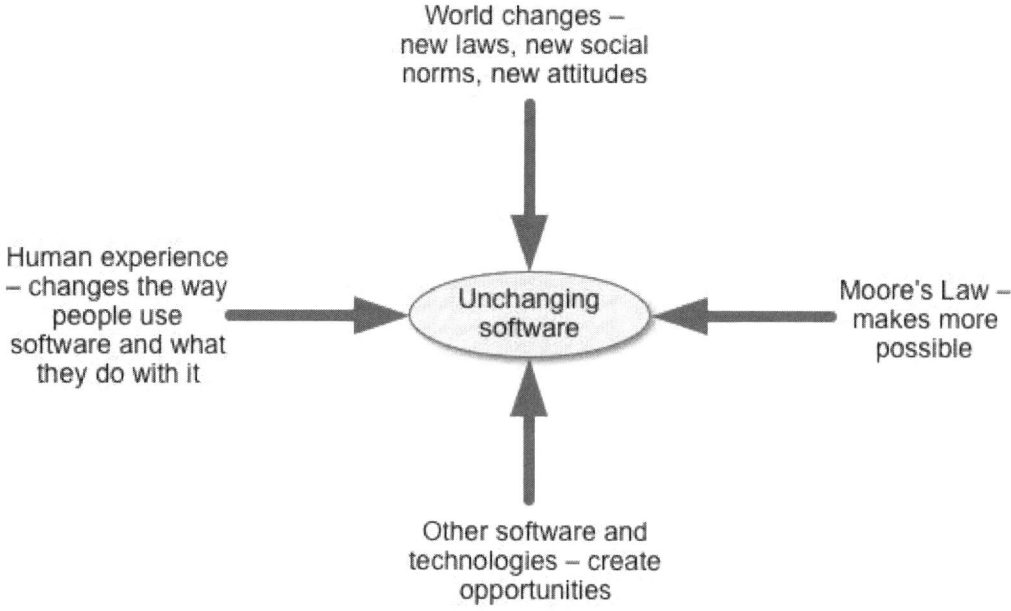

Some of the forces demanding change in supposedly unchanging software

Software lives

A mindset that says that 'the software is finished' does not allow for such changes. Failing to see software platforms as living and changing assets that need continuous investment induces decay as others advance. Organizations combat these changes by launching 'projects' on their software platforms. But these 'projects' have problems, as I will discuss.

In particular, funding is only available for specific changes, not for ongoing evolution and updates. 'Project thinking' provides large sums of cash, occasionally, for specific work on software. 'Asset thinking' would provide regular small sums of money for continued development.

Two specific problems arise from project thinking. Firstly, to complete a project it is common for its scope to be cut. The work may begin with the best intentions, but as time and budget run out, work is cancelled. This directly impacts the ability of the software to age gracefully.

Magnifying this problem is the tendency for many projects to be brought to a close by consciously ignoring known defects and accepting poor quality – what developers often call *technical debt*, but which is better considered as *technical liability*. This is akin to consciously deciding to leave part of the Forth Bridge unpainted just to finish on schedule.

Project thinking magnifies these tendencies, because such internal properties are hard for non-programmers to see and understand. As a result there is little awareness of the costs that Project A might dump onto Project B.

In software poor quality increases costs. By leaving defects and liabilities in the code base, the next set of changes are rendered more expensive and slower. Over time the lack of investment takes a toll: each successive set of changes takes longer and is more expensive.

Eventually the engineers complain, and sometime afterwards the budget-holders recognize the problems. But by this stage the liabilities are significant and it is questionable whether the required quality can be restored. Discussions about a total software replacement start – but the risks of replacement are immense.

Secondly, it is not uncommon for gaps to exist between projects. Sometime the gap can be months or even years. Gaps also exist in staffing: staff turnover is high in the IT industry, and when a project ends staff may well change employers. Even if the same staff work on the same code and product, there is no guarantee that they will remember the details after even a short break. In either case the result is the loss of the tacit knowledge essential to software work. Again this makes future work more expensive and slower.

Ceasing development work on a software system is akin to abandoning work in an underground mine. When work ceases, water and gas fill the workings, making it difficult or perhaps impossible to reopen the mine.

It is important to realize that neither problem is inevitable. Tools and techniques exist to keep software malleable, and knowledge can be retained.

Software is an asset

Software is an asset to the business that owns it, but it cannot be a static asset. Software ages and decays because the world around it changes. Consequently it needs ongoing funding to counteract asset decay.

Rather than treating work on software as a defined project, software needs to be treated as an asset that requires continuous maintenance, enhancement and refinement. Keeping the code base as good as it can be – *technical excellence* – actually ensures that costs are reduced and flexibility is enhanced.

This does not mean that funding should be handed over without justification: governance has a place. Teams receiving funding should be able to explain what they have done, what they plan to do and how both will benefit the business.

The accountancy profession has long recognized software as an asset. Unfortunately the accountancy profession still thinks in terms of projects. I'll talk more about accounting later: it is complicated, and an area where accountants need to be involved with creating the solution.

3. Higher purpose

I believe that this nation should commit itself to achieving the goal, before this decade is out, of landing a man on the moon and returning him safely to the earth. President John F Kennedy

...a computer on every desk, running Microsoft software. Bill Gates

Beat Xerox. Canon Group

...to organize the world's information and make it universally accessible and useful. Google

Goal, mission, vision, objective, BHAG (*Big Hairy Audacious Goal*)[1], MTP (*Massively Transformational Product*)[2] – call it what you will, but the underlying idea is the same: *a higher purpose.*

Organizations and people are motivated and inspired when they have a higher purpose. Organizations and people work better together when they share a common higher purpose.

In the Continuous Digital model each team is a miniature business in its own right, so each team needs a sense of higher purpose. In addition to the overarching organizational purpose, there needs to be a team-level shared higher purpose.

Survival is not enough: organizations are akin to organic life – they want to survive; they want to live; they want to grow. But survival alone, while necessary, is not enough. Organizations and the people in them need a higher purpose to motivate and focus on.

Over the years various authors have suggested different names and forms for this higher purpose; some are given above. While the details differ, the essential element is the same: something bigger than the individual, something that gives meaning, something to aim for, something against which to measure progress.

---

[1]*Built to Last: Successful Habits of Visionary Companies*, Collins and Porras, 1994
[2]*Exponential Organizations*, Ismail, 2014

Not money

Human beings don't only want comfort, safety, short working hours, hygiene, birth control and, in general, common sense; they also, at least intermittently, want struggle and self-sacrifice, not to mention drums, flags and loyalty parades.
George Orwell

Few people are motivated by money in anything other than the short term. Making money – creating revenue, making profits, enhancing return on investment – are objectives best pursued indirectly. Experience has shown that when organizations only focus on making money, things go wrong: think of Enron, Lehman Brothers and countless less famous examples.

The economist John Kay goes further in suggesting that directly targeting profit impedes the propensity to do good and generate profit. Kay cites numerous examples, such as the British chemical company ICI, which successfully generated profits for decades while it aimed at:

'...serving customers internationally through the innovative and responsible application of chemistry and related science.'

In 1997 ICI restated its higher purpose as:

'...to be the industry leader in creating value for customers and shareholders through market leadership, technological edge and a world competitive cost base.'

Ten years later ICI was gone[3].

Even the one-time champion of 'shareholder value', Jack Welch, has described single-minded pursuit of profit as "The dumbest idea in the world."

Making money is necessary for businesses and individuals, but more importantly, money is information. Healthy cash-flow shows a business that it is doing well, and failure to make enough revenue to cover costs tells a business that it needs to change or pack up.

Modern commerce has developed a mass of 'financial engineering' techniques that allow money to be extracted from an organization. Unfortunately these techniques dilute the informational value of money for the underlying business. That a company can pay large dividends while the core business rots demonstrates the prowess of financial advisors and obscures the underlying issues.

---

[3]*Obliquity: Why our goals are best achieved indirectly.* John Kay, 2017

Obliquity

*Obliquity describes the process of achieving complex objectives indirectly...
oblique approaches recognize that complex objectives tend to be imprecisely defined and contain many elements that are not necessary or obviously compatible
with each other, and that* **we learn about the nature of the objectives and
the means of achieving them during a process of experiment and discovery**[4].
John Kay, 2017

Kay's concept of oblique goals is not only attractive for technologists, but describes in one
word the whole *raison d'être* for software development. Developers start with a necessarily
fuzzy goal because the goal exists in a fuzzy world, but our machines do not tolerate fuzziness;
they know only the finite states of one and zero. If the problem is already sufficiently precisely
defined, then the computer can already solve the problem.

'The computer is very good at solving the problem we have specified and asked it
to solve, but less useful when we are not quite sure what the problem is.' Obliquity,
John Kay, 2017

Almost by definition the activity of instructing the computer to solve a problem is oblique,
fuzzy, ill-defined and requires one to learn about the solution and the problem.

Software development is inherently the work of turning oblique and fuzzy objectives into
specific systems. In doing so engineers deploy an armory of tools that seek to clarify the
problem in hand and focus attention and effort, while engineers offer up potential solutions
that may do more to help understand the problem than to provide a solution.

Embracing Kay's call for obliquity opens this author to the charge of hypocrisy, because
I have written much on defining, specifying and quantifying work. But in truth software
development always begins with oblique problems. Iterative software development is the
act of repeatedly focusing on the problem and potential solutions in order to create better
understanding. It is because problems software engineers address are inherently fuzzy and
oblique that one must constantly attempt to clarify the problem and solution. It is through
repeated and iterative attempts to define and specify the problem and solution that one
advances towards both a solution and the problem.

When technologists are able to specify problems and goals in specific terms, then solutions
can be crafted. Given a sufficiently precise problem statement, crafting a solution can be
trivial. However, specifying the problem is far from trivial.

---

[4]Emphasis added.

Organizations and teams

That organizations need a higher purpose is well-established, but what is less well-established is that teams need their own higher purpose.

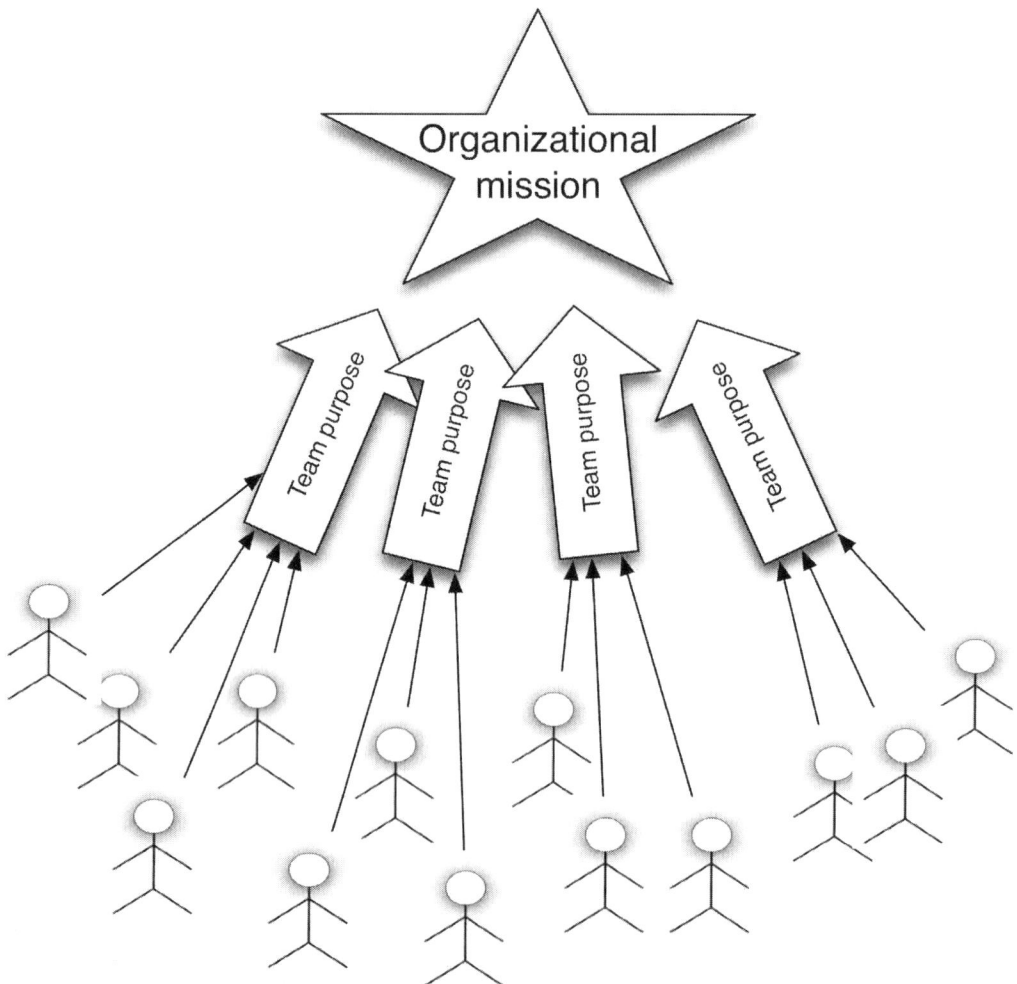

Individual aims build towards teams' higher purposes, which build towards the organization's higher purpose

While grand organizational – even national – goals may be highly motivating, they can also be very remote. While an oxygen tank designer deep in the bowels of Grumman Aerospace might understand how their work builds towards putting a man on the moon, does an accountant deep in the bowels of Google understand how their analysis of expenses helps to organize the world's information? Teams need to have their own higher purpose, and they need to understand how that builds towards the ultimate higher pursue of the organization.

Given that authority is devolved to the team, and that the team is expected to both decide what to do and execute it, then it is not possible to govern a team on the basis of "Have they delivered X?", because the team decides what X is. Assessing effectiveness and progress is tricky.

Knowing both team and organizational higher purpose allows one to frame questions of effectiveness and progress in terms of the higher purpose, for example "Has this release contributed to the team's purpose? To the organization's purpose?"

Scale

Each team needs its own higher purpose.

This is especially true when a team needs to work with other teams in the organization. Since all teams ultimately share the organizational higher purpose, team-level aims should not be too dissimilar.

When an organization is small there may only be one team. The organization's higher purpose is the team's higher purpose. Life is easy. But with growth there will come a point at which teams need their individual sense of purpose. In the first instance it would seem rational to hand these teams a predetermined higher purpose. Indeed this might be necessary in order to establish a team in the first place.

Where a team is following the 'amoeba model' and splits into two teams, it is entirely possible that the two teams share a common purpose at least initially. Over time their higher purposes may diverge.

Mutable

Although a team may be given – or inherit – a higher purpose to start with, teams need ownership of that higher purpose. Therefore each team needs to have the authority to modify their higher purpose over time. As they are part of a larger organization, such changes need to be undertaken in harmony with the organization.

A team intending to modify its stated higher purpose would consult with others – its customers and other teams with which it works. The organization's governance board is probably the ultimate arbiter of whether a proposed change of purpose can be made, although a team should probably avoid getting into a situation in which the board says "No".

If team members start to doubt their higher purpose and are unable to question and ultimately change their purpose, then they may be compelled to leave the team.

This might even be desirable – if one individual finds they are no longer motivated by the higher purpose, it may well be a sign that they should move. This is perfectly natural – individuals grow and change throughout their lives, and what they want and what motivates them changes over time.

However, if multiple team members find the higher purpose no longer motivates them or seems irrational, it may well be sign that the purpose needs revising. Again it is natural that over time teams' higher purposes will mutate and change – after all, the world around them is changing, technology is advancing, and sticking doggedly to a purpose that has become outdated is detrimental.

If team members are to truly believe in their higher purpose, they need to 'own' the purpose; if the team collectively owns the purpose, then it is allowed to change it. One of the privileges conferred by ownership is the right to change property. If 'owners' cannot change their purpose then they are not true owners.

Individuals

Each member of the organization should have a sense of mission. Inamori Kazuo[5]

Only when team members understand and share the team's purpose does it make sense to talk about individual goals or objectives. Indeed one might even ask: *if the team is the basic work unit, and if one is striving to create effective teams, then surely the team goals are individual goals?*

I'll leave that as an open question for discussion. However, if you decide that individual goals still have a role to play, it follows that individual objectives should not only be aligned with team and wider organizational goals, but should actually be *derived from* team and organizational goals.

---

[5] *Amoeba Management*: Kazuo Inamori, 1999

Project completeness

In the project model completion of the project is the goal. However, such an objective leads to goal displacement and damages profitability in a digital world. Still, individuals and organizations need meaningful and achievable goals.

Quantifying goals can be a great aid to determining whether they are met. However, sometimes it might be better to avoid quantification: set an oblique goal, make the goal something to strive for, and thus avoid attempts to 'game' the target. The problem with quantifiable goals is that while they appear objective, the goals can be met by oblique means, which undermine the goals' validity. This is highlighted by *Goodhart's Law*[6].

Closure

One of the advantages of the project model is that it allows individuals and organizations to achieve closure. Humans like closure: it provides a satisfying psychological safety. Something is done, complete, finished. That the continuous model deliberately avoids closure is itself something of a problem psychologically. However in the commercial world closure often creates problems.

> 'This shop is closed.'

Shops that close on Sundays can be an inconvenience – one cannot satisfy one's immediate needs.

> 'This shop has now closed.'

Shops that close and cease trading can be an even bigger disappointment.

Business closure is normally a bad sign – businesses want to live and continue!

Unfortunately organizations sometimes meet their goals, their BHAGS (big hairy audacious goals), their objectives, or complete their missions. Upon achieving their goals, both Canon and Microsoft faced existential questions and suffered commercial turbulence for several years. NASA too struggled in the years after Neil Armstrong became Kennedy's 'man on the Moon', and the final three Apollo missions were cancelled.

---

[6]https://en.wikipedia.org/wiki/Goodhart%27s_law

While one might sidestep such a problem by defining the higher purpose as something that is never complete, such an approach may be self-defeating if individuals feel that the aim is never achievable.

This is definitely one of those 'nice to have' problems. However it is one that should not be ignored indefinitely. The solution requires flexibility in the goal: once the goal is achieved, the organization needs to be capable of mutating it or adopting a new goal. The same should also be true of teams that achieve their higher purpose.

Finally

At an individual level a higher purpose helps to enroll and motivate team members. At an organizational level the teams' higher purposes allow the organization to coordinate disparate teams and assess effectiveness.

The organization's ultimate goals and objectives serve to coordinate teams and add to individuals' own sense of purpose.

Oblique goals provide the team with latitude to innovate and allow problems to be reformulated as solutions emerge. Oblique goals better match the nature of technology work: creating the specific from the vague and interfacing the exact world of machines to the fuzzy world of people.

4. Team-centric development

Divide the organization as necessary into small units, and rebuild it as a unified body of small enterprises. Entrust the management of these units to amoeba leaders to cultivate personnel with managerial awareness. Kuzuno Inamori[1]

Rather than organize work around a series of temporary projects, work needs to be organized around stable streams. These streams are not just aligned to the business: they *are* the business.

Stream teams are the mechanisms by which the business delivers to its customers. An individual team may be responsible for an entire product or service, or a team may be one of several supporting a product. For a large software product each stream might represent an entire subsystem; such a subsystem would need to represent business benefit in its own right.

There may be several related teams working on a product line, or several teams supporting related service offerings. The teams might be organized around customer journeys or value streams, around business lines, or around any other segmentation criteria the organization uses. The key point is that the teams are an intrinsic part of the business.

When a business expands it may initially expand a stream team, but there comes a point at which it makes sense to split the team into two sub-teams, each representing a stream in its own right.

For example, an online retailer might start with a single stream team. As the business and the team grow, there comes a time when the team should split in two, amoeba-style. After the split one stand-alone team maintains the catalog side of the operation, while the other team looks after everything else.

These splits continue: the next split might see a checkout team emerge to concentrate on payments. Splits do not need to be symmetrical: a team of 12 might split into a team of eight and a team of four.

In preparation for a split a team might need to temporarily overstaff some roles. For example, each team might need its own *product owner*: in the months prior to the split a second product

---

[1] *Amoeba Management: The Dynamic Management System for Rapid Market Response*, Kuzuo Inamori, 1999

owner may be added, so that when the split happens both teams have someone in-role on day one.

Each stream team stands alone, and, importantly, each can clearly see what difference they make to customers. After a split each new team starts with the same DNA and the same processes and thinking as the original team. Over time they will diverge; not only is this accepted – it is celebrated as a source of greater adaptation and learning.

Stream teams are stable. People will leave the team occasionally: people retire, babies come and, Heaven forbid, some people dare to change employer! People might switch to different teams, or be part of a group that is split out. But new people will join the team – indeed, the team probably needs to be in permanent recruitment mode just to keep up with departures and organic growth. Hopefully success will mean that a team needs and can justify more people. New team members also bring new DNA and new ways of looking at things, and can offset some of the inevitable *groupthink* that will occur.

On the whole, however, the team is stable: the team retains the same people. The team is also cross-functional: people on the team are multi-skilled even if they have specializations. The team is staffed so as to be able to see a piece of work from start to finish.

Governance centers on the stream and the stream team. Each team may even be its own accounting unit.

Streams need to be as independent of each other as possible. As with software, each stream should be lightly coupled and highly cohesive – they should minimize dependence on other streams and maximize their own independence. This might mean duplicating functionality and code in some places, and it means that teams should forget about reusable code – 'reusable bad, reused good' should be the mantra.

Conway's Law

If this all starts to sound familiar, it should – Conway's Law is at work:

> *Organizations which design systems... are constrained to produce designs which are copies of the communication structures of these organizations.* Melvin Conway[2], 1968

---

[2]*How do Committees Invent?*, Conway, M. E., Datamation 1968. Also Wikipedia:https://en.wikipedia.org/wiki/Conway's_law

Streams and their teams are akin to functions in procedural programming: functional decomposition enshrines hierarchical organizations into code. Stand-alone self-contained teams, with a public interface (and private organization), are a better match for object-oriented systems.

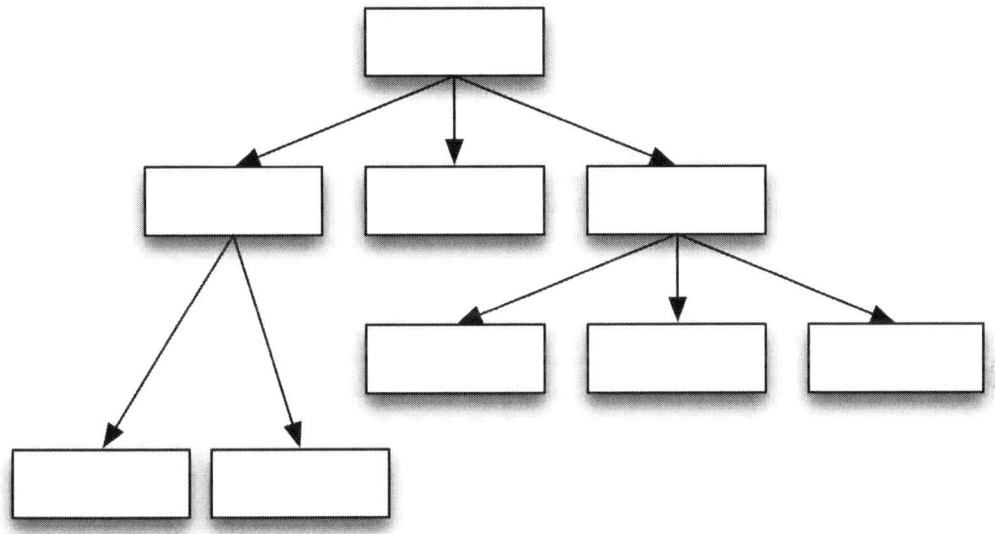

Structure chart or organization chart?

Procedural programming led to hierarchical system decomposition into layers, for example a database layer, a business layer and a user interface layer. Each layer had its own team, and project managers ran around trying to coordinate work across teams.

Object-oriented programming should give us independent cooperating teams that embody a business service. Hierarchical organization of enterprises is still the norm, however. This results in a mismatch between the system design and organization design, thereby violating Conway's Law and creating conflict.

Stream working draws on good software design. Each team is free to vary the way in which it works. Each stream will probably work initially much as its originating stream. Over time, though, the team may change working processes and practices, or even technology. Because each team is autonomous, it can do what it considers best, unhindered by other teams.

Like a class in object-oriented programming, the team is free to change its internal organization as long as its external interface is unchanged. Teams will need to spend time collaborating with other teams, and a well-defined interface and regular tests help here. Sometimes team interfaces will need to change, but over time such changes should become less frequent.

Amoeba teams

'Management by all' gives all employees a sense of achievement. Kuzuno Inamori

Successful teams will grown over time – they can pull in resources as they need and can justify. When teams become too big they may split into two teams, like the amoebas in biology textbooks. Each of these teams may grown and split further. But unlike the amoeba this process is reversible: if two teams find it hard to justify their costs, they may choose to merge into one smaller team.

Each team is a self-contained business unit with a business objective. It is staffed to fulfill its mission and is responsible for all decisions in its field. Importantly, each team is part of *the business*. These are not technology teams 'aligned' to a business unit: they are an integral part of that business unit. It may be that most of the team members are not actually technologists: they may be call-centre operators, logistics clerks, bankers, but to undertake and improve their work they just happen to need colleagues who are technologists.

Of course there will be teams that consist almost entirely of technologists and support many colleagues who are not themselves technologists. Technologists may even form a small sub-team within the larger business team, and there may be other specialist sub-teams. However a business unit organizes itself, it must keep a clear view of the customer and understand how the whole team contributes to the customer experience, and how any payment the customer makes finds its way to the team.

The amoeba has already inspired a management model that embodies these characteristics – a model that originated outside software technology. *Amoeba management* at Kyocera was described by Kuzuno Inamori[3]. Writing in 1999, Inamori reported that Kyocera had over 3,000 amoeba business units.

In amoeba management each team is its own business unit and is responsible for its own profit and loss. This does not mean that there are only customer-facing teams. 'Back office' amoebas also exist and have their own profit and loss accounts, even when they are hidden from customer view.

Inamori discusses amoeba teams working in research and development, logistics and other areas. These exist to allow other teams to do their work of delivering products and services to the customer. The different teams must come to an agreement about how the money they earn is apportioned between them.

---

[3] *Amoeba Management: The Dynamic Management System for Rapid Market Response*, Kuzuo Inamori, 1999

Minimally viable teams

All teams begin life as an MVT – a minimally viable team. If successful, and if justifiable, the team may grow, amoeba-like.

Initially an MVT is probably staffed by two or three people. One person alone is not enough, as they need to have someone to talk to, someone to bounce ideas off, someone to collaborate with, someone to act as a foil, and someone with whom to share the work, the pain and the joy.

Two people could be a team, one representing a more analytical side, someone with a business orientation. The second member might be a more technical person, someone better at synthesizing a solution. Yet it is arguable that if two is a team, what sport has teams of two? There are sports such as doubles tennis and two-man bobsleigh, but these are not blessed with the name 'team'. Teams begin with three people.

So an MVT is most likely three people. Each person is dedicated full-time to the stream. Their initial task is to work out what the mission is and how they might go about solving it. Those who created the team will have passed the team some sense of mandate or higher purpose, but the team needs to both understand this and make it their own.

While the team may have been passed a problem to solve, a true understanding and definition of the problem will only emerge over time as solutions are examined. The solution and the problem are understood and even defined in parallel.

The team will need to bootstrap – that is, self-start. Perhaps it might begin by interviewing stakeholders and building a prototype. In building the prototype the team will enhance its understanding of what is technically possible. It might then show the prototype to stakeholders to improve their understanding of the problem. The first checkpoint is a portfolio review (described later), where the team must show what business benefit it has delivered and what it intends to do next.

Those familiar with Conway's Law will see that MVTs are aimed at avoiding 'architecture by staffing': for example, assigning a database administrator to a team guarantees that the resulting product will use a database whether it needs one or not. MVTs start small and grow as they need to. Staffing a team with more than three people risks premature decision-making. In time the team will grow, or cease. Keeping the team small keeps both options valid.

Value-seeking teams

Teams exist both to pursue a higher purpose and to deliver value to the organization. The higher purpose should guide the search for value; if these two objectives are in conflict, the team will have problems that need to be addressed.

Each team should be seeking out value to deliver to customers and to the teams they work with, and at the same time builds to the higher purpose. Teams and work do not stop just because the team completes all the work it had earlier thought of: part of the team's task is to uncover more work in its designated area.

For a software team this means that its area of work should be creating value for the business, be it a software product or service. If the team identifies enhancements that will make its product or service more valuable, it should undertake them.

Importantly this means that all teams must contain skills, not just to build enhancements, but also to identify the need for enhancements. Such skills may be concentrated in one person, perhaps a Product Manager, but responsibility rests with the whole team. Even the humblest team member may contribute to the search.

Deadlines over end dates

When teams are stable and continue from one piece of work to the next the idea of an end-date becomes questionable. This is especially true when considering the case for value: later chapters discuss value and time in more detail. If revisiting a piece of completed work or releasing less soon produces extra value, then the team should do so.

While predetermined end-dates become a thing of the past, deadlines should not. Humans are very good at working to deadlines, so deadlines can be beneficial. Since different deadlines produce different values, there are likely to be several deadlines where before there was one end-date.

In fact deadlines based on value delivery are a far more useful tool than estimation. Humans are very bad at estimation but very good at meeting deadlines, even if the work gets done the night before! Teams should harness this foible to their advantage.

Continuity

Business lines and teams are expected to continue: unlike many of the features they build, teams do not come with a use-by date. The assumption is that *teams will explore and find more valuable work as they do their work.*

Teams are set up as part of business lines with the expectation that while they are delivering business benefit, they will continue. Should they not deliver business benefit they may well be disbanded, redeployed or redirected. Hence the need for governance and portfolio management, discussed later.

Continuity helps teams to control and improve their working practices. It allows team members to know where others are strong or weak. Most of all, continuity safeguards the tacit knowledge that underpins the teams' work.

When a team has continuity it is expected to ensure that its products – source code and operating processes – are also built with continuity in mind. For example, teams are discouraged from carrying too much technical liability, as this will hinder their future ability to respond.

Stable not static

While a team aims for stability and continuity, it is only natural that some people will leave the team while others will join. One can expect success (more business benefit) to result in more joining than leaving.

Over time teams will need to change: shrink, grow, add new skills, reduce other skills. How teams reach such decisions is an open question, but 'stable' does not mean unchanging.

As products and business mature the skills mix needed to work effectively will also change. This may mean that some skills are removed from teams. People may need to be released from teams, and new people added with additional skills – either completely new skills or those that bolster capacity in existing skills.

Sometimes teams will be able to train existing members in new skills. At other times releasing existing members and recruiting new members will be the right solution. As with growth, it is best if teams can come to such decisions themselves. However the nature of such decisions means that such changes are often more obvious to those outside a team than within it.

5. Work to be done

Over and over, people try to design systems that make tomorrow's work easy. But when tomorrow comes it turns out they didn't quite understand tomorrow's work, and they actually made it harder. Ward Cunningham

Stories, user stories, product backlog items, use cases, tickets, jobs to be done – day-in, day-out, most teams just do work. The items of work may come from pre-existing requirements documents, or they may arise dynamically from customer feedback, analyst investigation or ideas from the team or from many other sources.

Work also comes from projects. Where projects exist they are big bundles of *work to do*. Projects are simplest when there is a one-to-one relationship between teams and projects: one team does one project. But often teams have to work on multiple projects simultaneously, and project work often gets divided between teams. Still, the project is just 'work to do', and has to compete with other work a team may need to do.

The work items may take user story form: *As a... I want to... so that....* They may be more informal stories or more formal use cases; they may even be bug reports. They may be called 'product backlog items' or simply 'tickets'. They may be organized as a backlog, two backlogs or even more. Some backlogs might be disguised, perhaps as a bug list or a roadmap, and some might be hiding in pots dotted around the office. But at the end of the day it is all work to be done.

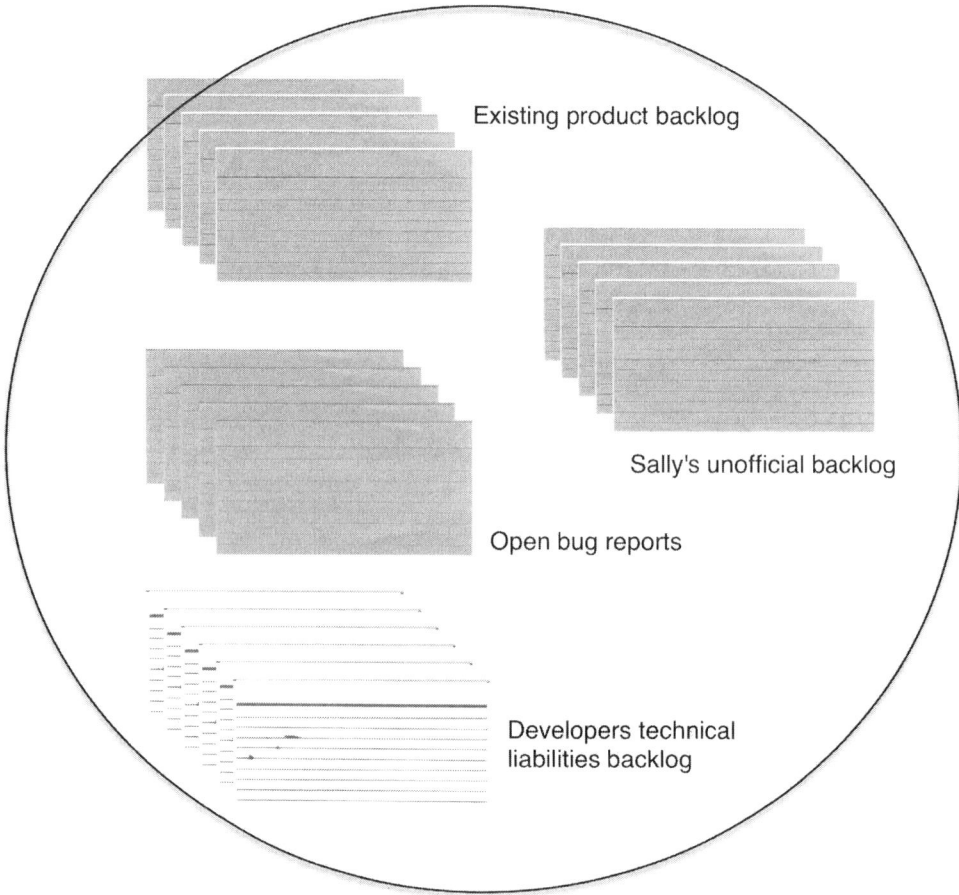

One backlog or four? It's all work for the team to do.

There is a team and the team has a capacity to do work. There is no bug-fixing fairy who will fix the bugs when team members are asleep; if the team doesn't use some of its capacity to fix bugs then they won't get fixed[1].

There is work to be done: whatever name the individual items are given, whatever structure (or lack thereof) they are held in, and whoever finds it, there is work to be done. The team exists to do that work.

It is very easy for a successful team to get lost in the day-to-day activity of 'doing work', particularly when customers find the work valuable and things are going well. However, as the previous chapter described, teams need a higher purpose, both as a motivator for

---

[1]Neither is there a requirements fairy or a testing fairy.

individuals and for organizations to undertake governance and coordination.

There is seldom a shortage of work to be done: the problem is not usually "We have nothing to do", but "What should we do next?". Higher purpose is one criterion for filtering and prioritizing work to do. Value is another useful filter: teams should aim to maximize the value delivered. Again, teams need to decide for themselves what filters to use and what criteria to apply. Most of all, teams need to decide when not to do work: deciding what to pass over is often the most important decision of all.

Teams and products

There is a team, there is work to be done, the flow of work needs to be regulated and controlled so that the team can a) work efficiently, and b) deliver with some degree of predictability.

In the simplest model one team works on one product. In this case all the work undertaken by the team relates to the product. A more common scenario is that a team exists and undertakes work on an existing and continuing product. While some of this work, and periods of time, may be assigned to a particular project, this is little more than an accounting convention. More likely than not the team and the product will continue to exist beyond any particular project; the work will simply be accounted for under a different project label or a 'business as usual' label.

Another common scenario is that a team exists to work on a major product but must undertake ad-hoc work for other minor products. Rather than being dedicated to a single stream of work the team, or just individuals on the team, must slice its time between different streams of work.

Teams will be most effective when the variety of work is the smallest – that is, all team members work on the same code base with the same focus. This set-up will also provide the greatest degree of predictability when forecasting deliverables and schedule. The greater the variety of work, the less efficient and less predictable the work will be.

As a general rule teams should seek to work on fewer things but deliver them sooner, rather than work on many things that all take a long time: *short and fat over long and thin*.

Who does it?

New ideas appear and new work happens. When new work happens there are two basic options: direct the work to an existing team or set up a new team.

Where teams already exist the best option is to direct new work to the most appropriate existing team. Indeed teams are expected to find new work themselves and are staffed to do so. If Team A identifies Work X then it is quite natural that Team A will just do X.

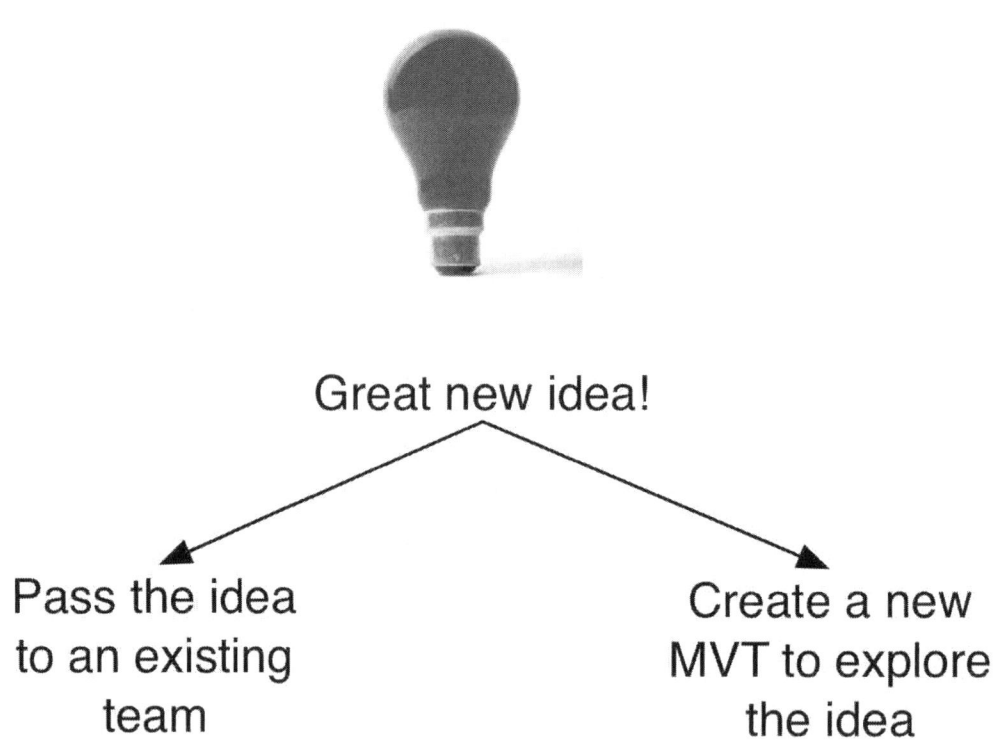

Great new ideas go to an existing team or a new team

Occasionally a team might identify work that is valuable but would be better suited to another team. In such cases the team simply passes over the work. There could be good reasons why the other team didn't do the work – it might have more valuable work in hand – but essentially the two teams can work out the best approach themselves. If the value of the new work is not competitive with other work the teams intend to do, then it should not be done.

What happens when work arises without an obvious home? It may still be worth directing it to an existing team, perhaps because the team has the resources and infrastructure available to look at the work quickly. Alternatively, a new team may be formed. New teams should always be formed as Minimally Viable Teams (MVTs).

Fail fast, fail cheap, learn, salvage

The decision about what to abandon is by far the most important and most neglected... No organization which purposefully and systematically abandons the unproductive and obsolete ever wants for opportunities. Peter Drucker, Age of Discontinuity, 1968

The mission of a minimally viable team is to fail: fail fast and fail cheap. Some information and even artifacts may be salvaged from this learning experience, but that is in the future. Some learning will be direct and some indirect; sometimes the most valuable learning is the learning that says "Don't do that".

Small teams are created for two reasons.

Firstly, a large team with a correspondingly large budget will immediately feel the need to justify its own existence. Even before the large team is formed the purse-string holders will look for evidence that the work will succeed in order to justify the money. Requesting such justification is reasonable, but:

a) It may be impossible to know if the work will succeed.

b) The quickest way to find out if the work will succeed is probably to start doing the work.

c) Creating the justification for funding decisions may well hinder later work.

Justification – analysis – takes time: because of cost of delay the time spent in analysis reduces the ultimate value. Rationally delaying decisions until more is known may well be the best course of action, but actually starting the work may be quicker and generate more value when successful.

If one attempts to find out the chances of success by analysis alone, the work has begun but it has begun a less efficient way. It is common to see big organizations that are only too happy to let analysts and architects start analyzing a problem but scared of letting anyone attempt to solve it for real. Yet often the richest route to learning is to actually attempt to solve the problem.

An MVT therefore is an exploratory team that aims to find out whether an idea makes business sense and whether it is technically achievable. In doing so it lays the foundations of long-term success.

Since most business initiatives fail, the aim is to quickly filter out those that *will* fail. If the team is too big, or too much money is committed too early, the team will lose the ability to fail. The 'sunk cost fallacy' makes it hard for corporations to kill expensive runaway projects.

The second reason for creating a small team is so that the team itself can decide how to undertake the work. If it is successful the team will grow, but prematurely growing the team hinders its ability to find small-scale solutions and the best architecture.

For example, suppose a bank decides to launch a new online service. Knowing this will be a large undertaking, they staff the project team with a solution architect, a database administrator, a UXD designer, three analysts, several SQL developers, several Java developers and a few more front-end developers. While that might be a reasonable staffing six months down the line, in the early days all these people need to find work for themselves to do. Each needs – perhaps subconsciously – inclusion, so any chance of creating a small solution is immediately lost.

Tolerate failure

> *Anyone who has never made a mistake has never tried anything new.* Albert Einstein

Sometimes things will go wrong. Sometimes development effort will not deliver value.

The software industry has a poor track record of forecasting where value lies and how long it will take to deliver that value. Rather than expending more time and energy on soothsaying it is often cheaper to tolerate cheap, fast, small failures. The failure will generate learning, and the learning is valuable.

Advances in technology and engineering tools mean that engineers can very quickly build new apps and functionality. Even if the work is not completed to release standard, they will know more about what is needed to take it to that level. It may therefore be more efficient to let two engineers try something rather than to have the engineers, plus several managers and analysts, debate whether it is possible to build the thing, the details of the thing, and estimates of how long it will take to build the thing.

Given such advances in technology there is a need to update process thinking and management models. It is now cheaper and faster to learn what is possible by doing rather than analyzing. There is still a role for analysis, but it happens in parallel with doing, or for a much shorter period at the beginning.

Even when work looks like failure, failure is subjective. Work may not deliver the intended value but still deliver useful learning: about technology, about the market, about what works. Value may be generated because something costly would *not* be done – experimentation can allow some options to be dismissed.

Companies need to be tolerant of failure, and when failure does strike they need to salvage what they can and move on. Every failure contains information, whether one learns from it or not. The key is, of course, to keep failures small – a few days of work as opposed to months or years – and avoid failures that would prove fatal.

Constraints breed innovation

Keeping a team small forces the team to think small and look for innovative solutions. If the team has plenty of capacity the tendency will be to think big: overstaffing leads to over-engineering. Speculatively staffing a team creates more problems than it solves.

When resources are limited, however, there can be a tendency to limit ambitions and grab the first solution that presents itself. Experience shows that the first idea is seldom the best: taking a little time (but not indefinite amounts) to consider options leads to more productive use of time.

The team needs a mindset that says *"We will think carefully about our options; we will try something quickly, see what happens, and refine our approach; we will search for the good solutions that are within our capacity without cutting corners."*

Using an initial minimally viable team enforces this approach; as the MVT pulls in more people and grows it needs to retain this approach and mindset.

6. Value

Price is what you pay. Value is what you get. Warren Buffet

Value is perceived benefit: that is, the benefit we think we can get from something.
Tom Gilb, Competitive Engineering Concept 269[1]

Teams, initiatives and work streams should be guided by the search for, and delivery of, value.

While that is easy to say, it raises a number of questions, not least of which is *what is value?* Defining value is hard, but exploring the details of how one creates value is harder, and maximizing value harder still. But that is no excuse to duck the issue.

I use the term *value* as shorthand for *benefit to the business* – that is, something that is valuable. What a business considers beneficial will itself be informed by the values the business and employees hold. (At this point there is a risk of creating circular definitions.)

Each team needs to decide what is valuable within its context. The values of its employer, stakeholders and individuals will all play a part in determining what is valuable to the team. So too will any higher purpose the team might have been given, or mission it has been asked to undertake.

Once the team has an understanding of what value is, it will need to consider how to create benefit and to whom to deliver it. These two questions are inherently interlinked, so the team may need to iterate several times to both understand what constitutes value and how it can create value. Where multiple teams work together on the same product or services, the teams need to have congruent understanding of value and how it is created.

Teams also need to communicate their understanding both to their stakeholders and, more importantly, to the governance bodies to which they answer. Governance bodies might hand down definitions of benefits to be delivered, value to be generated and stakeholders to serve. As atomic business units, amoeba teams might feel the need to challenge predetermined criteria and propose their own.

---

[1]*Competitive Engineering*, Tom Gilb, 2005

What is value?

While the term *value* tends to put ideas of numbers in one's mind, money is not the only potential benefit. Benefits may include learning, either by the team or the wider organization. Benefits may also include risk reduction – which might itself mean learning. Benefits may also include the delivery of one or more non-financial results.

For example, on a course I once had a civil servant who worked in the Department for Overseas Development. For them benefit could be measured by how many people in an area had clean drinking water, or whether children had access to education.

Benefit might also be progress towards some longer-term goal, possibly a strategic goal – although in many businesses such a goal may ultimately be financial. Benefit could also be some act of corporate social responsibility, although this might itself also build towards some ultimate financial goal.

Who benefits?

In considering benefit and value it is natural to ask *valuable to whom?* or *who receives the benefit?* Some readers will recognize this as the questions *who are the stakeholders?* and *what is their stake?*

Different stakeholders will interpret benefit differently. A busy manager might see a new expenses-tracking system as beneficial because it saves time, while the company accountant might consider it beneficial because it saves money. If the expenses system is hard to use, however, the company could pay in lost employee time as they struggle with it. A system that deters employees from claiming expenses might generate short-term benefits while also reducing long-term benefits through higher staff attrition.

One needs to recognize that there are different stakeholders and that different stakeholders will receive different benefits. Sometimes these benefits will be in conflict: the benefits to one stakeholder may come at the price of dis-benefits to another. To complicate matters, priorities change over time: a stakeholder who was not important before may become important later.

Finally, not all stakeholders are equal. Some are more important than others: many companies operate informally on 'decibel management' (he who shouts loudest) or practice HIPPO prioritization (highest-paid person's opinion).

Profit-maximizing organizations

For commercial organizations that aim to make a profit, especially those that conform to the economists' definition of a 'profit maximizer', there is a shortcut to value: money. When an organization sets out to generate profit then most decisions can be reduced to a simple *how much money does this make?*

While this shortcut may well be exactly the right definition, it can also be a trap. Such a definition has the advantage of simplicity, but that very simplicity hides issues. The expenses system above provides one such example. ICI, discussed in Chapter 3, provides another example of how reducing everything to the pursuit of more money, whether 'profit maximization' or 'shareholder value', can be misleading in the short term and damaging in the longer team.

Default to money

A good default answer to "What is value?" is simply "Money" – dollars, sterling, euros, rupees or some other currency. One of the roles of money is as a 'store of value'. Despite numerous failings, money serves as a measure and store of value. Many things, for better or worse, are reduced to money, and on the whole it works.

Most likely you are paid in money. You use this to pay for housing, to buy food, toys for your children, to donate to charity and to save for old age. Each of these is difficult to compare, but each can be reduced, imperfectly, to money.

Money has another attribute that is useful and frequently overlooked: money is information. When money flows in one direction, information flows in the other direction. For example, when you spend $10 on a pizza, you are giving the pizza seller information: that you consider their pizza to be worth $10. The pizza moves from them to you and $10 moves from you to them. You demonstrate, for example, that you are willing to forego a theatre ticket to eat this pizza, or that you will forego $10 of savings. The failure of money to flow may itself also contain information: by not buying a $20 luxury pizza, customers are saying they have better uses for $20.

Numbers

78.3% of statistics are made up on the spot. Anecdotal

People tend to believe 'facts' that include numbers more than they believe similar statements without numbers. The more precise the number, the more likely it is to be believed.

The word *value*, more than the word *benefit*, implies a cold hard number. Perhaps that is why it gets used more. But while it is very attractive to reduce every benefit to a number – a value – there are good reasons why some benefits should be left unquantified.

For a start, the very attractiveness and believability of a numeric statement may itself be misleading. Sometimes information needs to be presented with less bias; sometimes those receiving the information need to think – reducing complex issues to simple numbers can be an oversimplification. Sometimes the effort required to move from a non-quantified – that is, qualitative – assessment to a numerical version may not be justified.

It is certainly good to try to quantify things: we *should* try to quantify things. The rigor of numerical analysis is good, and the clarity of thinking it demands can itself be highly beneficial. But sometimes it is better to accept a qualitative statement. Sometimes it is simpler, and sometimes it adds more value, to leave things unquantified. After all, do you want to say "Can you put a number on that?" the next time your spouse says "I love you"?

Non-financial benefits

Some business benefits are not financial: some might deliver business benefit in the future and so are worth pursuing, even if they cannot be valued today.

It can be incredibly difficult to measure and quantify something. For example, a business can benefit from things it learns today that saves it money in the future. Hence it is important to recognize multiple different ways in which organizations can benefit:

- *Learning*. A team might not have delivered something, but they have learned about technology, the market or customers' needs.
- *Intellectual property*. Some learning leads to knowledge that is considered intellectual property (IP). Some of this IP may become a patent.
- *Learning by failure*. A team might have launched a new product and seen it fail. This in itself has value. The important thing is that the team moves on from this, perhaps by creating a new product that addresses the previous failure, or perhaps by disbanding the team and allowing resources to be deployed elsewhere.
- *Failure*. For every innovative success one can expect multiple failures. If teams are not failing with innovative products and services, one might question whether teams are being too risk-averse. Failure is a way of reducing the options available. The quicker non-viable options are removed the better.

- *Risk reduction.* For example, many cyber-security initiatives don't increase the bottom line directly, but they do ensure that organizations are less likely to fall prey to hackers.
- *Improved staff morale.* Staff morale can lead to higher productivity, to better staff retention or to improved recruitment.

This is far from a comprehensive list of possible non-financial benefits. The important thing in the portfolio review process is that a team can justify what it has done and relate it to the business strategy.

A sharp-eyed reader will note that several of these potential *benefits* are described in terms of *failure*. There is a potential paradox here: *can failure be beneficial?*

Failure is one of those words that English speakers are wired to interpret negatively. One might say that the word is not 'politically correct', and one might attempt to avoid the word so that positive aspects, such as learning, can be emphasized.

Yet faced with a failure, faced with something that didn't work the way one hoped, attempting to avoid the word or redefine its meaning, is intransigent. Rather than avoid the word, I suggest embracing it: accept that something didn't work, salvage what can be salvaged, and mark the experience down to failure. In time one may view the failure differently.

In truth failure and success are simply labels we attach to endeavors. Success feels good, but it contains the seeds of future failure because it tends to alleviate pressure to change. Failure, on the other hand, tends to be a motivator of change.

Non-profit organizations

Perhaps an apology is in order: not all organizations are out to make money and maximize profits. Life is easy in a revenue-earning, profit-maximizing enterprise; at the end of the day almost all decisions can be reduced to the (relatively) simple question: *which will make the most money?*

Lest we forget, such organizations form less than half of the economies of most advanced countries. Even in the USA the government sector (federal, state, city, military, NASA and so on) represents over a third of the total economy[2]. Add in the charitable sector, non-profit cultural organizations and the like, and the profit-maximizing proportion rapidly declines.

---

[2]Exact numbers for the US and other economies are hard to come by, because what one counts as 'government' spending is open to interpretation. Then there is a question of what to count: spending, number of employees, number of customers or some other metric.

Outside of profit maximizers the question of value mutates into a question of values. To put it another way, what does this organization value? Switching to the word 'benefit' helps a little: what will benefit the organization? For non-profit organizations the need to define what constitutes value/benefit is even more important, because there is no default answer. Many good answers are possible, but one needs to look for them.

Ironically, all these organizations have bought into the project model despite vast differences in values and objectives. All have subscribed to the 'on time, on budget, on features' mantra of success. When one considers how divergent these organizations are, this is at once both comforting and troubling!

Yet even within not-for-profit organizations a lot still comes down to money:

- Revenue raising is important to charities, and a lot of that looks very like the commercial sector.
- Non-profit organizations have costs just as the commercial sector does; in fact their need to control costs may be even greater.
- Non-profit organizations have missions to deliver benefit of some description to some target group.

In fact, non-profit organizations may find it easier than profit-maximizers to define what they are trying to do, and what constitutes benefit to the organization, for the very reason that the default option (money) is not available. Because non-profit organizations are forced to define *why* they exist, the benefits they set out to deliver, and who they intend to benefit, they may already have an understanding of what is valuable.

Staff in the non-profit sector who understand why their employer exists and how it brings benefit may well have greater motivation than staff in the for-profit sector. After all, how many readers get out of bed in the morning thinking "Gee, I'm really looking forward to making more profit for my company and shareholders today"?

A workaround

However you define value, it is worth noting that the things you do to identify and increase value are largely the same. A software change that truly generates business benefit will generate business benefit whether or not it is measured.

For example, value can be increased by releasing smaller parts of a software system earlier. In making small parts available earlier, two things happen. Firstly and perhaps most obviously those who use the small part will be able to provide feedback. Such feedback is useful in its own right, because it helps you to decide what you build next. It is also useful because it might cause you to *not* do something.

Secondly, and more importantly, if using the small part creates benefit, it creates benefit irrespective of how that benefit is measured. If that small part of the system generates revenue for the business, that is of benefit. Alternatively, it might improve the quality of the final product without bringing in more revenue. For example, in a healthcare system it might improve the care patients receive, or allow more patients to be examined.

In other words, many of the tools and techniques that can be used to increase value when value is measured in financial terms can also be employed when value is measured by other means.

Not having a watertight definition of value need not be an obstacle to increasing value. Certainly it might make life harder, but it should not stop progress. Indeed, as the earlier discussion of *obliquity* and Goodhart's Law show, watertight targets can create problems too. In fact the unit by which you measure value is secondary: the important thing is that improvements are enacted to increase value, and that the results are monitored.

One workaround for value is to create your own currency to measure it. *Business points* are one such currency. Business points are akin to the *story points* used by many agile teams to estimate effort. Business points can be assigned to potential pieces of work in the same way that effort points are assigned: estimation. Similarly, after the work is complete business points can be used to evaluate the benefit delivered.

While analysis can be used to assess business points, other techniques are also possible, such as simple estimation. Business points can be estimated, perhaps using the same 'planning poker' technique used for effort.

Assigning business points to a piece of work, even when they are estimated, allows tools and techniques to be brought to bear. Changes that will increase the notional business points are also likely to increase the real business benefit and value delivered, irrespective of how such things are ultimately measured.

Thought experiment

Imagine for a moment that a piece of work has a business benefit of €1,000,000, but assume too that you and your team have never heard of the euro. You have no idea what this currency is or how it operates; consequently your team has no way to put a value on the work.

Despite not knowing anything about euros, your team could still attach a value to this work item. Say you attach a value of $200,000. Now you can reason about the work: you can think about how you might release some of the value early, how you might increase the value, or how you might determine its priority relative to other pieces of work. Despite not knowing the work's true value, you can nevertheless bring a range of techniques to bear on the work.

For example, the team might be able to increase the work's value by 50%, to $300,000. Back in the 'real world', despite not knowing the work's actual value, these techniques will have increased the value by 50%, so the work is now worth €1,500,000. So knowing the absolute value is less important than behaving as if you know it.

Conclusion

While I can talk about what value might be, and I can highlight the importance of considering disparate stakeholders, I cannot define 'value' in anything other than abstract terms, because each team and organization is different.

For profit-making organizations it should be relatively easy to create an initial definition of value: money. Consider money to be the default answer to the question "What is value?" until you have a better answer. (Although you may want to define whether it is revenue – money in the door, free cash-flow – surplus cash, profit as defined by your accounting conventions or some other measurement.)

The important thing is that teams and organizations need to decide what is beneficial to them. What does the organization consider valuable?

Once benefit has been defined, even if it is a rough working definition or business points, teams and organizations can set about delivering and increasing benefit.

7. Summarizing the alternative model

Perhaps the most important complementary innovations are the business process changes and organizational co-inventions that new technologies make possible.
Brynjolfsson & McAfee[1]

The digital revolution demands not only that businesses reconsider the products and services they offer: they must also reconsider how these products and services are provided – the business processes and operating practices. This in turn demands that managers and executives reconsider how they think about and conceive the business: its products, services, processes and practices. Unleashing the full benefits of digital requires executives to both learn new mental models and, more importantly, unlearn models.

It has long been recognized – although perhaps too frequently overlooked – that the full benefits of technological change can only be realized when accompanied by business process change. However, technologists and their managers tend focus on processes changes needed by their own users rather than themselves. Technological change also demands that technologists reconsider their own processes and practices.

The project model, and specifically the traditional 'waterfall' model, may well have been appropriate when developing Cobol systems for mainframe computers served by green-screen terminals. However the technologies of information technology have themselves changed.

If your development initiative involves writing Cobol for Z-Series mainframes with a hierarchical database, then maybe you can stay with a waterfall project model. But if you are writing a mobile app with Ruby, Python, Scala, Objective-C or some-such on a Unix system with a NoSql database, then quite possibly your processes also need to change.

Digital is more than computers, more than hard-core tech. Digital includes all the things technological advances have made possible: 'big data', artificial intelligence, the Cloud, cellphone networks and smartphones, drones, sensors, the Internet of Things, social media, the gig economy – the list is endless.

---

[1] *The Second Machine Age*, Brynjolfsson & McAfee, 2014

At a basic level there needs to be recognition that projects are not the only way to organize work. Once this understanding is in place one can think about a new model. This new model is *Continuous Digital*, and it is capability-based: capabilities based on knowledge and skills to exploit software for business benefit in a world of digital business.

In the Continuous model software is an asset, an asset that requires change. Change is ongoing: software lives, so the stop-go project model needs to be rethought. 'Software as an asset' cultivates a continuous value-delivery mindset. Call it *product orientation, business as usual* or *business lines* if that helps. Modern businesses are dependent on software, so modeling your organization so that it is good at creating software has clear business benefits.

Today's businesses are technology businesses, and technology *is* the business. The technology may include more than software, but software is guaranteed to be a large part of it.

Continuous flow, continuous improvement and continuous delivery are not temporary. Benefit needs to be continuous too.

The unifying theme of everything discussed so far is to push decision-making and authority downwards to the team so as to make teams independent, responsible units for delivering business benefit. *Trust the teams.* Treat each team as its own business unit, its own amoeba. Release the teams from assumptions and constraints placed on them before they are born. Let the teams explore and discover the constraints themselves: because technology is changing, the constraints are also in a constant state of flux.

Emergent: strategy, products, design

Although not explicitly stated, it should by now be clear that viewing business strategy, products and software design as emergent properties, rather than preordained and planned artifacts, is essential under this model.

Key points

- The business is technology, and the technology *is* the business.
- 'Software as an Asset'. Software lives and changes: living software requires change because the world around it changes.
- Software needs human help to change; humans need knowledge to change the software; knowledge is valuable.
- Software teams are best organized as amoeba teams within business streams[2].

---

[2] The terms *Ameoba team* and *stream team* are interchangeable.

- Each amoeba is an independent value-seeking team. Each team delivers identifiable business benefit.
- Stable teams grow and split like an amoeba, but unlike an amoeba they sometimes shrink and merge. New teams start as *minimally viable teams.*
- Failure is normal when attempting innovation and change; adopting a 'fail fast, fail cheap, learn and salvage' approach is often appropriate.
- Governance should be through iterative portfolio review based on benefit delivered and strategy.
- Funding should follow a venture capital-style model.

These topics are managerial in nature and do not directly describe how the team does what it does. How teams do what they do in reality can vary greatly: they could run a strict Scrum model, or take a Kanban approach. They might even decide to take a more traditional approach; although I am unsure how they would implement that, I am open to the possibility that it might happen.

To keep things simple – that is, to save me from having to add a lot of detail and use a lot of *ifs, buts* and *maybes* – I am assuming that teams will take an iterative approach. More specifically, I assume that teams will follow my own hybrid method, Xanpan. Full details of this XP-Kanban crossover method can be found in my earlier book *Xanpan – Team-Centric Agile Software Development.* In fact at one point I thought of calling this book Xanpan XL. Any reader looking for more details on how teams should work day-to-day is referred to Xanpan.

II Interlude

Kurt Lewin argued that 'nothing is as practical as a good theory'. The obverse is also true: nothing is as dangerous as a bad theory. Sumantra Ghoshal[3]

Digital business demands new mental models and new reflexes. Management models and reflexes that originated during the industrial era are poor guides in the digital age.

Less sooner is worth more than *more later*. Technology is not something that happens off to the side: it is an integral part of business. Ceasing technology enhancements is nonsensical; requests and opportunities to enhance technology need to be welcomed just as new customer opportunities are welcomed.

Simply exploiting economies of scale will no longer work. Much digital work exhibits diseconomies of scale.

Higher quality is cheaper and faster than low quality.

Before exploring the Continuous Digital model in more detail, some foundations need to laid.

---

[3]*Bad Management Theories are Destroying Good Management Practices*, Sumantra Ghoshal, Academy of Management Learning & Education, 2005, vol.4 no.1, 75–91

8. Diseconomies of scale

Whenever a theory appears to you as the only possible one, take this as a sign that you have neither understood the theory nor the problem which it was intended to solve. Karl Popper, Philosopher, 1902–1994

Without really thinking about it you are not only familiar with the idea of economies of scale: you expect economies of scale. Much of our market economy operates on the assumption that when you buy or spend more you get more per unit of spending. The assumption of economies of scale is not confined to free-market economies: the same assumption underlies much Communist-era planning.

At some stage in our education – even if you never studied economics or operational research – you will have assimilated the idea that if Henry Ford builds a million identical black cars and sells a million cars, then each car will cost less than if Henry Ford manufactures one car, sells one car, builds another very similar car, sells that car, and continues in the same way another 999,998 times.

The net result is that Henry Ford produces cars more cheaply and sells more cars more cheaply so buyers benefit. This is *economies of scale*.

The idea and history of mass production and economies of scale are intertwined. I'm not discussing mass production here, I'm talking *economies of scale* and *diseconomies of scale*.

Milk is cheaper in large cartons

That economies of scale exist is common sense: every day one experiences situations in which buying more of something is cheaper per unit than buying less. For example, you expect that in your local supermarket buying one large carton of milk – say four pints – will be cheaper than buying four one-pint cartons.

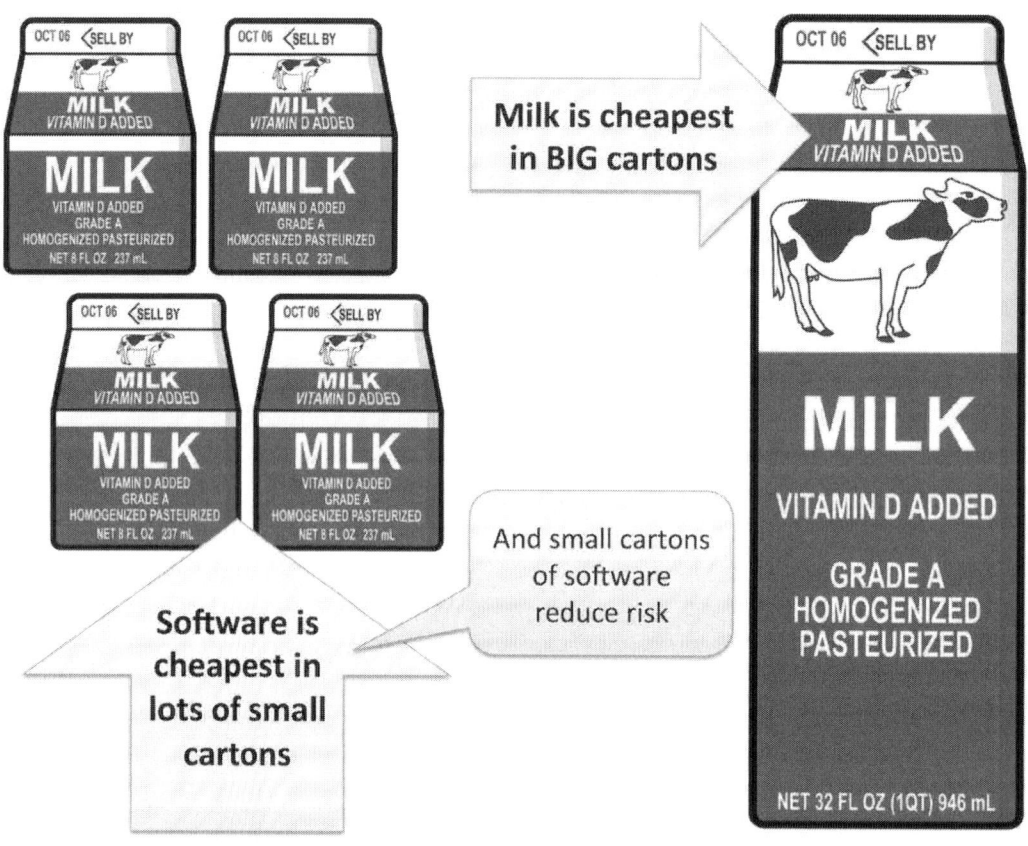

Small cartons of software are cheaper and less risky

So ingrained is this idea that it is newsworthy when shops charge more per unit for larger packs complaints are made. In April 2015 *The Guardian* newspaper in London ran this story:

UK supermarkets dupe shoppers out of hundreds of millions, says Which?

Examples raised by Which? include Tesco flagging the 'special value' of a six-pack of sweetcorn when a smaller pack was proportionately cheaper, and Asda raising the individual price of a product when it was part of a multi-buy offering in order to make the deal more attractive[1].

---

[1]*UK supermarkets dupe shoppers out of hundreds of millions, says Which?*, 21 April 2015, https://www.theguardian.com/business/2015/apr/21/uk-supermarkets-dupe-shoppers-out-of-hundreds-of-millions-says-which

Economies of scale are often cited as the reason for corporate mergers. Buying more allows buyers to extract price concessions from suppliers. Manufacturing more allows the cost per unit to be reduced, and such savings can be passed on to buyers if they buy more. Purchasing departments expect economies of scale.

I am not for one minute arguing that economies of scale do not exist: in some industries economies of scale are very real. Milk production and retail are examples. It is reasonable to assume such economies exist in most mass-manufacturing domains, and they are clearly present in marketing and branding.

But – and this is a big 'but'...

Software development does not have economies of scale

In all sorts of ways, software development has diseconomies of scale. If software development was sold by the pint, then a four-pint carton of software would not just cost four times the price of a one-pint carton, it would cost *far more*.

Once software is built there are massive economies of scale in reselling (and reusing) the same software and services built on it. Producing the first piece of software has massive marginal costs; producing the second identical copy has a cost so close to zero it is unmeasurable – Ctrl-C, Ctrl-V.

Diseconomies abound in the world of software development. Once development is complete, once the marginal costs of one copy are paid, then economies of scale dominate, because marginal cost is as close to zero as to make no difference.

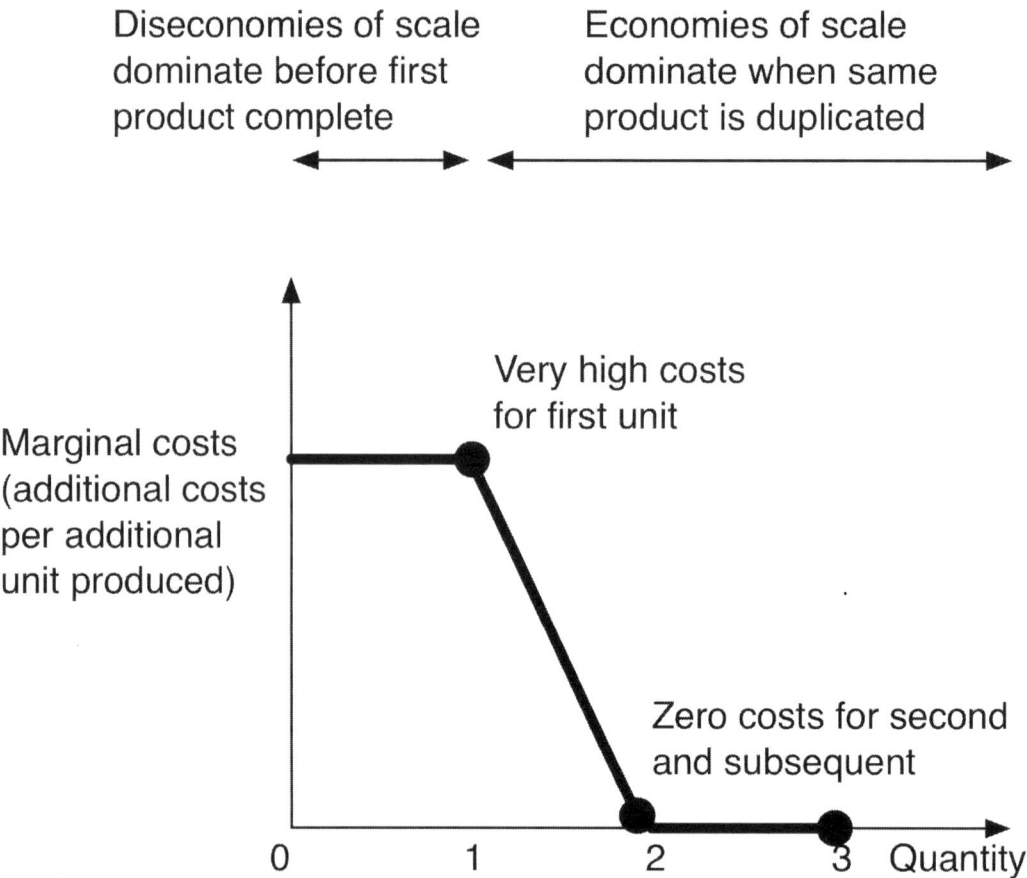

Diseconomies of scale and high marginal costs give way to economies of scale and negligible marginal costs

Evidence of diseconomies

Software development diseconomies of scale have been observed for some years. Cost estimation models like COCOMO actually include an adjustment for diseconomies of scale. But the implications of diseconomies are rarely factored into management thinking – rather, economies-of-scale thinking prevails.

Small development teams frequently outperform large teams: five people working as a tight team will be far more productive per person than a team of 50, or even 15. The Quattro Pro development team in the early 1990s is probably the best-documented example of this[2].

[2]*Organizational Patterns of Agile Software Development*, Coplien & Harrison, 2005

A more recent study of open source software development stated that:

> 'We find strong evidence for a negative relation between team size and productivity. ...we further conclude that all of the studied projects represent diseconomies of scale, exhibiting diminishing returns to scale[3].'

The more lines of code a piece of software has, the more difficult it is to add an enhancement or fix a bug. Putting a fix into a system with a million lines of code can easily be more than ten times harder than fixing a system with 100,000 lines.

As much as software engineers love the Lego-brick analogy, software does not scale like Lego. Software exhibits power-law characteristics[4]. Some parts of the system become more central. They are connected to more parts and changed far more often. Making multiple simultaneous changes to these parts is difficult, so changes must be sequenced. Consequently bringing more people to bear on the code does not make change happen faster – it happens more slowly.

Experience of *work in progress* limits shows that doing less at any one time gets more done overall.

Projects that set out to be *big* have far higher costs and lower productivity per deliverable unit than small systems. Capers Jones' 2008 book contains some tables of productivity per function point that illustrate this. It is worth noting that the biggest systems are usually military, and they have an atrocious productivity rate, not to mention horrendous schedule slips. The Airbus A400 transport was reportedly four years late and €5 billion over budget, while the Lockheed F35 fighter is reportedly seven years late and $163 billion over budget[5].

Testing

Testing is another area where diseconomies of scale play out. Testing a piece of software with two changes requires more tests, time and money than the sum of testing each change in isolation.

When two changes are tested together the combination of both changes needs to be tested as well. As more changes are added and more tests are needed, there is a combinatorial

---

[3]*From Aristotle to Ringelmann: a large-scale analysis of team productivity and coordination in Open Source Software projects*, Scholtes, Mavrodiev, Schweitzer, Empirical Software Engineering volume 21 issue 2, April 2016, pre-print version available https://www.sg.ethz.ch/media/publication_files/paper_bQeEC8G.pdf

[4]*Understanding the Shape of Java Software*, Gareth J Baxter, James Noble, Marcus Frean and Ewan D. Tempero, Proceedings of the 21th Annual ACM SIGPLAN Conference on Object-Oriented Programming, Systems, Languages, and Applications, OOPSLA 2006, October 22-26, 2006, Portland, Oregon, USA

[5]https://en.wikipedia.org/wiki/Lockheed_Martin_F-35_Lightning_II#Program_cost_overruns_and_delays

explosion in the number of test cases required, and thus a greater than proportional change in the time and money needed to undertake the tests. But testing departments regularly lump multiple changes together for testing in an effort to exploit economies of scale. In attempting to exploit non-existent economies of scale, testing departments increase costs, risks and time needed.

If a test should find a bug that needs to be fixed, finding the offending code in a system that has fewer changes is far easier than finding and fixing a bug when there are more changes to be considered.

Working on larger endeavors means waiting longer – and probably writing more code – before you ask for feedback or user validation when compared to smaller endeavors. As a result there is more that could be 'wrong', more that users don't like, more spent, more that needs changing and more to complicate the task of applying fixes.

Cost of delay

Waiting is an interesting case because it has a cost. The longer it takes to deliver a product, the greater the *cost of delay*[6]. For example, the more time the product spends in development, the greater the costs, the more time it spends in development, the less time it spends in the market, the less time it is in the market before competitors arrive, and so on.

(To my mind *cost of delay* would be better called *benefit foregone* or *value foregone.*)

Those who have worked on agile teams that use small stories, or user stories, will have noticed that small stories flow through the system and are delivered sooner than large stories. For this reason agile teams often want lots of small stories rather than fewer larger stories. Unfortunately they are often met by product managers who claim that "The customer wants all or nothing. The customer will not accept anything less than everything they asked for."

Cost of delay means that delivering something sooner, even if it is smaller, may well be worth more than delivering a big thing later. Even if creating the big thing enjoys economies of scale – which is doubtful – and is cheaper per unit (line of code?) than a small thing, the revenue lost because of late delivery needs to be considered.

Batch size

Software development works best in small batch sizes. There are a few places where software development does exhibit economies of scale, in which case large batch sizes make sense, but on most occasions diseconomies of scale are the norm. (Reinertsen[7] has some figures on batch

---

[6]Don Reinertsen discusses cost of delay in depth in his book *Principles of Product Development*, 2009.
[7]Don Reinertsen discusses cost of delay in depth in his book *Principles of Product Development*, 2009.

size that also support the diseconomies-of-scale argument.)

This happens because each time you add to software work the marginal cost per unit increases:

- Add a fourth team member to a team of three and the communication paths increase from three to six.
- Add one feature to a release and you have one feature to test; add two features and you have three tests to run: two features to test plus the interaction between the two.

In part this is because human minds can only hold so much complexity. As the complexity increases (more changes, more code) our cognitive load increases, mental processing slows down, people make more mistakes and work takes longer.

Economies of scope and specialization are specific forms of economies of scale and again, on the whole, software development has diseconomies of scope and diseconomies of specialization:

- Teams should focus first and broaden later when they have a working product.
- Generalists are usually preferable to specialists: technologies that demand in-depth expertise should be avoided if possible.

However, be careful: once the software is developed then economies of scale are rampant. The world switches. Software that has been built probably exhibits more economies of scale than any other product known to man. In economic terms the marginal cost of producing the first instance are extremely high, but the marginal costs of producing an identical copy (production) are so close to zero as to be zero: Ctrl-C Ctrl-V.

Think diseconomies, think small

First of all you need to rewire your brain: almost everyone in the advanced world has been brought up with economies of scale since school. You need to start thinking *diseconomies of scale.*

Second, whenever faced with a problem where you feel the urge to 'go bigger', run in the opposite direction: go smaller.

Third, take each and every opportunity to go small.

Fourth, get good at working 'in the small': optimize your processes, tools and approaches to do lots of small things rather than a few big things.

Fifth – and this is the killer: know that most people don't get this at all. In fact, it's worse...

9. Diseconomies and risk

Only those who will risk going too far can possibly find out how far one can go.
T. S. Elliot, poet, 1888-1965

There is another problem with undertaking large packages of work: taking on larger work packages increases risk.

Suppose 100ml of milk is off. If the 100ml is in one small carton then you have lost a litre of milk. If the 100ml is in a four-litre carton you have lost four litres.

Suppose your developers incorporate one bug a year that slips through testing and crashes the users' machine. Suppose you know this, so in an effort to catch the bug you do more testing. To keep testing costs low you need to test more software, so you do a bigger release with more changes – economies-of-scale thinking. That actually makes the testing harder, but...

Suppose you do one release a year. That release blue-screens the machine. The user is now seeing every release you make crashing their machine: 100% of your releases create problems.

If instead you release weekly, one release a year still crashes the machine, but the user sees 51 releases a year that don't. Less than 2% of your releases create problems.

Consider testing too. Suppose the team does one change a week. With a single release, final testing cannot occur until the end when all combinations of changes can be tested together. Thus testing is more complex, and if a defect is found it could be in any of 52 changes.

Alternatively, if each change is tested and released, then testing is simplified and each test occurs on a released build. Any problems found are confined to the most recent change. Source code management is simplified too.

A project example

Imagine you have a large piece of work, let's call it Project A. The project is worth £1 million and you believe it has a 30% risk of failure and that the risk is evenly distributed across the entire duration of the work. Thus the risk weighting is £300,000.

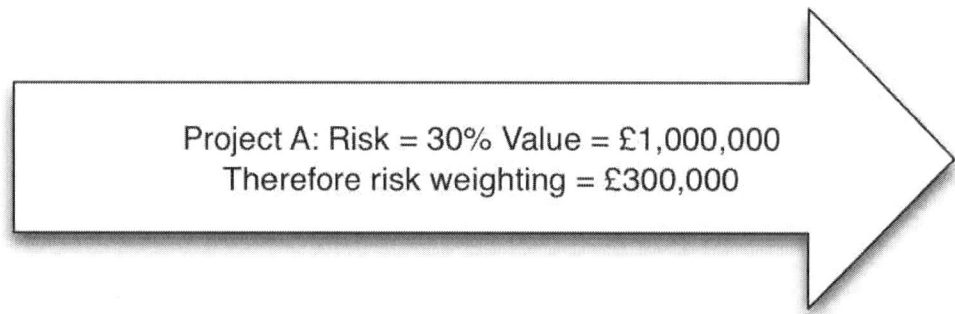

Risk on one large project

Now consider splitting the work into two smaller pieces of work, Project B and Project C. Each is worth half the original value and carries half the risk. Consequently, each has a risk weighting of £75,000.

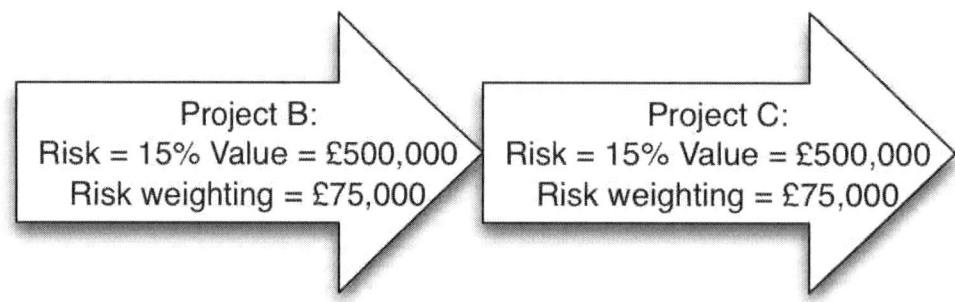

Risk on two smaller projects

In practice Project C might still depend on Project B, but if Project B goes wrong then Project C can be canceled before any more is spent. Alternatively, if Projects B and C can be split so that there are no dependencies, then each can succeed or fail on their own terms without endangering the other.

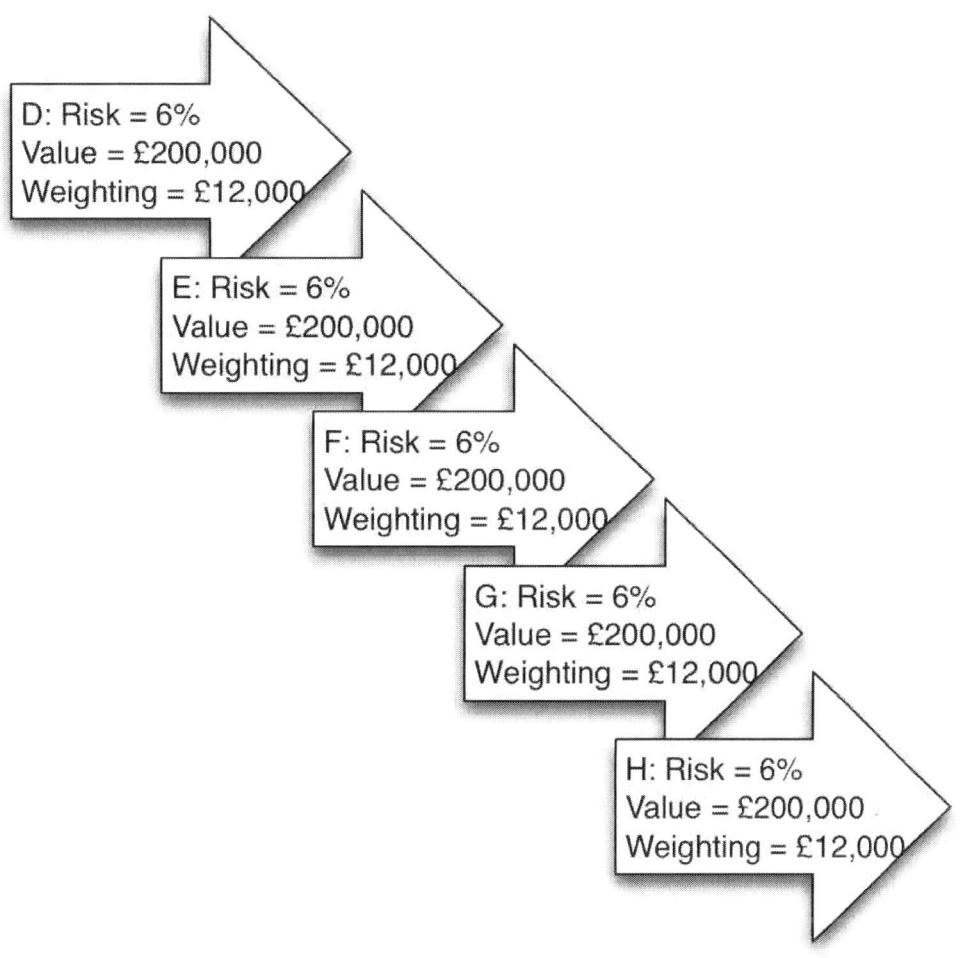

Risk on five smaller projects

The approach can be carried further. Suppose instead Project A is split into five pieces of work, E, F, G, H and I, each one carrying a fifth of the value – £200,000 – and a fifth of the risk, 6%. Each now has a risk weighting of £12,000. The total risk is now 5 x £12,000 = £60,000. By dividing the work into five pieces the risk weighting has been cut five-fold.

While risk is unlikely to be evenly distributed, the argument still stands. Teams should aim to spread risk evenly over the course of work. It is unlikely to be evenly distributed to start with: over time teams need to learn to reduce risk and spread it more evenly.

Some risks are associated with the start of work, such as an immature team or an invalid business case. Teams should aim to expose and address these risks early rather than tolerate them until they do damage. Other risks gravitate towards the end of the work, for example testing and deployment: such risks need to be brought forward.

Conclusion

Hopefully the message here is clear: recognizing diseconomies of scale and working on lots of 'small' reduces risks. Small and regular releases expose early hidden risks sooner. Small regular releases also allow the team to experience tail-end risks sooner.

10. Living with diseconomies

It is difficult to get a man to understand something, when his salary depends upon his not understanding it! Upton Sinclair, American writer and politician, 1878-1968

Unfortunately, economies-of-scale thinking prevails. People assume economies of scale apply without thinking.

In any existing organization, particularly a large corporation, the majority of people who make decisions are out and out economies-of-scale thinkers. They expect that going big is cheaper than going small and they force this view on others, especially software technology people.

Many senior people got to where they are today because of economies of scale and many of these companies exist because of economies of scale; if they are good at economies of scale they are good at doing what they do.

Consider banking, for example. Banking, both retail and investment, exhibits many economies of scale. These occur in marketing, where the same brand may offer many services, and in cross-selling: sign a customer for a current account, later sell her a loan, then a mortgage, then life insurance.

Economies of scale occur in capital funding too. Some have even argued that size alone, while making banks riskier, also makes their funding cheaper, because governments must underwrite 'too big to fail' banks[1].

There are those who claim that modern banks are disguised software companies. Yet those individuals who reach positions of authority in a bank will do so because they are good bankers rather than good technologists. Consequently they will have spent a career exploiting economies-of-scale thinking. When confronted with technology concerns they will cling to that which has brought success in the past: economies of scale. Inevitably this will place them in conflict when faced with a problem that requires the reverse mindset.

In the world of software development this mindset is a recipe for failure and under-performance. The conflict between economies-of-scale thinking and diseconomies-of-scale working will create tension and conflict.

---

[1] *The Bankers' New Clothes*, Admati & Hellwig, 2013

And projects...

Part of the problem with projects is that they are – almost by definition – large batches of work. The administrative work involved in creating a project, getting it approved, bringing the resources together, making the resources work together effectively and then at the end unwinding all the temporary structures means that the project model only makes sense when projects are large.

Complicating matters, it can be hard to disentangle costs of the organization from actual development costs. Some organizations demand that all work is conducted under the project model; consequently, whether the initiative is small or large, two weeks of effort or two years, both initiatives require the same preparation, paperwork and approval.

In the language of economists both initiatives have fixed costs (the start-up costs), but the longer initiative will have lower average costs, because the same fixed start-up costs are amortized over more production units. However, because the larger initiative requires more coordination, the marginal costs per unit will be higher. Consequently it can be hard to do true cost comparisons between endeavors.

Companies seem to like projects: projects imply change and change implies growth. This is much more attractive than 'business as usual'. But the need for projects to be large means that small is not an option, and therefore the stakes are high and the risks large.

Unfortunately software development lacks economies of scale. Time and time again building software in the small is more efficient than doing so in the big.

> *Software is cheapest in small quantities*

There is an inherent conflict between the best way of running a project and the best way of organizing software development endeavors.

Making small decisions

In part big-batch projects are an attempt to maximize the value of the most precious limited resource: senior management time. Getting time with a senior manager is difficult: their interest in discussing anything less than $10 million is negligible (replace this with a relevant figure for your organization). So why bother them with small pieces of work? You are more likely to get a few minutes of their time to approve a $10 million project than to discussion 100 small $100,000 pieces of work.

For software development to exploit the rampant diseconomies of scale, executive authority needs to be devolved downwards so that small decisions get made efficiently when needed, rather than batched into single big decisions.

Optimize for small

Diseconomies of scale mean organizational structures need to be reconsidered. Individuals, teams and organizations need to learn to think small. They need to start looking for *small*:

> Teams need to organize themselves for lots of small.

> Organizations, teams, processes and practices need to be optimized for small.

Because of diseconomies of scale it is necessary to rethink the traditional economies-of-scale-based organization structures and create structures and processes that are optimized for small. Only by optimizing for small can organizations and teams exploit diseconomies of scale.

Work processes need to be optimized for small pieces of work – small batch sizes and small items. This means that big activities (such as set-up, teardown, one-off reviews) need to be removed. Things that are expensive and which get minimized (like sign-off and final test cycles) need to be removed or rethought so that they can be efficient in the small.

Each of those small pieces of work needs to demonstrate potential value and be evaluated later for value delivered.

Kelly's Laws

I have two personal laws:

> *Kelly's first law of project complexity:* Project scope will always increase in proportion to resources.

The more people, time and money you have, the more your project will attempt to do.

> *Kelly's second law of project complexity:* Inside every large project there is a small one struggling to get out.

Look for the small piece of work struggling to get out, then work to deliver that early.

What if?

I increasingly wonder where else diseconomies of scale rule? They can't be unique to software development. In my more fanciful moments, I wonder if diseconomies of scale are the norm in all knowledge work.

Even if they aren't, as more and more work comes to resemble software development – because of the central role of individual knowledge and the use of software tools – then I would expect to see more and more examples of diseconomies of scale.

11. Schedules

85% of companies do not quantify cost of delay. Reinertsen, 2009[1]

Six months' delay can be worth 33% of lifecycle profits. McKinsey/Reinertsen, *Electronic Business*, 1983

"When does the customer need it?" is a far more important question than "When will the developers have it ready?" Business needs should drive schedules, rather than engineering estimates. Time is but one constraint of many that engineers need to work within.

The task in hand is *not to build the best solution possible, but to build the best solution possible within the constraints.* Understanding the constrains is part of the work.

Engineers need to create solutions that fit within business schedules. That does not mean cutting corners or shipping with bugs or technical liabilities. It is the art of the possible and it's what engineers have always done.

Work should be guided by business benefit. Since benefit changes over time, that means that one needs to understand how the value created changes with different delivery dates. (It also means 'yesterday' and 'tomorrow' are not particularly useful demands, as a later chapter will discuss.)

Once one starts discussing business value, it is a logical next step to ask *does value change over time?*

In most cases one can assume that 'sooner means more money, more revenue', but continuing this train of thought, one can ask "Does revenue decline with time?" and "Is there a date beyond which there is no revenue?". I like to sketch dates against value or revenue in a graph I call a *time-value profile* – examples follow later.

The changing value over time is usually called *opportunity cost of delay*, since later delivery dates usually mean less value and/or more costs. Indeed, I don't think 'cost of delay' is the best name for this idea: I'd rather it was called something like 'benefit foregone through delay', but 'cost of delay' is the name we have.

---

[1] Don Reinertsen discusses cost of delay in depth in his book *Principles of Product Development*, 2009.

Once the discussion shifts to the value unlocked by different delivery dates, it should become clear that development schedules should be driven by value rather than by developer estimates. Effort estimates are merely an engineering tool to explore different options. Deadlines should come from the anticipated commercial results.

Rather than saying:

> "How long will X take to build?"

One need to ask:

> "Given that there is M money to capture, in timeframe T, what can we build for that much money in that much time and have a respectable profit left?"

Time and money are inherently linked. Everyone gets that more time creates more costs, but fewer people get that more time probably means less revenue.

To rephrase the question:

> "How much of X can we build in time Y and how much of the total potential value M will that capture?"

Worked example

Let me give an example to show how a cost of delay analysis – with value estimates – can be used to substitute for effort estimates. So here goes, I'm putting on my economist hat... let's set up the scenario.

Image it's Christmas, and at one of those family gatherings you see Uncle George, who works for a successful start-up. George says the back-end he has been working on is great and has a nice REST API. The start-up wants to grow an ecosystem and the company is about to open up the API to third-party apps. For a few months from 1 February the start-up will pay a small finder's fee to third parties for each customer they bring to the platform.

Back in the office on 2 January you make some calls and find everything Uncle George said is true. In fact the start-up is falling over itself to help: they are desperate for apps and customers. You have an opportunity and you have at least a four-week head start on any competitor.

Some quick 'what if' calculations tell you there is €10,000 a week to be made. But you also know that as competitors come into the market the finder's fee will decline. As you have a four-week head start you probably have four weeks from the start of February before your revenue starts to fall off.

Further analysis leads you to conclude that competitors will steal increasing chunks of your revenue: you think it will decline by €1,000 a week after February. Thus you can draw the following graph:

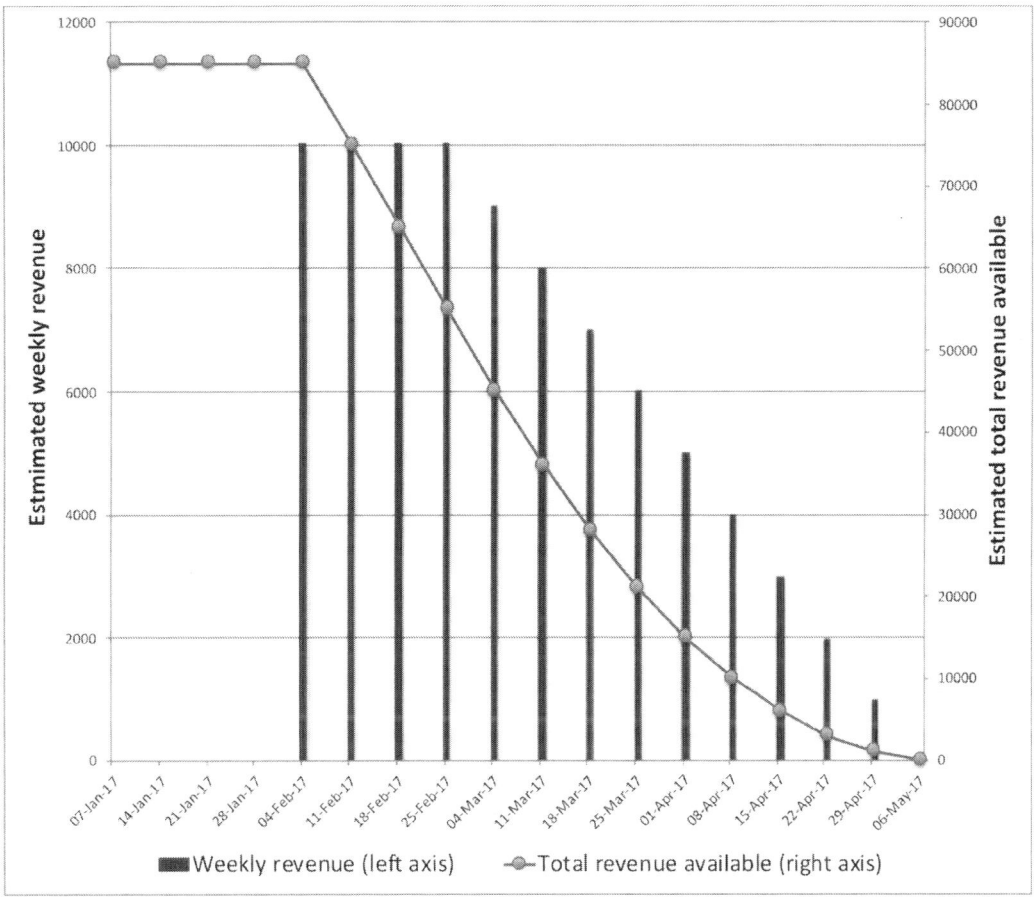

Time-value profile showing the change in value over time

Week ending	Weekly revenue	Total revenue available
7-Jan	0	85000
14-Jan	0	85000
21-Jan	0	85000
28-Jan	0	85000
4-Feb	10000	85000
11-Feb	10000	75000
18-Feb	10000	65000
25-Feb	10000	55000
4-Mar	9000	45000
11-Mar	8000	36000
18-Mar	7000	28000
25-Mar	6000	21000
1-Apr	5000	15000
08-Apr	4000	10000
15-Apr	3000	6000
22-Apr	2000	3000
29-Apr	1000	1000
6-May	0	0

The blue bars show the weekly revenue, while the red line shows the total lifetime revenue, the lifetime being from the start of February to early May. What happens after May is uncertain, so to play it safe you have assumed no revenue at all.

Note that this chart uses two axes: the one on the left is for the blue bars, the one on the right for the red line. The red line is important: it shows the maximum revenue you could make, and so forms an upper boundary.

It doesn't matter whether you release your product tomorrow or on 31 January: there is no extra revenue to be made during January. As long as you have a product in the market on 1 February you can start to capture some value. If you have a fully functional product then you can capture €10,000 a week.

The delivery date is important: earlier is better, but so is the amount of product. Since revenue declines from March onwards, delivering something smaller sooner may well make more total revenue than delivering more later. Less (functionality) may well mean more (revenue).

As you can see, releasing a product at any time before the end of January will result in €85,000 of revenue in total. After this, the later the product is released, the less revenue it will make. *Your deadline is not a binary event: it is an elastic range of options that each produce a different outcome.* The graph and chart show how revenue changes with different dates.

Time is money, but money is both cost and revenue: the longer you spend developing your product, the greater the costs. More importantly, though, if the product is not in the market by 1 February you are losing revenue. The longer you go without a product, the greater the costs and the lower the revenue.

This is a simple model: like any good economist I have confined my analysis and assumed that all other things are equal. Specifically I have assumed that other competitors do not spot the opportunity before 1 February, that your product could grab the entire market on day one without a ramp-up time, and that even launching in March, when there are other competitors in the market, you can still grab sizable market share on day one.

Every model requires certain assumptions; the assumptions made here do not invalidate the model. The reader is encouraged to create their own model where they can relax these assumptions and consider the results.

Adding effort estimation

This analysis does not use any effort estimates, but does use value estimates. Once one understands value it is logical to consider costs next.

In the first instance, armed with this analysis, you go to your development team and instead of saying:

> "How long will it take to build this?"

You say:

> "Given this analysis, what can we build in the next four weeks that can capture some of this value?"

It is not a question of "Can you build X?", but "What can you build in this time for this much money?"

Ideally the team would deliver a fully functional and perfect product in time to capture all the value. Since this is not possible, the aim is to capture some (hopefully lots) of the value.

Let's suppose that you and the team quickly envisage a product, one that can be rolled out in stages, say 10% per week. Even the first 10% will be useful. Let's assume a perfect correlation between the percentage of product built and the revenue captured and add this to the model.

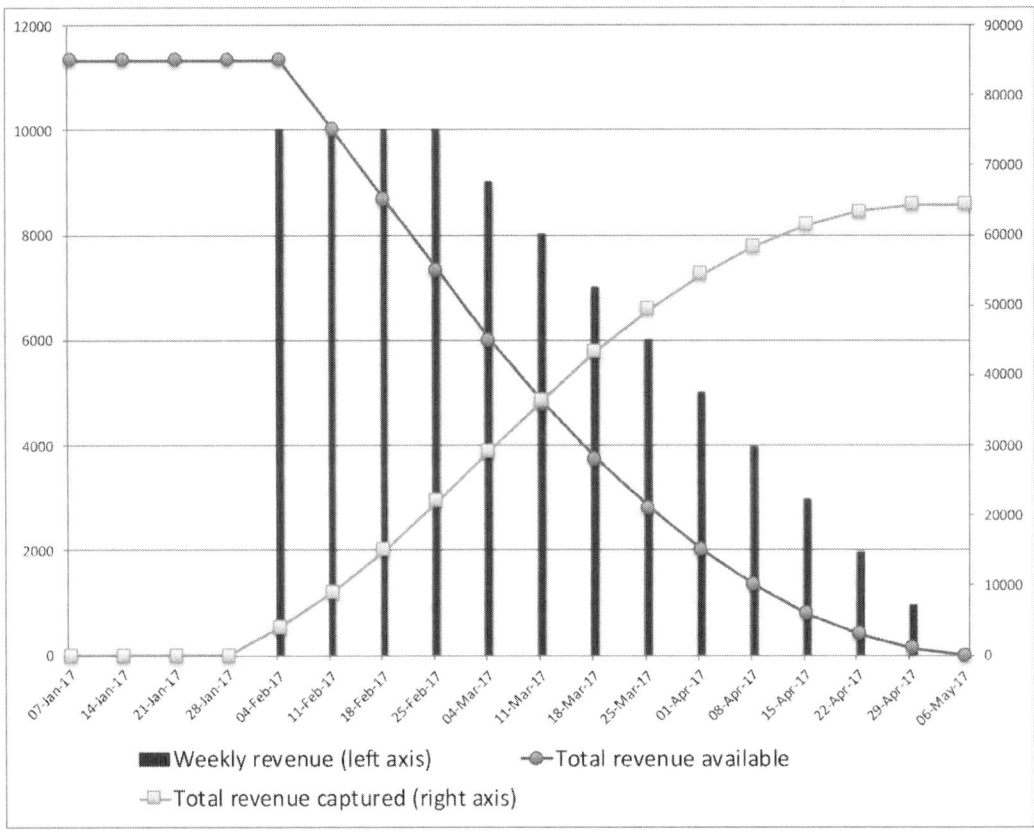

Value and revenue over time

Week ending	Total revenue available	Total revenue captured
07-Jan-17	85000	0
14-Jan-17	85000	0
21-Jan-17	85000	0
28-Jan-17	85000	0
04-Feb-17	85000	4000
11-Feb-17	75000	9000
18-Feb-17	65000	15000
25-Feb-17	55000	22000
04-Mar-17	45000	29200
11-Mar-17	36000	36400
18-Mar-17	28000	43400
25-Mar-17	21000	49400
01-Apr-17	15000	54400
08-Apr-17	10000	58400

Week ending	Total revenue available	Total revenue captured
15-Apr-17	6000	61400
22-Apr-17	3000	63400
29-Apr-17	1000	64400

Notice that in this model it is impossible to capture all the €85,000 of potential revenue, because the product cannot be ready in full on 1 February. If you wait until the product is 100% complete before releasing it, it will be mid-March and you will only make €28,000 in total. This contrasts with the €64,400 you could make by launching with reduced functionality earlier – that is, launching a smaller and incomplete product earlier allows the capture of €36,400 more.

I could have relaxed some of my assumptions and enhanced the model, but I'm keeping this simple. You can also play 'what if' games: for example, what if you halted development at the halfway point?

> If development halted at the beginning of February at 50% done and the product remained in use until May, then it would generate €41,500 of revenue (64% of the total that could be made).

> Plus there would be savings in development costs. More importantly, releasing people early might allow them to work on other initiatives with a higher return on investment.

Higher development costs do not invalidate the model. They may invalidate the business case for building the product, but the model is independent of the numbers. Having such a model allows value and costs to be compared overt time. After all, the product only has an anticipated lifespan of three months. Once March arrives the product revenues are falling, so why would you continue to invest?

There are many directions in which you can take this analysis and I'm not denying that effort and cost estimates have a role to play in a complete analysis. However, benefit estimates and cost of delay analysis can be performed without any effort estimates: when value analysis is available it can be used to inform the effort estimation process.

Analysis costs too

Time-value profiles and cost-of-delay analysis open up new techniques to complement the many that already exist. However, while it is always rational to request 'more analysis',

analysis is not free. Typically analysis is conducted up front before development begins. Therefore the clock is already ticking, and cost-of-delay is creating additional costs by doing the analysis.

To put this another way: the cost of analysis is not just the analyst's time or the research reports they need to buy: analysis also costs because it delays the release of the product. When analysis turns into paralysis, these costs are rampant.

Therefore work with rough analysis to start off with; use estimates and approximate numbers. If these numbers look good then begin development and continue to refine the analysis.

Once the team is in development then cost estimates will be more accurate, and once the product begins shipping market value estimates can be tested with real customers.

When a business case is strong, where the return on investment is clearly high, then it is worth taking more risk. In contrast, when the business case is weak or marginal, it might be better to avoid the initiative altogether.

Summary

Time-value profiles allow you to assess the impact of different delivery dates, and from these teams can work backwards to find what can be built in the time available. More importantly, it allows tradeoffs to be visualized and discussed.

The underlying aim is to deliver a little something sooner: a little something will allow some of the potential value to be captured. In capturing value early it will directly improve return on investment calculations. In addition, smaller early releases also allow for market validation and customer feedback, which can further increase value over the long term.

One might counter and say that it is better to delay launch and grab a greater share of the potential revenue later. Such an argument can be investigated and evaluated using a time-value profile. Each case needs to be examined individually. As much as I would like to say "Launch sooner and grab a smaller piece of a bigger pie", such advice does not hold in every case.

Delivering a smaller product earlier does not prevent the release of a bigger and more functional product later. The route to the bigger product will lie through the smaller one. Releasing a smaller product initially will also help to reduce risk, and reducing risk is valuable in itself.

12. Time-value profiles and elastic deadlines

Nothing in life is to be feared, it is only to be understood. Now is the time to understand more, so that we may fear less. Marie Curie

Once one starts to understand *opportunity cost of delay*, then the central question for development efforts changes from:

"When will it be ready?"

To:

"When do you need it by?"

Then:

"What is the difference in value from different delivery dates?"

There is nothing wrong with deadlines, but deadlines should come from business needs, not effort estimates that are magically transformed into deadlines. When deadlines are business-driven they are driven by the need to capture value, and the value that can be captured varies over time. Therefore:

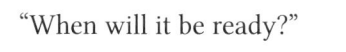 *Deadlines are elastic by value*

Different 'end' dates result in different values. Understanding the tradeoffs allows engineers and non-engineers to consider options, design solutions and commercial tradeoffs. There is no single 'right' design, approach or product offering: many are possible, and knowing the constraints allows one to choose appropriately.

Worked example

Imagine you run a software development team for a toy business. Two internal customers come to you and ask for similar but different products to be developed. Both customers, Alex and Si, present you with a story and an estimated value:

Alex's request. As a toy retailer I want an app that allows kids to select from my special range so that their parents can buy. Estimated value: $355,000.

Si's request. As a toy retailer I want an app that allows kids to make lists of toys they want so their parents can buy. Estimated value: $1,060,000.

Although these two stories look similar, let's assume that there is very little overlap and therefore no opportunity to combine any of the work.

Following frequently recommended agile practice, Si's request would be prioritized above Alex's and work would begin because it has a higher value. Now supposes that Alex complains:

"But my request is smaller, my story has a better cost-benefit payoff, it gives a bigger bang for the buck."

So your team take some time and analyze the work required for both apps. Leave aside for the moment that undertaking analysis would itself take time and would delay the start of work; leave aside too the question of whether such estimates are accurate. Your team comes back with:

Alex's request will take four weeks to build.

Si's request will take six weeks to build.

On this basis:

Alex's payoff: $355,000 / 4 = $88,750 per week

Si's payoff: $1,060,000 / 6 = $176,666 per week

Clearly Si's story represents the better value for money.

Alex doesn't give up easily, though, and next points out that the company doesn't need to choose between these two applications: it can have both! He points out that his request is aimed at the Halloween market, so the development team could do his request and then do Si's. Of course Si points out that his application is aimed at Christmas and is also time-critical.

It is now September 1st and both customers have modified their stories:

> *Alex's request.* As a toy retailer I want an app that allows kids to select from my special HALLOWEEN range so that their parents can buy. Value: $355,000. Time to build: four weeks.

> *Si's request.* As a toy retailer I want an app that allows kids to make lists of toys they want SANTA TO BRING so that their parents can buy. Value: $1,060,000. Time to build: six weeks.

Options

At this point the portfolio board has a range of options it could choose from:

A. Do Halloween and forget Santa

B. Do Santa and forget Halloween

In revenue and cost-benefit terms, if the company is to choose only one story to build then Si's Santa App is the one to build.

C. Do Halloween and then Santa

D. Do Santa and then Halloween

Potentially these options allow both Si and Alex to get what they want. But both options require more analysis.

E. Change the estimates

As silly as it sounds, people not only suggest this but do it when faced with such problems in real life. Changing the estimates might remove the immediate problem, but as with other 'kicking the can down the road' solutions, could well store up future problems.

Given the inaccuracies common in the estimation process, this strategy might not be as irrational as it initially sounds. Even so, changing estimates to fit the time available without corresponding flexibility elsewhere might simply increase risk, because it hides a potential problem.

Indeed, if estimates are to be changed to fit the desired outcome, one might question the point of creating the estimates in the first place – especially since the time taken to create the estimates could have been used more productively.

F. Do both and pray

Although seldom acknowledged or listed as a policy option, sticking one's head in the sand and hoping for the best is a common strategy, albeit one that rarely brings success.

G. Add more people

Obviously adding more people would increase costs, so more analysis would be needed. But before that analysis is undertaken there are more practical questions: could more people be recruited in time? Would they become productive enough quickly enough to make a difference?

The well-known Brook's Law[1] states:

> 'Adding manpower to a late software project makes it later.'

Even trying to recruit more people will create delay, because technical software recruitment usually requires existing technical staff to review resumés and conduct interviews, and such work takes them away from cutting code and developing product.

Since identifying and recruiting suitable new staff members is not guaranteed, such a strategy will increase risk: existing developer capacity will be surrendered in the hope of adding more capacity.

H. Parallel work

Unless more people are available, running the work as two parallel streams does not offer any immediate advantage. Indeed such an approach will make for more management work, and could create bottlenecks if two work streams require the same resources.

Asking individuals to undertake two different pieces of work (multitasking) is commonly thought to reduce overall effectiveness. Some parallel work might be beneficial, but more analysis would be required.

I. Reuse code

---

[1] *The Mythical Man Month*, Brooks, 1975

Were the development team to be an outsource provider, there would be questions of intellectual property rights that might prevent this option if Alex and Si were from different clients. However in the scenario described this is not an issue.

As before, more analysis is really needed to understand key issues. How much code of the Halloween app could potentially be reused for Santa? How much of the Santa app would still need development from scratch? More importantly, how much extra time would be spent building Alex's Halloween app for reuse? The effort estimates need to be revisited.

More importantly, linking the apps through a reuse strategy significantly increases risk. While the apps are considered separately or built in sequence, the second can proceed even if the first fails. However, where reuse enters the picture, the second app becomes dependent on the first: failure to complete the first app places the second at high risk.

There are overtones of parallel work in writing for reuse. Focus is diluted, as individual developers are asked to deliver towards two goals simultaneously. There is good reason to believe that 'second-guessing the future' leads to over-engineering.

Many of these options require more analysis. Such analysis takes time and will delay development work. As all analysis is based on assumptions and available data, should assumptions or existing data prove wrong, then the analysis will be flawed.

What is needed is a lightweight analysis technique that can be used with incomplete data. One such tool is a time-value profile, which builds on the idea of *cost of delay*.

Time-value profile

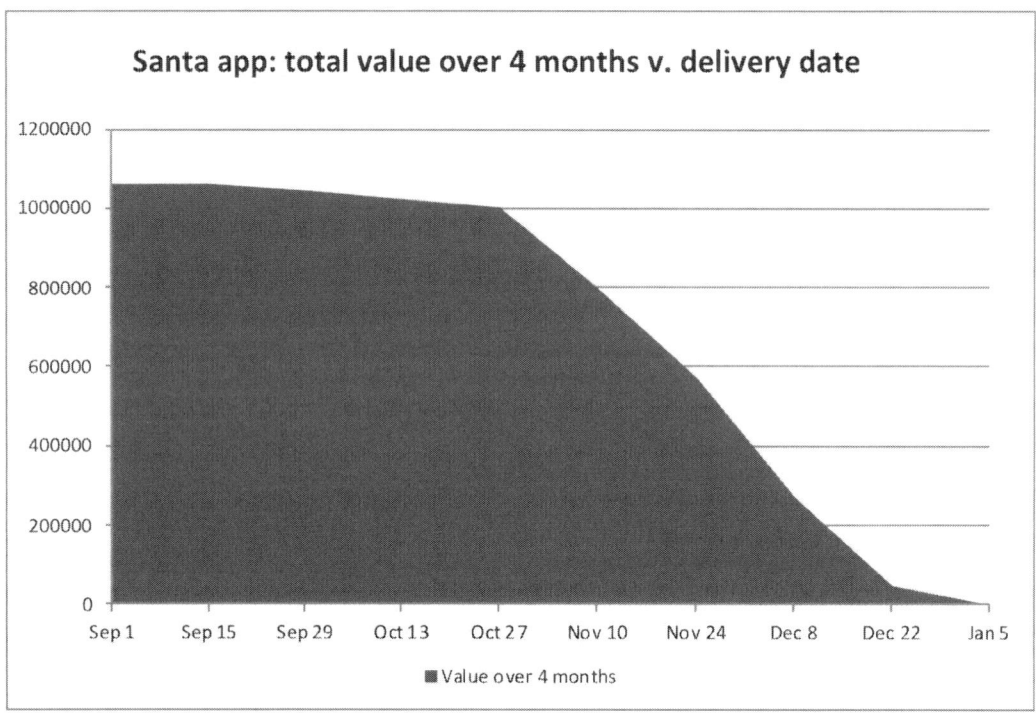

Time-value profile of the Santa Claus app as of 1 September

The first time-value profile graph shows the lifetime value of a product as it varies by delivery date. From this graph it can be seen that the stated $1,060,000 of value can only be recognized if the app can be delivered to market before 15 September. At any date after this date the revenue generated will be less.

To borrow from food retailing, you can think of this time-value profile as the equivalent of 'best before' and 'use by' dates. In food retailing some food is marked with a 'best before' date: consuming the food before this date delivers maximum taste. Food marked with a 'use by' date will not only taste bad, but may actually be harmful after this date, as in the case of shellfish.

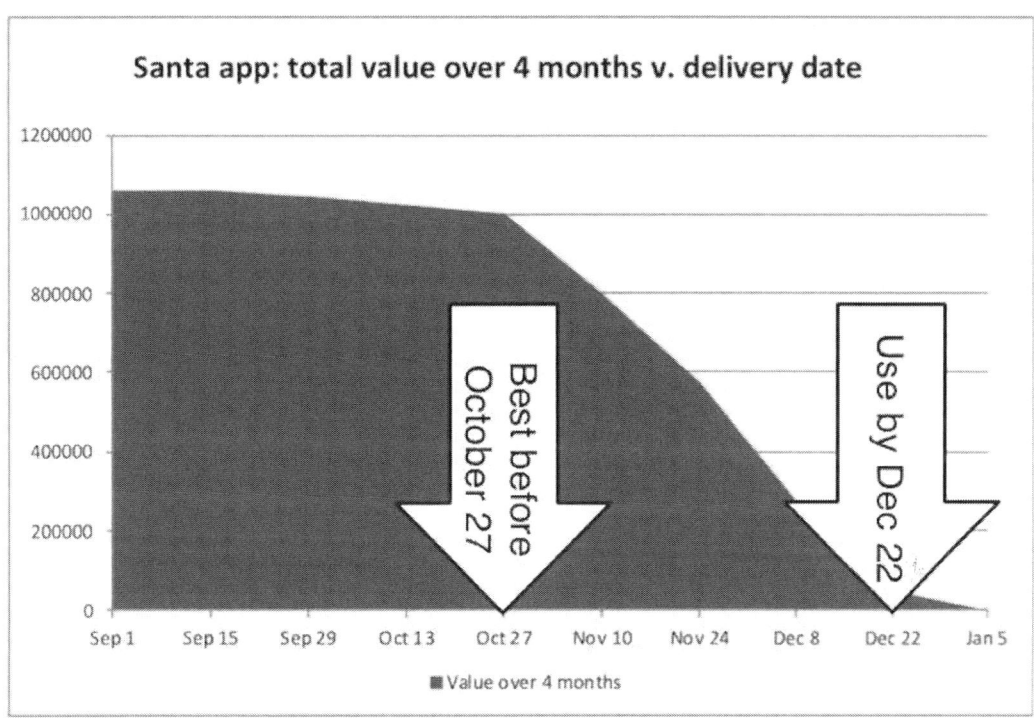

Time-value profile reveals best-before and use-by dates

From the graph it is clear that if work on Alex's Santa app begins immediately the app will be delivered before the critical 'best before' date and most – although not all – of the anticipated revenue will be realized.

Importantly, the graph also shows two more things. Firstly, it is not possible to recognize all the anticipated revenue unless it ships in the next two weeks. Therefore this figure needs to be revised downwards in light of the anticipated development time. Secondly, and more importantly, the graph shows that delivering the Santa app a little later is still worthwhile.

Time-value profile for Halloween

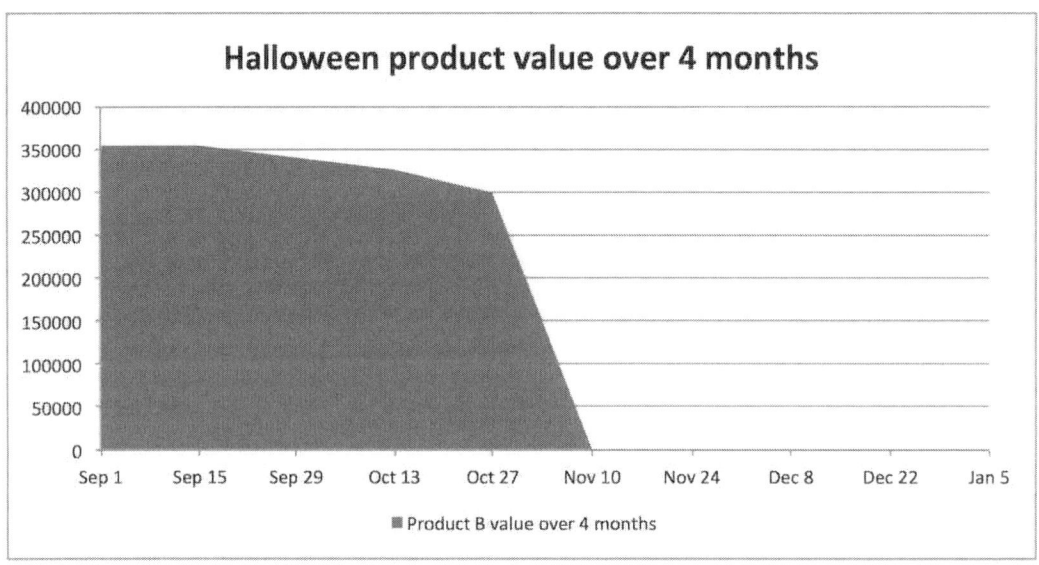

Halloween app time-value profile

Next look at the time-value profile of the Halloween app. While following a similar pattern, this app has a more dramatic decline. Again 'best before' and 'use by' dates can be imposed, but in this case there is little difference because the value decline is that much steeper.

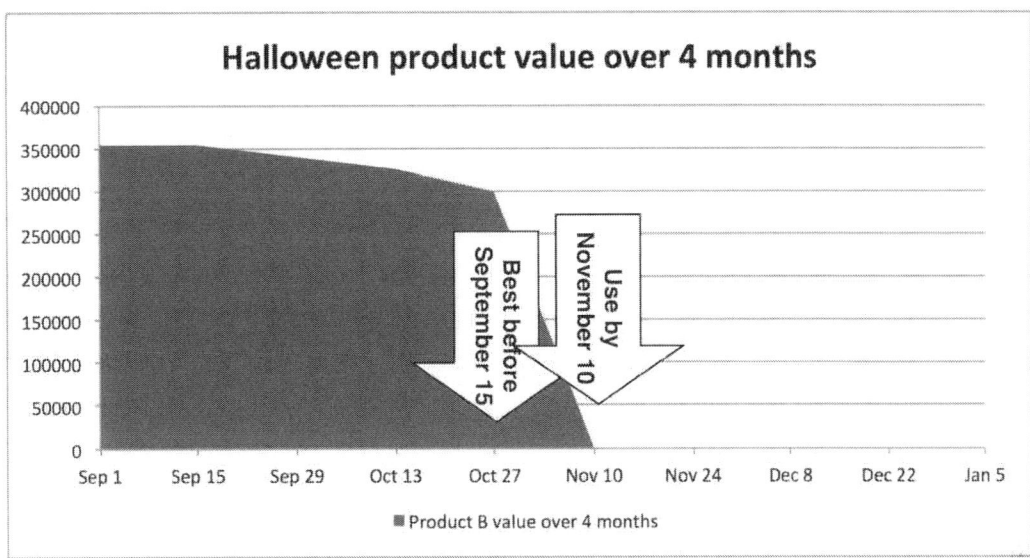

Halloween app best dates

When considering 'best before' and 'use by' dates for the Halloween app, the placement of the 'best before' date is a little subjective. 15 September is arguably the 'best before' date, because this is the last date on which the full value could be realized. However as most value is retained until end of October, a later date might also be considered the 'best before' date.

The answer is...

Using these graphs one can calculate what the value-maximizing options are.

Building Si's Santa app first – options B and D – will result in $1,025,000 of revenue. Even with the earliest possible delivery date the full potential cannot be realized. However most of the value can still be realized.

Unfortunately, once the Santa app is delivered, the Halloween app cannot be delivered for at least another four weeks – 9 November – by which time it would be valueless. Thus options B and D are actually equivalent.

Reversing the build order – options A and C – would see the Halloween app delivered on 29 September, and although it will not make the originally promised revenue of $355,000, it will capture $340,000.

With Halloween done, work on the Santa app can commence (option C) and delivery should occur by 10 November. By this date $225,000 of potential revenue will be foregone, but the app should still generate $800,000 when delivered.

Together the apps will generate $1,140,000, which is $115,000 more than the second-best option of only building the Santa app.

Hence one can conclude that:

> *Deadlines are elastic by value*

> *Different delivery dates generate different value*

Parallel build

Having established a model, several other options and consequences can be considered. For example, what if the Halloween and Santa apps were built in parallel?

As before, one needs to make some assumptions. Let's assume that the development team is divided into two equal parts and as a result both development efforts take twice as long:

- The Halloween app now takes eight weeks and will be delivered on 22 October. This would allow it to capture about $312,000.
- The Santa app would now take 12 weeks and deliver by 24 November, capturing $575,000.

In total a parallel build approach would capture $882,000, which is still less than the best option considered so far. Arguably this approach reduces risk, because both efforts proceed independently and the Santa app is no longer dependent on the Halloween app finishing on schedule.

However, one might also argue the counter-case, that with smaller teams both apps are at greater risk because they are less able to absorb variation and problems, for example inaccurate effort estimates, technical complications or disruption such as illness.

Again one can make different assumptions and calculate different values and different risk profiles. For example, if after completing the Halloween app the team merges with the Santa team and competes the remaining work in two weeks instead of four, the Santa app could realize $800,000, making a total of $1,112,000 – although again the risk profile would change.

Pre-work investigation

A more radical approach, and one that might be effective where effort estimates are unreliable, would be to spend some initial time in investigation or prototyping. The problem normally with this approach is that such planning or research has a habit of continuing for too long. Using these graphs you can see how much value needs to be traded for time.

For example, suppose the first iteration was used in prototyping and research. Let's assume a worst-case scenario in which this work did not produce any time-saving or revenue-enhancing result. As a consequence the Halloween app would not start build until 15 September and would complete on 13 October, with the resultant reduction of $25,000 in value.

Similarly the Santa app is delayed by two weeks, ships on 24 November and captures $225,000 less value. A two-week delay at the start of the work results in $250,000 less value being captured. Building the apps is still commercially worthwhile, but one can see that further delays would have more significant effects.

The question is: would undertaking two weeks of non-coding research generate more than $250,000 of value later?

This question may be further refined as: might two weeks of non-coding research generate options to enhance revenue, reduce costs or risk, that would be worth more than $250,000?

Depending on one's approach to risk and the potential upside from investigation, one might consider this is an acceptable option.

Costs

All models are wrong; some models are useful. George E. P. Box

The model presented so far is a simplification, as are all models. In particular the analysis has deliberately ignored costs in order to emphasize value.

Costs are important. However costs traditionally get a great deal of attention, while value receives far less. Perhaps because costs are easier to define and control, there is a natural tendency to focus on the solid.

It is relatively easy to add cost analysis to the time-value analysis so far. However, let me suggest that the opposite – adding value analysis after cost have been drafted – is problematic. When costs are 'known', cognitive biases seem to influence the value assessment.

Even in real life looking at value first allows the time-cost question to be reframed. For example, rather than asking the technical team "How long will this take to build?", it would be equally possible to ask the technical team "How much of X would we get in time T?", or "Given that we have four weeks to build something like X, could we do it?". Such questions are not only less confrontational, but are also open to discussion.

When time-value profiles are available one can also examine the effect of inaccurate estimates. The Halloween app in this example is expected to take four weeks to build. Even if it overruns by another four weeks it will still deliver the lion's share of the forecast value. However this will seriously impact the Santa app.

Armed with a time-value profile it becomes possible to work backwards to establish a development schedule and examine engineering tradeoffs. As discussed earlier, one option could be to release a smaller product to capture a small part of a large potential market. Alternatively, launching a larger product later could capture a large part of a smaller potential value.

Accuracy of time-value profiles

It is worth noting that time-value profiles do not need to be particularly accurate. What is important is the shape of the graph and the dates on which value changes.

Consider the first Santa Claus time-value profile above. It is unimportant whether the value that would be recognized by releasing on 1 September is actually $1,060,000, more, or less. It could be $2,000,000 or $500,000. While the actual numbers are useful for comparison with the Halloween app, what is more important is the 'best before' date, in this case 27 October.

Between the initial date and 27 October the value changes little: there is a slight loss over the month of October, but it is nothing compared with what happens during November, when each day of delay reduces revenue significantly. Similarly, once past 22 December the delivery date matters little.

Given that all estimates, whether they are of value or effort, are rough approximations based largely on judgement and therefore – almost by definition – inaccurate means that caution needs to be exercised. What the graph does show is some key dates. Analyzing how the value changes over time helps to expose important dates.

What is also shown is that the original value estimate of $1,060,000 is itself a time-dependent figure and one that is unlikely to be realized.

Assumptions and sensitivity

As already noted a number of simplifying assumptions have been made, as is common practice with economists. Making these assumptions has allowed an analysis model to be constructed. The reader is now free to relax any of the assumptions and rebuild the model, although I advise relaxing only one assumption at a time.

In doing so the model will remain but the range of outcomes will increase. Replacing my assumptions with your own will generate an alternative scenario with different graphs and numbers. As the assumptions are relaxed further the number of potential outcomes will increase. This is called *sensitivity analysis*: plug a range of different assumptions, with different numbers, into the model and see how the outcome varies.

Using sensitivity analysis you will find that some assumptions and variables make far more difference than others. Simply knowing which variables cause the greatest variation vastly improves the analysis.

Finally

As the old saying goes, "Time is money."

While most people are familiar with the idea that more time leads to higher costs, fewer think how more time often – although not always – results in lower revenues. In my experience the expression 'cost of delay' leads people to think about the additional costs incurred by late delivery more than the revenue foregone by late delivery.

Express shipping, increased staffing costs, perhaps temporary staff, fines and regulatory charges are easier to spot than sales lost because the product wasn't in the shops when the customer wanted to buy. Or the cost of allowing a competitor to get to market first[2].

Similarly most people see a deadline as a binary thing: the deadline is either met or missed. In fact deadlines are analog: different delivery dates result in differing value capture. *When* is just another parameter that accompanies *what*. The available time is one of the constrains under which software engineers work. Since there are many potentially different solutions to the 'what' question, 'when' is simply one of the constraints on selecting and designing a solution.

Rather than frame the discussion in terms of "How long will it take?", the discussion can be framed in terms of "What can be built within the available time?". Not only does this

---

[2]Don Reinertsen discusses cost of delay in depth in his book *Principles of Product Development*, 2009.

sidestep the question of estimates and their accuracy, but it allows for a fuller discussion of value and options.

Once you start thinking along these lines it becomes clear that delivery on different dates results in different values. Most of the time delivering something sooner generates more value – not always, but usually. However, delivering something sooner may mean delivering something with less functionality, and therefore something that delivers less value per unit.

Although the discussion in this chapter is couched in terms of value as money, value may be defined in other terms: children able to read, patients receiving treatment or families accessing clean drinking water.

Constructing time-value profiles and undertaking sensitivity analysis creates a framework within which engineers can work to produce a solution. After all, that is what engineers do best: solve problems within constraints.

13. I need it yesterday!

Yesterday all my troubles seemed so far away,

Now it looks as though they're here to stay.

Oh, I believe in yesterday.

Lennon and McCartney.

"Remember that user comments feature we've been talking about like *forever*?", Oliver cut in without even saying hello.

"Err... yes..." replied Doris, wondering what was coming next.

"Well I need it YESTERDAY": everyone could hear the capitals in his scream.

"OK, well we'd better find Peter, he's the product manager, prioritization is his call."

"Oh know that Doris, but I've been looking for him all morning and the one place he isn't is around here."

"I think he's with a customer, should be back after lunch, we can grab him at, say two?"

"Could we get one of your devs working on user comments ASAP now, since I can could have sold that to the Norwegians for a million yesterday?"

"Oliver, it's 11.30, I don't want to interrupt any of my devs in the middle of work. If – and its a big if – Peter was to agree by two-thirty then we are only looking at two hours of work, it's hardly anything."

"Lunch is for wimps. Two it is then."

....

"OK, what is so urgent that I have to delay my call with the US?"

"Peter, it's like this, I was with the Norwegians yesterday and if I'd had the user comments feature I could have closed a deal for $1 million. We have to begin work on it at once."

"Why didn't you?"

"Come on Peter, you know how Liz and the other devs behave when I sell features we don't have? They are a long streak of misery for weeks."

"Well, first, that doesn't seem to have stopped you in the past and second, as I've said before, you bring me a signed purchase order for a million and I'll move heaven and earth to do it. True, $900,000 doesn't get the same treatment, but a million is a game changer."

"So now can I have it?"

Peter picked up his pencil and started to draw a graph. "The thing is, Oliver, that deal was yesterday and that is, well, yesterday – it's past. Yesterday that feature was worth $1,000,000" – he deliberately said one million slowly – "and today, well...". He turned his pad around and pointed to the graph:

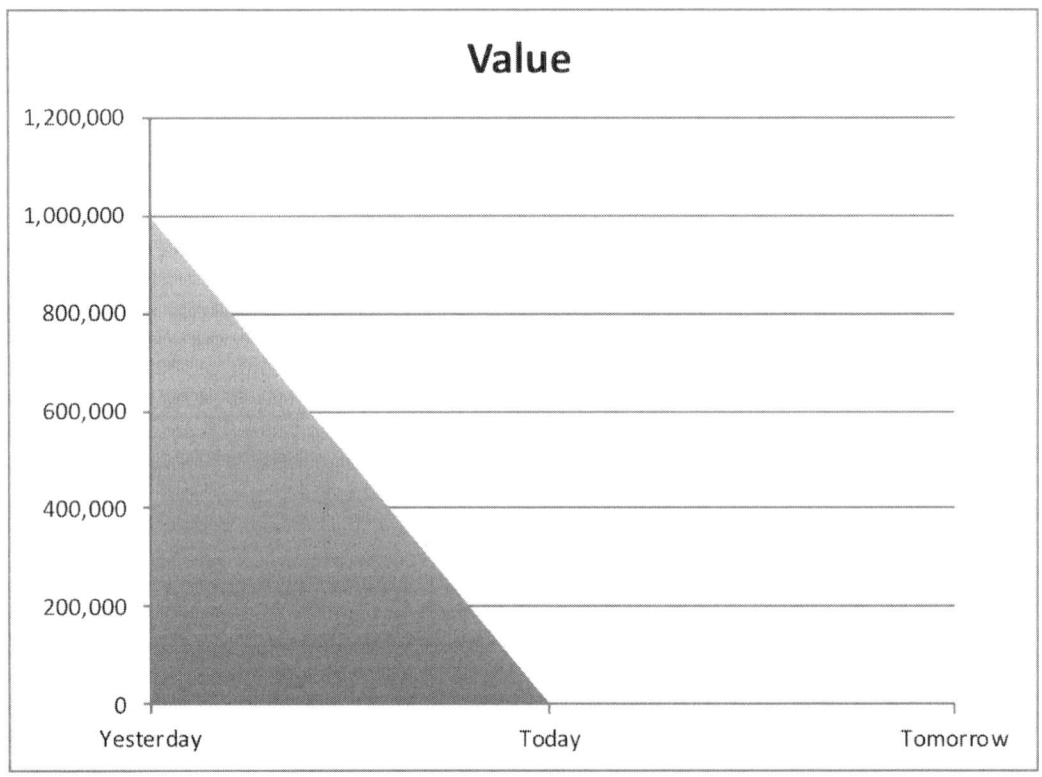

Yesterday it was worth $1,000,000, today $0

"Doris, please correct me if I'm wrong, but last time we checked we don't have a TARDIS?"

"Correct Peter, we wanted to build a TARDIS but..."

"TARDIS?"

"Time and Relative Dimensions in Space, don't you watch Dr Who? A time machine."

"Don't get all sarcastic with me, Peter."

"Well we can't go back in time and sign that deal, nor can we go back in time and build the feature you want, and so far you have told me nothing that suggests the feature is worth anything today or tomorrow."

"I have been saying for months that customers want comments, and more customers do still want them. Now I have been proved right. Our past decisions were wrong and we need to change things fast before another million slips through our fingers."

"Oliver, you are right." Peter was firm: "We have new information; we will consider it when we next conduct our prioritization. But I will remind you that all my discussions with customers still lead me to believe that while customers do want user comments, they want other features more."

"So I have no data that leads me to change my current prioritization. Plus, doing this for Norway would disrupt our plans and I would need to explain to Sharon why upload management is delayed. We all agreed last year to avoid doing customer 'specials', but for $1 million we'll break that rule and do a special."

"On that basis", concluded Peter, "I don't see the need to change priorities mid-sprint, and probably not even this quarter."

"What," Oliver was on the defensive, "if I can get the Norwegians back in the game?"

"You mean they might still pay a million?"

"Maybe."

"That would change the picture". Peter pulled his pad back and drew another diagram.

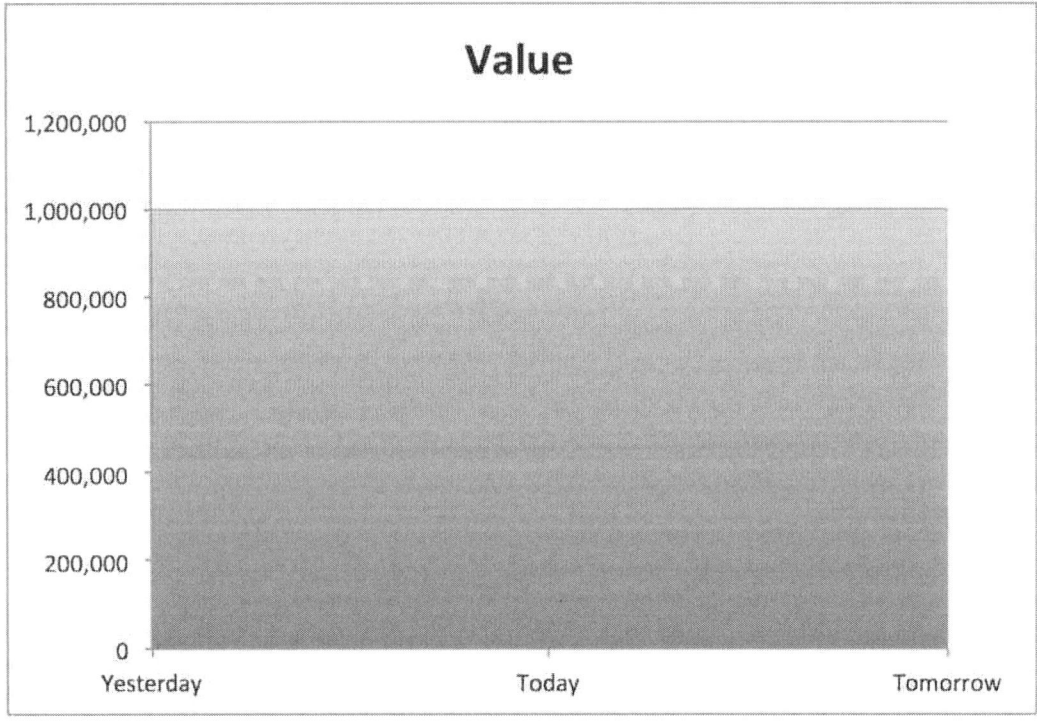

$1,000,000 yesterday, today and tomorrow

"So how long will it take to build?", asked Oliver.

"That's the wrong question." replied Doris, "The question is, how long have we got? How long would they wait? How long will it take them to get an alternative? And how much will they need to pay for it?" – Doris paused – "And it's not just how long will it take to build, it's what else will be displaced?"

"Oliver, get on the phone to the Norwegians, find out if they are still interested, find out when they would want to sign off, find out when they want to deploy. Find out what they do if we don't do it."

"OK Pete, and in return can Doris' engineers start work on it now?"

"No. We need to understand just what they want."

"For pity's sake, user comments are user comments, don't you guys use Amazon?"

"Oliver, Amazon reviews are different to TripAdvisor reviews, are different to Match.com reviews. Do you want moderation? Do you want user IDs? Do they want anti-spam? And so on. I'm not expecting, or would ever ask for a detail spec, but if my engineers have an idea of how much time we have we can start proposing options."

"OK, OK, OK, I'll call Oslo."

....

Two days later...

"Doris, thanks for making time." Peter handed Doris a simple Excel chart printout, "Oliver has had several conversations with the Norwegians and we've put together a new time-value chart, please see this."

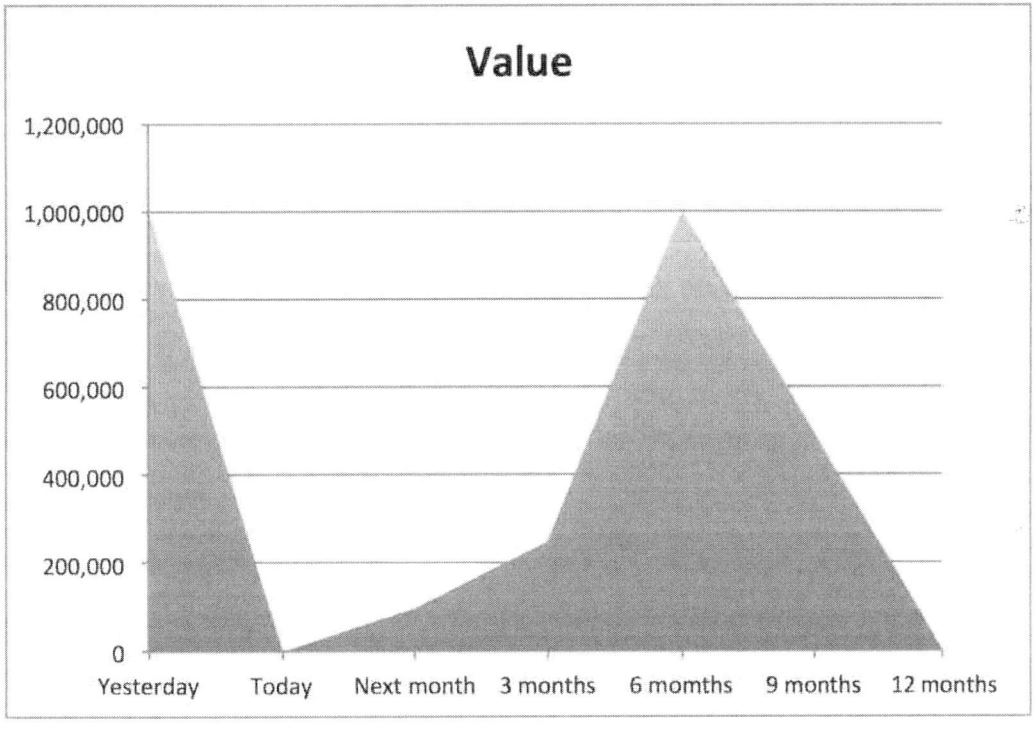

12 months value

"This is only based on the Norwegians. I'm still working on whether this will have an impact on other clients or deals, but even so it seems to pan out. I'll let Oliver explain."

"Thanks Peter. Three days ago I had the CEO in the room. He would have signed there and then, seems he wants the feature but nobody else on his top team do."

"No use crying over spilt milk", Peter put in.

Oliver made a face and continued "If I had the feature today, Olaf, their product manager, couldn't sign it off: he has to go through channels and it would take months so it's worthless right now – unless of course him or me happen to bump into the CEO on the golf course, which is unlikely in a Norwegian winter."

"Olaf has been told by the CEO to start planning to build their own user comments feature. He doesn't want to. If he has to then he thinks their project committee will allocate $100,000 next month. If however we can commit to the feature, and preferably show them something – anything – he can argue against his own project. Knowing that, I think I can get them to spend the $100,000 with us. A downpayment on an option, something to keep the CEO happy."

"Even if we had something next month they couldn't go live. Their controllers would want to review it and they would need to train their staff."

"Their next capital allocation period begins in three months. If we have something to sell by then we can sign them. I think we can get another $150,000 out of them in the first case: if we keep improving it then we can work up to the million."

"That's assuming, of course," Peter pointed out, "that Olaf and the execs don't persuade the CEO to dump the idea. If we build this thing in the hope the CEO will sign we might still get nothing."

"If we get them to pay a bit at a time we reduce that risk. I wouldn't be surprised if they dump the idea after $100,000 – this might only be worth $100,000 to us."

"I'm sure that won't happen, Peter." Oliver assured him. "If we can't deliver till later then it's entirely probable they will either build their own or shop for a third party. That means if we deliver late we will need to integrate with their solution – even if we just suck the data out."

"I now know that if I'd signed them when I was there they wouldn't have been able to pay until the next period anyway."

Doris tried her best not to smirk; "So Oliver, you're saying that we always had four months to build this thing?"

"I guess so."

"And let's get this right: we now have a few weeks to get a very basic proof-of-concept prototype, MVP, something... in front of them and another two months to get a simple thing working?"

"Yes, it looks that way", Peter replied for Oliver. "Really doing the work is getting us an option to play for the big money."

"And we can continue to iterate and build this thing up as we go?", Doris continued.

"That's the beauty of it; we can use them as guinea pigs, get their feedback, and hopefully use them as a reference customer."

"Cool," Doris smiled, "what are you waiting for?"

"You'll start today?", asked Oliver.

"No, I didn't say that" Doris replied, "but we will start soon; no point in interrupting the sprint when we are near the end."

"Umm..."

"If we change priorities now then seven days of work for France is left unfinished and unsalable. Customers are upset, devs are upset, Sharon is upset and our reputation for delivery is hit."

"Oliver," said Peter, "what are you waiting for? – get yourself to Oslo and get a signature."

"For $100,000? Olaf will give me that on the phone, getting $1,000,000 out of him $100,000 at a time is child's play, ten easy payments. Not sure if Sharon our CEO will be happy though, she likes big deals, impresses the investors."

"Sharon might not, but Sam the CFO will.", Peter shot back, "Sam likes smooth cash-flow, recurring payments, no surprises, says the investors do too."

For a man who had got what he wanted Oliver seemed reluctant to leave the room, but he eventually did.

"So we didn't need a time machine after all?", Doris mischievously asked Peter.

"Good thing too!"

"The thing is, Doris, demands for yesterday are pointless. We can never deliver by yesterday, we can only look to the future. If all the value was in the past then it's gone and it's never coming back. If there is value in the future we need to understand when."

"And that way my engineers know the constraints they are working within?"

"Exactly Doris, and thats what engineers do best."

14. Theory X, Theory Y and strategy

There is a great deal of talk about loyalty from the bottom to the top. Loyalty from the top down is even more necessary and much less prevalent. General George S. Patton

Agile, *Beyond Budgeting*, *Emergent Strategy* and *Continuous Digital* are all members of the same family, the 'Theory Y' family.

Traditional management, budgeting, strategic planning and 'waterfall' software development are firmly in the Theory X family. Theory X suggests that workers need to be actively supervised and their work controlled: workers cannot be left to decide and plan their own work, because they are intrinsically lazy and would choose to do as little as possible.

Therefore supervisors (managers) need to proactively manage the work and monitor what is being done, otherwise little or nothing would be done. To know what the workers should be doing the supervisors must have plans. Given the correct plans – which can be written by an elite cadre – implementation is simply a matter of ensuring that the plans are executed correctly.

Conversely Theory Y starts with the assumption that workers are not lazy, rather they are intrinsically motivated when offered meaningful work and high levels of autonomy. Thus Theory Y thinking demands that workers have the authority to make real decisions. Failure to allow them to make meaningful decisions undermines the very motivation on which Theory Y is predicated.

Pushing authority down to workers has other advantages apart from worker motivation, although the benefits to productivity and effectiveness of higher motivation should not be underestimated.

Both Theory X and Theory Y have significant ripple effects. One's view of budgets, strategy, projects, personnel (also known, rather crudely, as *human resource management*) and operations are all influenced, if not shaped entirely, by which theory one subscribes to.

Historically management thinking and action has often been predicated on Theory X. Today's business leaders follow previous generations of leaders who drew on hierarchical military and church models, which are inherently Theory X-based. Many – probably most – managers learn their craft, not in school, but by observing others.

Now, in the early years of the twenty-first century, with massive computer power doing much of the hard work, the question business leaders face is whether Theory Y represents a more effective model. While some businesses attempt to graft elements of Theory Y into their inherently Theory X-based cultures others, usually completely new companies, embrace Theory Y models.

Grafting elements of Theory Y onto a existing Theory X organization inevitably creates tension. Long-term coexistence of both is unlikely – in time one or the other will win out.

Tim O'Reilly[1] has even suggested that today's programmers are the new managers. Rather than instruct people in what to do, programmers instruct machines in what to do and how to do it.

Theory X and Y

'Theory X and Theory Y are theories of human motivation and management. They were created and developed by Douglas McGregor at the MIT Sloan School of Management in the 1960s. These theories describe two contrasting models of workforce motivation applied by managers in human resource management, organizational behavior, organizational communication and organizational development. According to the models, the two opposing sets of general assumptions of how workers are motivated form the basis for two different managerial styles. Theory X stresses the importance of strict supervision, external rewards, and penalties. In contrast, Theory Y highlights the motivating role of job satisfaction and encourages workers to approach tasks without direct supervision.' Wikipedia[a]

[a]https://en.wikipedia.org/wiki/Theory_X_and_Theory_Y

Business strategy

Business strategy itself is a form of design. Broadly speaking there are two schools of thinking on business strategy; also broadly speaking, these two schools line up behind Theory X and Theory Y.

Before continuing the discussion of business strategy, it helps to take a slight detour through strategy assumptions.

---

[1]*Managing the Bots that are Managing the Business*, Tim O'Reilly, MIT Sloan Management Review, Fall 2016

Strategy as a plan

For classicists, profitability is the supreme goal of business, and rational planning is the means to achieve it. ...the features of the classicist approach: the attachment to rational analysis, the separation of conception from execution, and the commitment to profit maximization. Richard Whittington[2]

The idea of strategy as a plan – an ultimate goal and a plan for reaching the goal – is probably the dominant school of thought in business strategy. This school of thinking sees big decisions made by an elite cadre. The cadre decides the objective and the broad approach to meeting it, then hands these designs off to another cadre that plans its implementation. The second cadre takes the decisions from the elite and plans their execution. When the plans are complete they are handed off to those who must implement the plans.

Does this sound familiar?

Waterfall software development actually has its roots in the 'rational' approach to business strategy in vogue after 1945.

While advocates of agile software development like to start their story with Royce's 1970 'waterfall' paper[3], a better place to start the story might be 1961 at the Pentagon. Defense Secretary Robert McNamara introduced the *Planning, Programming and Budgeting System* (PPBS), an inherently top-down planning process. Starting with the objective (fighting Russia on the plains of Germany), all expenditure was controlled towards this end. Unfortunately for America, the country found itself fighting a very different war.

Emergent strategy

While the 'strategy as planning' school may be the best-known view of business strategy, it is not the only one – indeed there are several.

Another school of thought sees business strategy as an emergent process that results from learning within the organization. While the elite may make some decisions, these decisions are themselves derived from what is happening in the organization and what is being learnt.

Organizations exists in a changing environment: competitors are actively seeking to undermine the organization, customer tastes are changing (and may not really be known anyway),

---

[2] *Theories of Strategy*, in *What is Strategy and Does it Matter?*, Richard Whittington, 2001. Reprinted in *Strategy for Business*, Mazzucato, 2002

[3] *Managing the Development of Large Software Systems*, Winston Royce, Proceedings of IEEE WESCON 26, 1970

new information is arriving all the time and individuals are learning. They are processing all this information, changing their models of the world. As a result no strategic plan can be perfect or static.

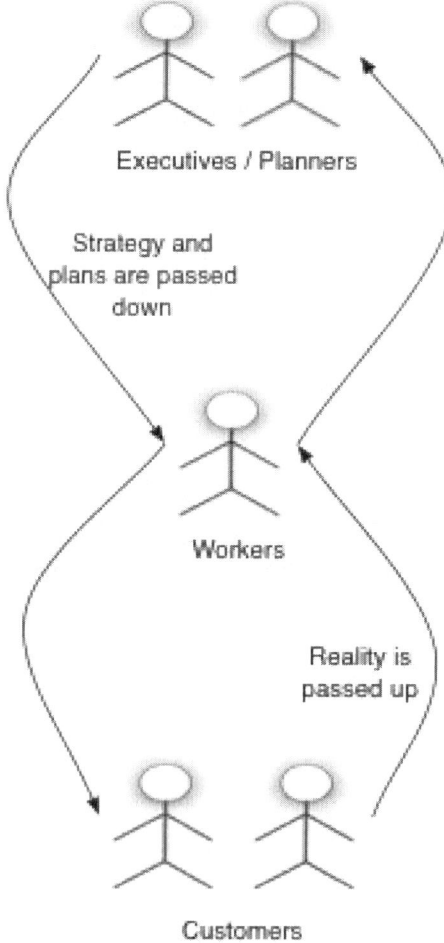

The business feedback loop

Because the elite at the top of the organization are the staff furthest removed from day-to-day operations – customers, markets and competitors – they have less information than those doing the work.

'In middle management, you may very well sense the shifting winds on your face before the company as a whole and sometimes before your senior management does. Middle management – especially those who deal with the outside world, like people in sales – are often the first to realize that what worked before doesn't quite work any more; that the rules are changing.' Andy Grove[4]

There is a big feedback loop at work. Planned strategy assumes near-perfect knowledge, while emergent strategy feeds off what actually happens.

Perhaps the best known proponent of this school of thinking is Professor Henry Mintzberg. In his book *The Rise and Fall of Strategic Planning* he dissects the ideas of the strategy-making process. He questions both the act of planning and the idea that strategic plans 'only' need executing. (Anyone versed in the waterfall versus agile debate will find the parallels between strategic planning and software construction uncanny.)

Yet Mintzberg also recognizes the role of some deliberation. Elsewhere he has written:

> 'Our conclusion is that strategy formation walks on two feet, one deliberate and the other emergent. ...managing requires a deft touch – to direct in order to realize intentions while at the same time responding to an unfolding pattern of action. The relative emphasis may shift from time to time but not the requirement to attend to both sides of this phenomenon.' Mintzberg and Waters[5]

Strategy perspectives

One's preferred model of business strategy often comes down to one's own perspective. One's perspective often comes down to personal experience, or even choice.

Clearly planned strategy falls within the Theory X camp, while emergent strategy aligns with Theory Y. Those who start with the belief that workers are lazy will automatically tend towards planned strategy, while those who believe in intrinsic motivation will tend towards emergent strategy.

Which view of strategy you hold will be informed by your own experiences and the organization you work for. Some organizations are clearly command-and-control strategic-planning and executing organizations. For some of these organizations these policies work and deliver good results. Other organizations find success through distributed decision-making, a tolerance of failure and emergent designs and strategies.

Which is 'best' is a question of opinion. Indeed, even the definition of 'best' is subjective; one may well argue that, rather than choosing between these two approaches in order to achieve

---

[4]*Only the Paranoid Survive*, Andy Grove, 1997
[5]*Of Strategies Deliberate and Emergent*, Mintzberg and Waters, *Strategic Management Journal*, 1985

some definitive 'best', as human beings we define 'best' in terms of our world view. It is the means rather than the end that informs our definition.

In truth Theory X and Theory Y, planned strategy and emergent strategy, are just two points on a spectrum – perhaps the extreme points. All organizations, and all of us as individuals, are somewhere on this spectrum.

Conflicts arise when an organization tries to stand at multiple positions on the spectrum. For example, a hierarchical bank with a planned strategy will undermine its own roll-out of self-organizing agile software development teams and sooner or later find conflict.

Perhaps the question should really be *which of these approaches are going to produce the greatest value?*

But since what we *value* is again defined by our world view and personal approach, the question of X or Y must itself be answered before value itself can be defined. One may not like this circular problem, but it is one that exists.

Emergent design

Software design – or, to use a grander title, *software architecture* – parallels business strategy. Design and strategy form frameworks into which other decisions fit. Like strategy it is traditionally described and taught as a top-down hierarchal activity, but in reality it is as much, if not more, an emergent phenomenon.

While design and strategy are commonly thought of as forward-looking and entirely rational, an alternative view sees them as retrospective processes. Strategy and design attempt to explain past rationales and missteps. Both strategy and design are as much stories told to explain what happened as they are plans for the future.

Removing the central controlling and decision-making will reduce the homogeneity of decisions. While some may see this as a disadvantage, others will see advantages in greater diversity.

In terms of software design, service design and organizational structure this results in an emergent design process and emergent decisions. Multiple heterogeneous decisions will result in a variety of 'designs' that may even be incompatible.

Such incompatibilities might not be a bad thing: each example might cater for one specific problem, customer segment or market opportunity better than a homogeneous approach. While the costs of supporting two incompatible approaches could be higher, the resulting value might be even higher.

Where incompatible designs are not justified, the organization and its processes need to allow for changes to homogenize designs. Heterogeneous designs should be tolerated until such time as a optimal design becomes clear. Think of it as a form of natural selection. Once the optimal design emerges, additional work needs to happen to homogenize the design.

Over time the optimal design may change – today's optimal solution might be a local optimum; as knowledge increases a better solution might become apparent. Indeed in a fast-paced environment it might be better to tolerate variety simply because there is no clearly optimal solution.

Variety has other advantages, especially in a rapidly changing environment: variety offers greater fault tolerance and robustness, and variety provides greater learning opportunities.

Volkswagen

A few years ago Volkswagen decided to limit car production across its various brands to just four common platforms. VW Golf models used the same platform as VW Beatles, Audi A3s, Skoda Octavias and Seat something-or-others; the VW Passat shared another platform with the A4, a Seat and so on.

Although the initial cost of creating common platforms was high, it saved money after introduction. Economies of scale allowed for common parts and common tooling.

But... Volkswagen had also locked together the product lifecycles of the cars using the same common platform. When the time came to replace the platform, costs rocketed: not just one car had to be redesigned and introduced to the market, but four or five. Safety issues could effect more platforms, and product recalls could be much bigger. Customers noticed too: why buy an expensive VW when it was little different than a cheap Skoda?

Patterns

Both strategy and software design can be seen as largely pattern-based activities. Patterns represent recurring responses to recurring problems within a context. While no two responses may be identical, there is an underlying pattern of cause–response.

It is only in hindsight that patterns can be recognized. Decision-making may be guided towards an existing (known) pattern or towards a deliberate and planned approach. In time a new approach, if it proves useful, may itself become a pattern.

Patterns are generative – one leads to another – and evolving. When a pattern recurs modifications and variations are inevitable; just as in evolution, beneficial modification will emerge. Also as in evolution some modifications will not be successful and will die out. However, without variations patterns are likely to die as the context they exist within changes. As with evolution, it is not necessarily the most adapted business strategy or software design that is superior, but that which shows the greatest adaptability.

For evolution to succeed, variations are necessary. When organizations centralize decision-making, either about business strategy or software design, they restrict modifications. Without modification there will be no evolution. Forward movement depends on a superior mind – a business strategist or software architect – to direct change.

The promise of patterns is to allow those who do the work, the ordinary worker, to control their work. Architect Christopher Alexander[6] originally proposed patterns as a way for individuals to participate in design and construction of their homes and environment. Software and business patterns offer the same hope to programmers and workers. Of course, that means that individuals must learn the patterns.

Finally

> *Plans are worthless, but planning is everything.* Dwight D. Eisenhower, US President

As Eisenhower's famous quote recognizes, plans have their uses, but planning itself has far greater benefits. Traditionally plans are a means of control, budgets doubly so. If workers are to be freed of command and control, then plans and planning needs rethinking.

Planning itself is useful mostly as a form of learning. It allows those doing the planning to rehearse the future and potentially avoid issues or enhance benefits. In so doing planners build a shared understanding.

Many in the technology community mistake schedules for plans. Scheduling and forecasting are but two aspects of planning: scheduling is itself a form of control, while forecasting can be a learning exercise. However planning is far more than creating a Gantt chart with Microsoft Project.

Software designs are plans. Interface designs are plans. User journeys are plans. Roadmaps are plans, of a sort. Architecture is a plan, and probably a form of planning that is more emergent than predicated.

---

[6] *A Timeless Way of Building, Christopher Alexander*, 1979. See also, *A Pattern Language*, 1977 and *The Oregon Experiment* 1975.

Not all plans are bad. Plans as a means of rehearsal and coordination are good, but plans as a means of control are not so good. The trick is to keep the positive aspects of planning without the negative aspects of plans. To do this, planning needs to be a collaborative, inclusive and democratic learning exercise.

Planning has rapidly diminishing returns and plans decay rapidly. The mantra is not 'no planning', but planning that:

- Is frequent and short,
- Is collaborative and shared,
- Incorporates the latest learnings, and
- Isn't scared of reversing the decisions of yesterday.

That means the whole team planning for 30 minutes each day, rather than a designated planner planning for eight hours one day. It means coders and testers spending an occasional 20 minutes together at a whiteboard, rather than an elevated expert spending days producing formal documents.

For any organization in transition – from classical to agile, from Theory X to Theory Y – there will be conflicts as one part of the organization adopts different perspectives and values from other parts. When the other part of the organization is more senior, the conflicts will be more severe.

Some of these conflicts will be transitional, but while transformation is less than whole the conflicts will persist.

15. Planning

Failure to plan is planning to fail. Project manager maxim, source unknown

Our conclusion is that planning is a centralizing process, discouraging the very commitment it claims so earnestly to require. Mintzberg[1]

So the real purpose of effective planning is not to make plans but to change the microcosm, the mental model that these decision makers carry in their heads. de Geus[2]

In the Continuous model planning is seen as a learning activity. The aim is to capture the benefits of planning while avoiding the negative side-effects.

Some readers may be surprised to see the Continuous model embracing ideas such as planning and objectives, balanced score cards, governance and even estimation. These are simply tools and techniques that can be used in a project context, in a Continuous project-less context, and quite probably in other contexts too. When overused, goal displacement occurs.

Planning is a tool that deserves particular attention. Planning takes many forms. For example:

- Scheduling
- Forecasting
- Software design
- Test design and creation
- User interface design
- Refactoring

Software engineers tend to associate 'planning' with the first of these items, which is typically done by 'managers'. The latter items are undertaken by coders and testers. In truth schedule

---

[1] *The Rise and Fall of Strategic Planning*, Henry Mintzberg, 1994
[2] *Planning as Learning*, Arie de Geus, Harvard Business Review, 1988, 66, 70

planning is just one form of planning, several of the other forms being blessed with the name 'design'. Like other forms of planning, design is a forward-looking learning exercise.

Planning is useful in all its forms, but it is not a benign activity. Planning has benefits but also has liabilities. Negative side-effects can hinder the ability to do work.

Continuous Digital recognizes planning as a learning activity. As such a little bit of planning is useful. However planning has rapidly diminishing returns: after a little bit of planning, learning slows. At the end of a day's planning the planners are not learning as quickly as they did in the first hour.

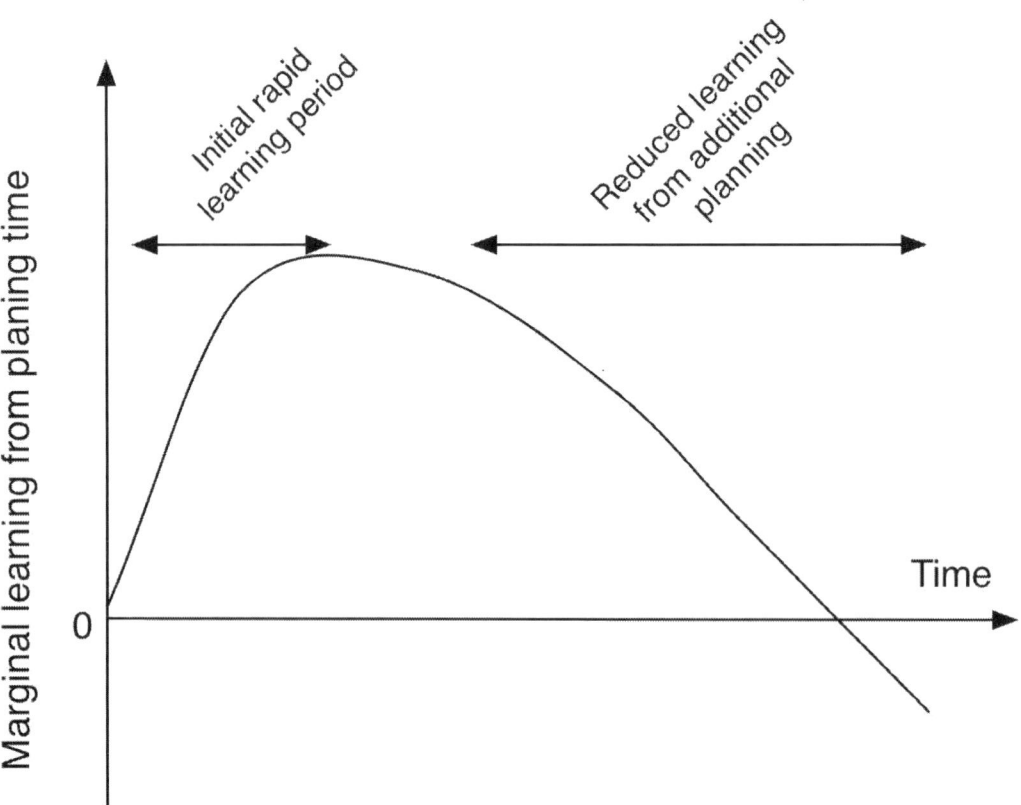

Initial planning can produce very rapid learning, but as diminishing returns set in additional planning becomes less valuable

In the extreme, when planning drags on, when it is measured in days rather than hours, planning can actually reduce knowledge. Planners repeat discussions, add more and more detail, or speculate about unlikely scenarios. In all cases less will be learned and less will be remembered. Prolonged planning makes these problems worse, because the act of planning usually precedes doing. In an effort to get the 'paper' plan right, the act of doing is delayed and even put at risk.

Delay itself causes more problems: the *cost of delay* phenomenon means that value is reduced while simultaneously requirements continue to change[3].

Doing is learning too

Planning is learning, but doing is also learning: there is no cutoff point when learning ceases. The longer planning takes, the later the doing will start, and therefore *learning from doing* will be delayed. When planning there rapidly comes a point at which more can be learned, and more rapidly, by doing.

Iterating between planning and doing is more valuable still. Interleaving planning and doing allows learning from doing to be fed into later planning sessions, which themselves inform doing and so on.

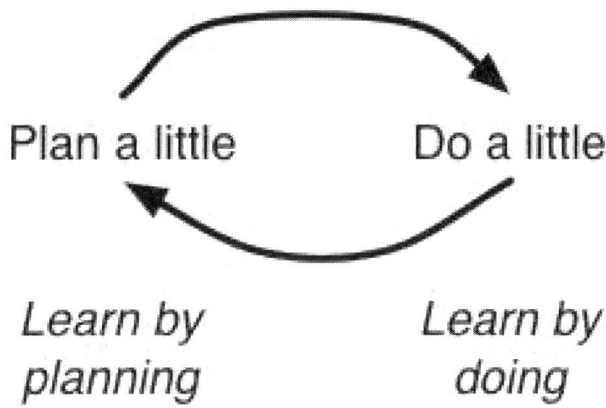

Iteration between planning and doing

Taking time after doing to plan allows for reflection and adjustment. The same idea appears again and again, usually in slightly more complicated forms and names: PDCA cycle (Plan Do Check Act/Adjust), Deming or Shewhart cycle, OODA (Observe Orientate Decide Act), Decision Cycle, Red Green Refactor and so on.

When doing results in a usable artifact then the artifact can generate further learning, for example by showing the artifact to others and getting their feedback, or by putting the product into the market and observing (potential) customer reaction.

---

[3]In *Applied Software Measurement*, 2008, Capers Jones suggests requirements and specifications change and grow at the rate of 2% per year.

Plans are *transient objects*, even product artifacts can be transient objects; such objects facilitate learning but are themselves discarded. In the same way that children play with soft toys and dolls to learn about the real world, plans and (prototype) products facilitate learning.

Money is itself feedback. In some ways money is the best feedback, because not only does it benefit the recipient directly, it also demonstrates what the spender is prepared to surrender in return for your product.

When an artifact can be sold for money, two things happen. There is an immediate feedback loop, because the money shows that others consider the artifact valuable. There is a similar second feedback loop within the organization through the financial control system. In both cases money is feedback.

The question is, *what is the fasted way to learn?*

Given a blank sheet of paper, the fastest way for a team to learn might well be to engage in two hours of planning. By hour three the quickest way to learn might be to go and talk to some customers. After an hour talking to customers, the quickest way to learn might be to build something.

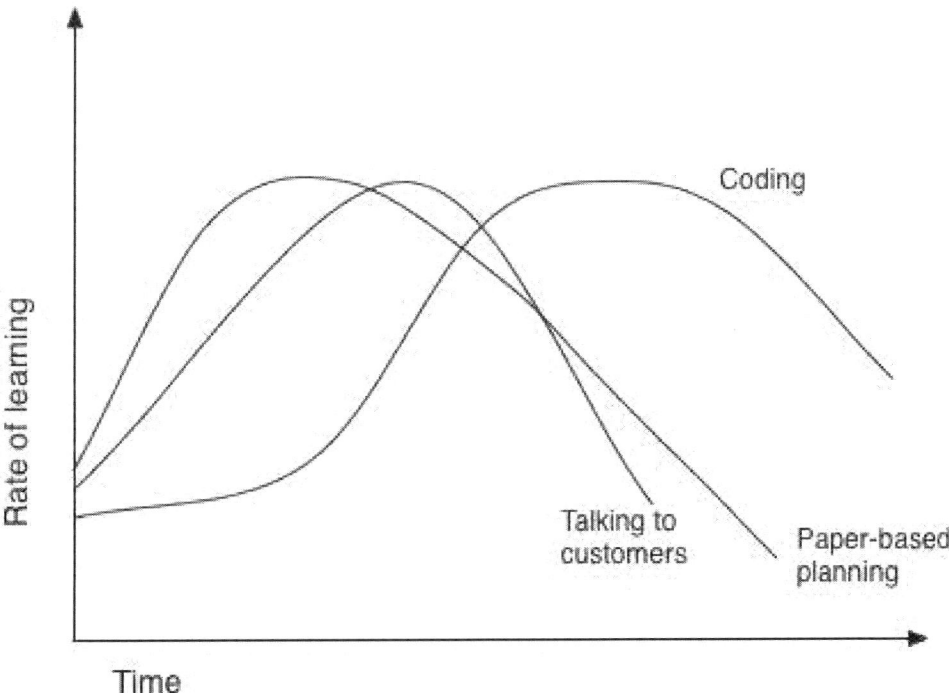

To maximize learning, use different activities at different times

The trick is to maximize learning. As different activities experience peak learning at different times, teams need to switch between them – or at least to change focus and iterate. Sequencing activities can also increase learning: for example, showing customers a prototype might create more learning than simply talking to the customers without an artifact.

Problems

While some planning is an essential part of Continuous Digital, excessive planning is not. Planning should be conducted in short collaborative bursts and then tested with action. Planning sessions should be measured in hours, not days.

Planning is not the benign activity it is usually seen to be. Not only does planning have diminishing returns, but excessive planning can be damaging. Nor should one forget that planning itself costs money: planners are often among the elite in an organization. As such their time costs more and the opportunity costs – that is, the value they could produce elsewhere – are higher.

I vividly recall a planning meeting I attended at a large retail bank. There were over a dozen other attendees: programme manager, project manager, several business analysts and several architects, all from the bank, plus an account manger, analyst and architect from the supplier. This was one of many similar meetings to plan work that would be done by a team of ten or fewer developers.

The financial cost of one such meeting would easily exceed the cost of the development team. The meeting was conducted without the benefit of doing, so learning was lower. In addition, any decisions made had to be communicated to the delivery team, an extra cost.

When economies of scale hold such meeting might be justified, but when diseconomies of scale prevail such meetings can only be the product of bureaupathology.

Cost of delay

Perhaps the largest financial problem with excessive planning is the cost of delay. Since planning is normally a precursor to action: longer planning periods delay the delivery of the final product. Such planning is effectively a batch process that must be concluded before flow-based development can begin.

The (usually) unspoken assumption is that time spent in planning saves time (and/or money) later. In an uncertain world – with rapidly advancing technology, competing demands and problems that are only understood as solutions are created – such an assumption is almost certainly erroneous. Upfront planning that is uninformed by doing is by necessity done with imperfect knowledge.

Delay to the final product increases costs and usually reduces benefits. Not only are benefits delivered later, but feedback from customers and users is delayed and so compounds the problem.

There is a need to reduce the batch size in planning. Instead of lots of planning up front, it is better to have a little bit of planning often, interweaved with doing. The total amount of planning may well be greater, but it is only undertaken – and paid for – as it is needed.

Goal displacement

In some places plans themselves become the actual goal. This seems particularly true of organizations that outsource work; the organization itself exists to commission others to do the work. Thus the goal of the employees becomes the plan that others will enact. The reader can use their own experience to decide for themselves what the goal of the outsourcer should be.

Reducing commitment

Plans reduce commitment in two ways. While project planners frequently blame others for deviation from a plan – "The programmers aren't good enough!" – such failures are really failures of the planners. Had the planners been better, had they sought more information, they would have known that the programmers were second-rate.

Armed with additional information the planners could have incorporated countermeasures into their plans. Ultimately all failures of implementation of a plan can be attributed to deficiencies in the plan itself, and by implication poor planning on the part of the planners.

When all problems can ultimately be traced to *the plan*, what is the incentive for anyone to commit? Since the planners anticipated lazy workers, there is no point in workers being anything other than lazy.

Secondly, because planning is traditionally conducted by a small cadre of planners and designers, the majority of workers are excluded. They are consigned to a secondary status with less responsibility than the planning cadre. This is hardly a recipe for encouraging commitment.

Such planning models might have worked in traditional factory environments with a high degree of repetition – compliant workers undertaking manual processes. Software development and other knowledge-based industries are quite different. Worker expectations have also changed.

Communication cost

When planning is conducted by one group and passed to another group for execution, there is an additional handover cost. The first group, the planners, need to communicate all they have learned to those who are undertaking the work.

Clearly this costs in time. Time is needed for the planners to prepare documentation and deliver presentations, but time is also needed for the doers to read the documentation, attend the presentations and assimilate the information.

In his book *The Living Company*, Arie de Geus suggests that when the planners and doers are the same people, plans are put into action sooner and with greater success than when the two groups are separate. Extra time taken in planning is more than made up, because action starts and ends sooner.

Centralization, command and control

Another direct result of using a small planning cadre is an automatic tendency to centralize decision-making – mostly in the hands of the planners. The planners or their proxies have a vested interest in holding the workers to the plan.

The promise of planning is that a core group can produce a plan that can be delivered by a larger workforce. Inevitably delivering to the plan requires that those not involved with the planning are controlled in such a way to deliver the plan.

Illusions, creep and flexibility

The very existence of a plan creates the impression that the outcome is highly likely to happen. After all, if the plan did not have a good chance of success, why is it being offered as a plan? What planner would honestly say to an executive "After several weeks of in-depth planning we have produced a plan that we believe has a 25% chance of success?"

Even when the chances of success are low there is an incentive for the planners to overstate the probability of success. Alternatively they may engage in ever more planning, thus enlarging the plan in order to obtain more certainty, incurring more costs both directly and through delay.

However some initiatives are inherently risky and prone to failure, for example developing highly innovative technology. Such endeavors benefit from more flexibility in their delivery, but flexibility may be hindered because of the very existence of a plan.

Right or wrong?

Consider an innovative technology initiative. The work reaches a point at which a decision is required. Imagine that the 'right' decision is clear to all, but that such a decision will deviate from the plan. Staying consistent with the plan requires the 'wrong' decision to be made.

While it may be obvious to you and me what the team should do, there may be expectations that the team should follow the plan. At the very least it is possible to imagine the team taking the 'wrong' decision for the sake of adherence to plan.

Of course 'right' and 'wrong' are seldom clear-cut. When right and wrong are ambiguous, the chances that the team will make the 'wrong' decision is greater. Deviating from the plan now opens the team to criticism and even punishment (censure, overtime, lost bonuses). Conforming to plan, even in the face of considerable doubt, is the safe option.

Pressure to conform may be greater still when the planners are a separate group. In the event of following the plan, 'blame' can be attached to the planners. Conversely, taking the 'right' decision risks censure for not following the plan. If the team are uncertain as to 'right' and 'wrong', it is far safer to stay with the plan even if team members have doubts.

The plan has in effect created a precedent and exposed the delivery team to *the principle of the dangerous precedent*.

Planning is useful

Despite these issues planning is useful – it's just not useful in the way that most people normally perceive planning. The plans themselves are less important than the process that leads to the plans.

In planning the planners forge a common language, a common world view and mindset. The process of planning will take the planners on an exploratory journey in which they (should) consider different possibilities, different outcomes and different ways of achieving those outcomes. By talking through these possibilities, they not only come to a consensus view, but mentally rehearse alternatives. So when reality inevitably deviates from the plan, their minds are already prepared. In planning the planners might not have considered exactly the scenarios that unfold in reality, but the very fact that they have mentally explored alternatives will have prepared their minds.

The planning process is itself an act of learning. The plans are merely an attempt to codify what has been learned. Unfortunately in presenting the plans the side conversations and alternatives are usually omitted, preventing the plan's readers from learning what the planners learned.

Even if planners attempt to capture all the details of the planning process, they will still fail. Firstly they will fail because they will not recognize the tacit knowledge they have learned and so will not communicate it. Secondly they will fail because the reader can never experience the same mental preparation as the planners.

Once one accepts planning as learning, it follows that learning should be experienced by as many of a team's members as possible. Sharing the learning experience becomes key to preparing the team for action. It therefore follows that planning should not be restricted to an elite cadre of architects, designers, managers and so on.

Planning should be conducted on a *just-in-time* basis. It should not attempt to look too far into the future, lest dangerous assumptions and precedents are created. Planning should aim to generate learning and knowledge across the team and so create a shared outlook.

Most of all, planning should be an iterative process interwoven with doing: learning by planning, learning by doing.

Back in the USSR

Never forget: if plans and planning were the answer, all of us would today live in some version of the Soviet Union. Communist governments put their faith in plans – hence the term *the planned economy*. Grand five-year plans – which were, amazingly, achieved in four years!

In its efforts to eliminate deviation and stay on plan, the Soviet Union even resorted to managing the weather. Indeed, Russia is still a world leader in weather control.

While the Soviet Union produced some truly significant computers – Elbrus and Kronos to name just two – engineers working within a five-year plan could not keep pace with Western technological advances based on Moore's Law, the doubling processor power every 18 to 24 months. For a Soviet computer scientist, processing power was eight times greater at the end of the plan than at the start.

Such is the world today: all plans risk being outpaced by advances in technology. Planning is useful, but too much planning may be worse than too little planning. The solution is to iterate between planning and doing. Planning should be little and often. Planning informs doing and doing informs planning. The life expectancy of any plan should be measured in months, if not weeks or days.

Moore's Law

> *Moore's Law is the observation that the number of transistors in a dense integrated circuit doubles approximately every two years. The observation is named after Gordon Moore, the co-founder of Fairchild Semiconductor and Intel.* Wikipedia[4]

Those working in technology are well aware of the power of Moore's Law and the force it creates, not just for technological change, but for organizational and global change. However the true magnitude of the change still escapes many.

---

[4]https://en.wikipedia.org/wiki/Moore%27s_law

Consider a ten-year cycle of Moore's Law, which would include at least five doublings of CPU power. The final doubling, in years eight and nine, will deliver a greater increase in power than the sum of the previous eight years of increases (four doublings).

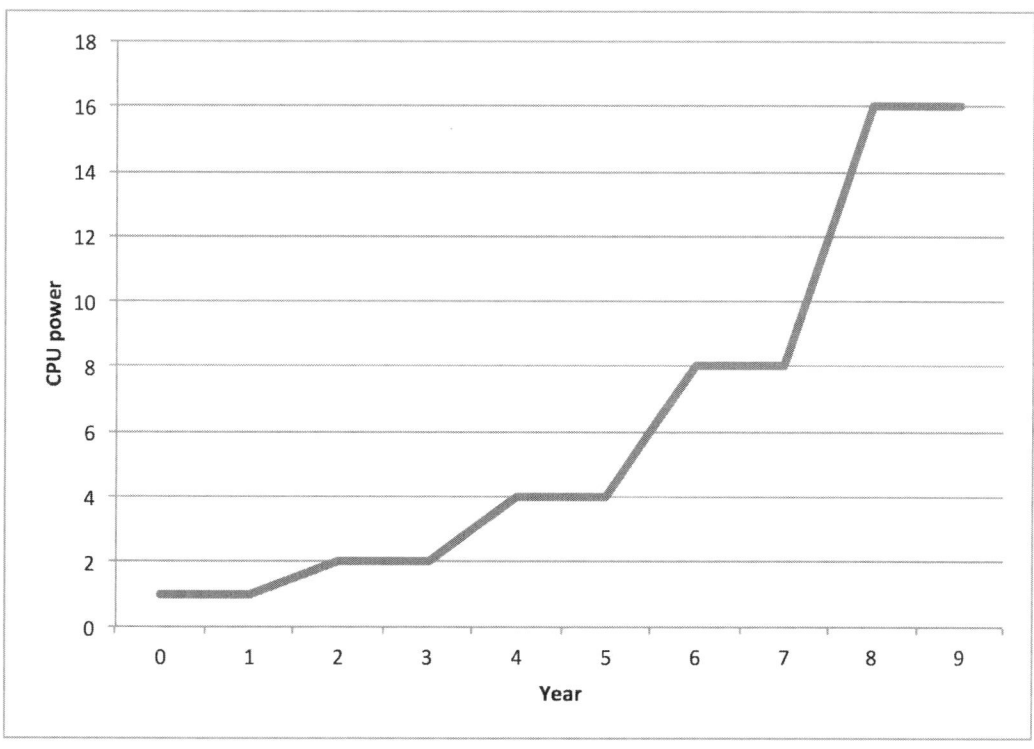

CPU power doubles every two years

The fifth doubling in year eight produces 16 times more power than was available in year one. The previous eight years increased power by 15 times (8+4+2+1). In the next year, year ten, processor power will double again.

Increasing CPU power in its raw form makes machines run faster, so processor-intensive activities complete faster. More importantly, it allows more advanced tools to be used. Consider how many tools now work with human-readable text files (for example XML): such luxury was unimaginable when I began coding on Z80 and 6502 microprocessors.

With increasing CPU power the range of problems that humans can address with machines increases. Similarly, the opportunity to redesign businesses and business processes increases at an accelerating pace.

The technological advances unleashed by Moore's Law create forces with the power to change organizations, companies and the global economy. Look at the changes to the global economy produced by Google alone between 2000 and 2010.

What plan could possibly keep pace?

Finally

While all of these issues can be addressed with more planning and more detail, the plans that result would be pretty much indistinguishable from the desired end product. Any plan of sufficient detail would itself be the end product.

In a rapidly changing world of accelerating technology, conflicting demands and problems that are only understood as solutions to them are devised, there are two obvious responses:

> *Option A.* An approach with extensive planning is conducted before the doing begins.

> *Option B.* A 'make it up as you go along' or 'muddling through' approach.

The real question is, *how does one achieve the desired end state as quickly – even efficiently – as possible?*

In all likelihood the best approach lies somewhere between Option A and Option B. The Continuous model positions itself firmly closer to Option B: short bursts of collective planning interleaved with doing in an iterative model.

16. Piecemeal growth

Gall's Law: A complex system that works is invariably found to have evolved from a simple system that worked. A complex system designed from scratch never works and cannot be patched up to make it work. You have to start over with a working simple system. John Gall, 1975[1]

When born babies are fully operational humans. Not only do they have all the external characteristics in miniature – arms, legs and so on – but the insides are also miniature versions of adults'. They have tiny lungs, a tiny heart, liver, two kidneys.

It is true that they need help from others at first, but they are fully working humans. Mothers and fathers invest in their mini-people, and once they start eating solid food they are fully functional people.

Some time afterwards they become economically active and contribute to society. The age at which children start earning depends on societal norms and has increased as society has developed. Humans grow. Similarly most businesses start small and grow (or fail).

Attempts to start large companies seem to fare little better. Iridium offers one such example. The original Iridium Satellite LLC was a large company born out of Motorola to operate a worldwide phone service using 66 satellites. The company failed less than a year after starting operations. However a second, smaller company, Iridium Satellite LLC, has succeeded in salvaging the assets and operating successfully.

Successful software, like babies and successful businesses, grows. As it grows, it changes. The same principles need to govern the design and development of software: gradual growth of a working whole.

When embarking on a new endeavor the first goal is to get a small piece of software working. Once a small system is working it can, provided it is found to be beneficial, be added to: it can grow. The enlarged system should work and be beneficial. If it does not, it should be fixed before any further growth is allowed.

Little by little the system will grow.

This idea appears again and again in software literature in different contexts and under different names: 'prototype', 'proof of concept', 'walking skeleton' and 'minimally viable

---

[1]*How Systems Really Work and How They Fail*, John Gall, 1975

product' are just some of the names. While each term has a specific usage, the idea is the same: *start small and grow.*

After each growth the system is usable – something Kevlin Henney calls *Stable Intermediate Forms²*. At each stable point the sponsors of the work have the option: continue with more work (and more cost), or cease at this point and take the benefit as is.

Invariably the software that runs the world today has followed this path. The latter-day Microsoft Word is far bigger and more feature-rich than the version that first appeared in 1983. Much of today's cyber infrastructure began life as much smaller systems: the software used for tax collection, bank payments, airline reservations and more is decades old.

Despite being built on old technology, these systems have grown because they are successful in doing their jobs, but they have often outlived attempts to replace them wholesale with new and larger systems. Yesterday's constraints forced 'small', even if at the time these endeavors looked large.

Small advances

> *By piecemeal growth we mean growth that goes forward in small steps...*

> *In the case of the environment, the process of growth and repair that is required to maintain morphological integration is far more complex. Repair not only has to conserve a pre-ordained order, as it does in an organism, but must also adapt continuously to changing uses and activities, at every level of scale.* Christopher Alexander³

The physical design and construction of buildings is often used as a metaphor for software design and development. Such a metaphor is wrong in many ways, but in one way the method works.

Successful buildings are never done. Indeed, unsuccessful buildings are often unsuccessful because they cannot adapt and need to be replaced. Successful buildings change over time; the more adaptable they are, the more utility they offer.

---

²*Stable Intermediate Forms*, Kevlin Henney, 2005, Proceedings of the Ninth European conference on pattern languages; also https://www.researchgate.net/publication/221034431_Stable_Intermediate_Forms_A_Foundation_-Pattern_for_Derisking_the_Process_of_Change
³*The Oregon Experiment*, Christopher Alexander, 1975

When the environment – physical, social, economic or even meteorological – around a building changes, some building change too, or as Stewart Brand says, they *learn*. Those that don't or can't fall into disuse and are eventually demolished.

I write these words sitting in a railway station built for steam trains by Isambard Kingdom Brunel. The station has acquired overhead cables to support electric trains, as well as countless coffee shops and bike stands. Right now new platforms are being dug under the station in its latest expansion.

Buildings have a surprising habit of changing. The Musée d'Orsay in Paris is a wonderful art museum located in a former railway station. The Albert Dock in Liverpool '…was considered a revolutionary docking system because ships were loaded and unloaded directly from/to the warehouses[4]' when it opened in 1846. Today it is home to three museums, at least one hotel, apartments, shops and more.

Often dismissed as mere maintenance, the changes that occur to physical buildings and to software after they become economically active are among the most important additions made.

> 'Maintenance, in this light, *is* learning.' Stewart Brand[5]

As Brand has pointed out, once one accepts that a building – or in our case software – is never 'done', then one's approach to initial construction changes. It becomes natural to design and build for future additions.

Democracy

There is another and perhaps more important reason to embrace starting small and piecemeal growth.

Working in the small allows individuals and small groups to exercise autonomy and authority. Small groups of people become masters of their own realm. This brings technical benefits, because the group can devote its entire attention to a small piece of work. More importantly, it provides genuine authority and responsibility.

Traditionally when working in the large an elite group is elevated above the average worker. This elite group is entrusted with major decisions that direct the software architecture and constrain the authority of those implementing the system, the programmers. As with

---

[4]https://en.wikipedia.org/wiki/Albert_Dock
[5]*How Buildings Learn*, Stewart Brand, 1994

physical construction, software engineering uses the title *architect* to describe the individuals who are elevated and tasked with making decisions others will follow.

Elite design disempowers the programmers who actually do the coding by undervaluing their skills. Experienced programmers know that small details can have big implications for a whole design. In contrast, an elite group cannot devote itself to the details of the choices it makes.

An elite group nevertheless makes decisions that constrain the decisions of the implementors in two ways. In the first case those in the design group are given more authority by the organization: they are put on a pedestal. In the second case the design decisions they make take away decisions from the implementors. Together this is an act of disempowerment.

Conversely, when design decisions are devolved to a small team of equals, authority is devolved too. Those that do the work have real power, and with power comes responsibility.

The role of senior designers – *architects* – changes. Rather than being the custodians of grand plans, they become the shapers of thought processes, guardians of the language of design, and with that comes the responsibility to educate those with less experience.

Economics

The same phenomenon is at work in national and global economics. The logical rationale of the Communist planned economies failed to deliver improvements in living standards equivalent to those of free-market economies. Adam Smith's 'invisible hand' proved more successful at allocating resources and increasing output despite lacking any master plan.

While Governments can set many of the parameters and rules for markets, and maybe even encourage some activities, central planning is at best suboptimal and at worst an outright failure.

Today, in 2018, the rise of new technology and the events of the last ten years are leading many to again question the 'invisible hand'. However the experience of the last 100 years should stand as a caution: not only did central planning lead to poorer economic results, it created elites that placed little value on human life.

Fake it

'The picture of the software designer deriving his design in a rational, error-free way from a statement of requirements is quite unrealistic. No system has

ever been built that way, and probably none ever will. Even the small program developments shown in textbooks and papers are unreal. They have been revised and polished until the author has shown us what he wishes he had done, not what actually did happen.' Parnas and Clements[6]

At some point software engineers came to believe that, rather than starting with a really small working system and growing it, they would be better off creating *components* and then 'wiring' the components together.

This is akin to deciding that humans need a pump for blood, which requires a heart, so the heart should be constructed first. Since the blood must be oxygenated, lungs follow next. Gradually our baby can be constructed from modular elements. Each element performs perfectly in its own right but is useless without all the others.

To complicate matters further, software engineers decided that the architecture that governs the connections between the various components is more important than the components or the system as a whole.

Maybe the whole mistake came from reading descriptions of already working systems. When looking at a working system, even when describing a working system, one rationalizes how the pieces fit together and explain the logic. One does not describe all the mistakes, blind alleys and reworking that occurred on the way to finding the working system.

'Mathematicians diligently polish their proofs, usually presenting a proof very different from the first one that they discovered. A first proof is often the result of a tortured discovery process. As mathematicians work on proofs, understanding grows and simplifications are found.' Parnas and Clements[7]

Test-driven

When creating a new business, someone somewhere decides to invest time and money. It might be your own entrepreneurial endeavors using your own savings, or it might be the latest and greatest spin-off from 3M. To start with, time and money are extended, and may well be lost.

The first real challenge a business faces is to get more money; initial investments don't last for ever. The business must either:

---

[6]*A Rational Design Process: How and Why to Fake IT*, D. L. Parnas and P. C. Clements, IEEE Transactions on Software Engineering, January 1970.

[7]*A Rational Design Process: How and Why to Fake IT*, D. L. Parnas and P. C. Clements, IEEE Transactions on Software Engineering, January 1970.

- Use its initial finance to create a product or service that can be exchanged for more money.
- Persuade investors that ideas, plus the results of spending any initial money, have produced something worth investing in. Property rights to these ideas, or to future revenue streams, can then be exchanged for more money.

If the new business cannot generate more money then before long it will cease to be. (Babies also face a number of challenges during the first few hours and days of life, although in this case most of the challenges fall on the parents.)

The same approach can be used when building software: tests are set, and if the software passes the tests it can advance. If it cannot, then it will cease to be.

Some of these tests are set at a very high level; in a digital business the ultimate test of the software is to generate money for the business. But most of the tests set for the software are tiny: really, really small. Take this example:

```
def test_talk_fields(self):
        t = Talk()
        self.assertEquals(t.title, "")
        t.title = "Great talk"
        self.assertEquals(t.title, "Great talk")
```

The process of creating tests and enhancing the software is called *test-driven development*. Despite its name, it is really more of a design technique than a test technique.

At first the tests are small, written by programmers for programmers. There are also bigger tests, perhaps written by professional testers to demonstrate that the system is working. A demonstration to a potential customer is another form of test: *does it convince them to buy?*

The ultimate test is whether the software satisfies a need and delivers enough benefit to justify its own construction. The 'invisible hand' of the market sets the test: *will people give up something else for this software?*

One might say that it's tests all the way down:

- Will customers buy?
- Will the product manager accept the deliverable?
- Will the software tester find any defects?
- Can the programmer pass their own unit tests?

Fine-grained (unit) tests allow programmers to start ultra-small. Starting ultra-small allows them to harness diseconomies of scale and satisfy Gall's Law:

- Build something small, as small as possible.
- If it works and is useful, then grow it.
- Change what needs to be changed when it needs to be changed.
- Follow good engineering practice but don't second-guess what might happen in future.
- Repeat.

Refactoring

Refactoring is the term used by programmers to describe post-development design. That is, once a system or a piece of code is working, its design will be changed and improved. Naturally this will entail changing the code.

When the software code base is small refactoring is simple, almost so simple it doesn't need to be named. Similarly when businesses are small they restructure naturally as they grow, giving special responsibilities to new hires, opening new offices and so on. It is when software and business are big that refactoring becomes hard.

In code a good set of automated unit tests fortunately makes refactoring a safe activity. Unfortunately, if the tests don't exist, then refactoring is high-risk and many will advise avoiding it, as in the well-known engineering saying, "If it ain't broke, don't fix it."

Refactoring is predicated on the belief that the best time to produce a *good design* is when as much as possible is known about the system and what the design needs to support. Traditional design makes similar assumptions, but is predicated on the assumption that the moment of maximum understanding occurs after the problem has been studied but before coding begins. Advocates of refactoring believe that maximum understanding occurs *after* working code has been produced.

Since the act of refactoring (and additional usage) will further increase knowledge, it follows that subsequent refactoring may be required if the design is to incorporate all current knowledge. Therefore refactoring is not a one-time activity, but may be repeated periodically.

The act of refactoring has few parallels in building architecture. Prominent architecture tends to be restricted to new buildings: traditional 'up front' design dominates. Yet physical refactoring happens too. Take King's Cross station in London. Opened in 1852, the station has changed over the intervening years. One notable refactoring was the addition of a large green extension in the early 1970s. This 'temporary' extension was removed in 2012 when a new airport-like departures area was added on the side of the station. Of course airports didn't exist in 1852, so the idea of a departure area didn't exist either. Once the idea was known it became possible to retrofit an existing station.

Physical buildings do undergo refactoring, but because they are physically harder to change refactoring happens less often. Software should be 'soft': software has advantages over physical buildings because it can be changed easily. However, in order to see and embrace such opportunities, one must relax the physical building metaphor.

Finally

Given the inherent diseconomies of scale discussed earlier, starting small should be obvious, but there are other advantages to working in this way. Commercially there are several *pull factors* that encourage this approach:

- Risk is reduced because work can be canceled early if no usable products are produced.
- Risk is reduced because work can always stop with a working system.
- Return on investment is increased because something usable and beneficial is produced sooner.

There are other advantages to starting small and growing apart from diseconomies of scale. These may be considered the *push factors*:

- It is much simpler to get a small system operational and working than a large system.
- Errors are less likely in something small, and if there are errors they are easier to find and fix.
- Small allows for workers to make meaningful decisions and devote maximum attention to those decisions.
- Change and growth allow valuable learning to be incorporated into systems, learning that is only possible because the system exists.

This approach to digital development allows software to follow the same lifecycle as businesses: start small and grow with success.

More often than not a paper-based grand design is really a dry run, a prototype, plan, a learning exercise. Once actual coding begins reality quickly deviates from the plan as more is learnt. Attempts to force code to comply with an earlier plan result in failure, either of the paper plan or of the code.

'Software development is always through piecemeal growth and rarely through thorough design. Such planned development can lead both to technical problems because the future of a piece of software cannot be known and also to social problems because completely planned development alienates those developers who are not also the planners.' Richard Gabriel, 1996[8]

---

[8]*Patterns of Software*, Richard Gabriel, 1996

III Teams

Everyone thinks of changing the world, but no one thinks of changing himself.
Leo Tolstoy

17. Devolved decision-making

Plans are only good intentions unless they immediately degenerate into hard work.
Peter Drucker

Taken together the ideas set out in this book outline a different model of authority and decision-making. This model inverts the traditional model: the aim is to move decisions as close to the work as possible.

Traditionally decisions are made higher up the organization. If one considers an organization as an inverted tree with individuals as nodes, information and decision requests come from the nodes below, while instructions come from the nodes above. (The classic inverted tree beloved of computer scientists.) The nearer a decision-maker is to the root of the tree, the more sources of information they will have, as there are more nodes below them.

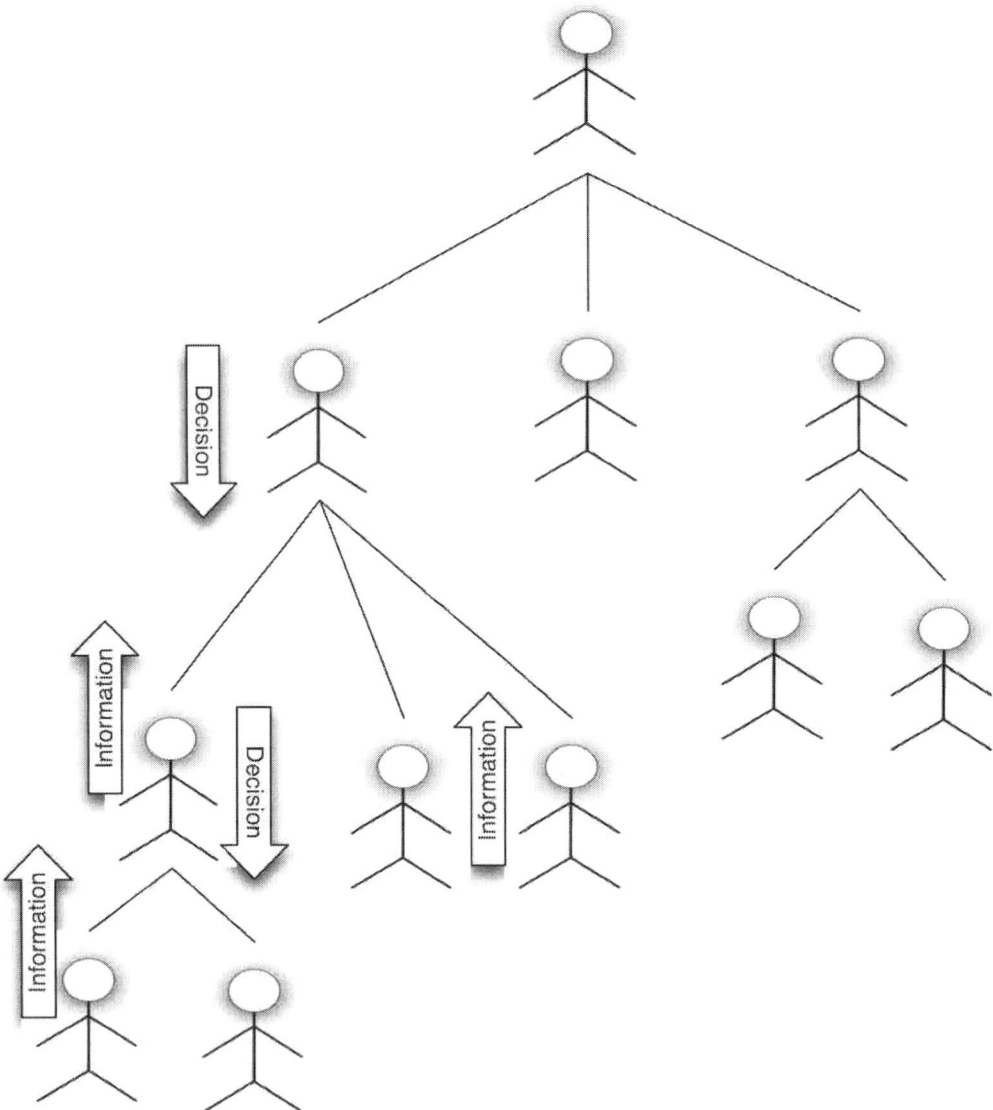

Information goes up, decisions come down

When a decision is needed at a leaf node, the request travels up the tree to the appropriate point, the decision is made, and the answer is passed back down. In the new model, however, decisions are pushed down the tree rather than up. Decision-making is largely inverted, with far more decisions being made by small cooperating groups at the leaf nodes. You can think of this as leveraging breadth rather than depth when decision-making.

Moving decision-making to leaf nodes offers several advantages. Firstly, the workers (leaf nodes) have greater motivation because they have decision-making power. The second advantage is one of speed. Removing the need for decision requests and the information required to make them to travel up the tree, and the answer travel back down, makes for a more rapid decision-making process. A more rapid decision-making process in turn accelerates work, and that in turn generates more value because delay is reduced.

When information and requests must travel up the tree, and a decision back down, there is inevitable information loss. As information travels up it degrades: it is retold, summarized, elaborated and manipulated. The decision-maker may have information from more sources, but information from each source will be lost in the process. Similarly, as decisions and explanations travel back down the organizational tree, information will be lost. Some scenarios may benefit from hierarchical decision-making, but many more will benefit from being devolved and made by those doing the work when the decision is needed.

When dealing with complex technology, perhaps the most compelling reason for devolving decision-making is knowledge itself. Those dealing with the relevant technology have more information, because they understand the technology and because the problem is immediately in front of them.

Further, as the speed of technology increases, the relative cost of delay also increases. When the speed of technology doubles, a delay of a day costs more, because the work that could have been done during that time is correspondingly greater than previously.

The downside of devolved decision-making is that the individual or group of individuals making a decision may not be aware of information elsewhere in the tree. Making all information available to all people would quickly lead to information overload.

While some decisions may still need to be made higher up the tree, there is much that can be done to move decision-making downwards so that those in possession of the relevant information contribute to the decision.

There are several ways to facilitate this and at the same time avoid information overload. The first is to recognize and encourage decision-making, not by individuals, but by groups. An individual faced with a problem and in need of a decision should be able to consult with others.

Such consultations may well span different levels of the tree: those in distant branches or several levels above (or below) can be included. Of course that means that such individuals need to be accessible and have the time to join discussions.

Zen'in keiei

When all workers participate in decision-making all workers become a type of manager. The Japanese retailer Uniqlo has long advocated an approach called *zen'in keiei*. This translates broadly as 'every person participates in decision-making'. Uniqlo have also described this as 'every employee adopts the mindset of a business manager, regardless of his or her position', and 'everybody is a business leader... everybody should feel accountability and ownership as a part of Uniqlo.' Such a philosophy fits well with the idea of amoeba teams.

Of course, if more people are going to be given more information and more authority, it will help immensely if these people are knowledgeable – skilled – in how to use such information and make decisions. Therefore, while this this approach means that much of what is considered 'management work' will be devolved to workers, simultaneously there is a need to ensure that those workers are able to use the information.

That may well mean that in addition to learning the latest programming and testing techniques, staff also need to learn about management. Paradoxically, having fewer management staff means that an organization needs more management knowledge and probably more management training.

Authority, not empowerment

Throughout this book the term 'empowerment', as in 'worker empowerment', is deliberately avoided. Instead I prefer to talk about 'devolved authority' and 'distributed decision-making'.

> 'The term [empowerment] indicated that the power remained with the manager. Truly empowered workers, such as doctors in a hospital, even bees in a hive, do not await gifts from their managerial gods; they know what they are there to do and just do it.' Henry Mintzberg[1]

Nor does this book make much use of the term 'self-managing team', even though the ideas being discussed are contemporaneous. The reasoning here is different. The term 'self-managing team' is historically ill-defined. Some authors use it synonymously with 'self-organizing team' and/or 'self-directed team', while others use the terms to mean something different.

[1] *Managing*, Henry Mintzberg, 2009

I have chosen to side-step this issue entirely. What is important is that real decision-making, which might be called 'managing', 'organizing' or sometimes 'directing', is devolved and authority passed to those doing the work who will normally work as part of a team.

Organizational structure

Organizational structure has a role to play where information and decisions are frequent and require specialist knowledge. For example, say a programmer and tester need to know more about customer motivation. It then makes sense to embed that knowledge in the team, so product managers should be part of the team. A traditional model would give such specialists an elevated position with more authority. In this new model, any additional authority is the result of specialist knowledge, not hierarchal position.

Work patterns too can be altered to ensure more brains are brought to bear on a problem or decision. In software development this sometimes manifests itself as *pair programming*[2] and *mob programming*[3].

Another approach is simply to share more information. Proponents of self-organizing teams are sometimes heard to say something like:

> "Managers gain their power from the control of information. Because technologies (e-mail, wikis, Slack, VOIP and so on) allow for the efficient distribution of information, the manager role is no longer required."

The problem here is one of information overload. Removing the manager as 'information hub' has its advantages, but using technology to make more information available to more people does nothing to increase humans' ability to read and assimilate all the available information.

Making more information available – especially when it is delivered using interrupt-based systems such as e-mail and Slack – makes the problem worse. Not only do individuals need to process more information, but their capacity for concentration and focus is reduced.

Rather than trying to squeeze vast amounts of information and knowledge into individuals' heads, a better approach is to help individuals to know who to ask when they need information. Merely letting people know that such knowledge might exist and who might have the information is a start. Indeed, knowing who-might-know may well be more important than knowing itself.

---

[2] *Extreme Programming*, Kent Beck, 1999
[3] *Mob Programming*, Woody Zuill and Kevin Meadows, https://leanpub.com/mobprogramming

Failure tolerance

If you want to succeed, double your failure rate. Thomas J. Watson Sr, CEO IBM

Organizations that trust employees to make decisions, that embrace decentralized and distributed decision-making and accept emergent design and strategy, also need to accept failure and mistakes.

Inevitably some decisions will be simply wrong. Others will be costly. Sometimes decisions and solutions will create conflict, and sometimes designs and strategies will not work as expected. If the organization does not tolerate – even celebrate – such failure, then employees will quickly realize that failure is not acceptable and should be avoided. While the organization may talk about devolved authority, failing to accept failure will erode autonomy, and people will seek approval from those who would condemn a mistake.

Conversely, organizations that can tolerate and celebrate failure benefit from employee motivation, innovation and rapid progress. This may come with increased cost, however.

Certainly some decisions are critical and care needs to be taken. But most decisions are not life-threatening. A 'wrong' decision will not put the company at risk.

The team mantra should be:

- Fail fast
- Fail cheap
- Learn
- Salvage

Fast decision-making adds value and maybe even innovation. But when a decision has costs – in money, risk, or some other measure – decision-making will slow. Decisions therefore need to be kept cheap, so they can be made quickly and reversed if needed.

Accepting that some decisions will not be as good as they could be, accepting that some will need to be reversed, accepting that some come with a cost, allows decision-making to be accelerated and authority devolved.

One powerful way to learn about decision-making is by studying one's own successes and failures. In order for this to happen, people must be allowed to make decisions, and make decisions that later come to be seen as failures or mistakes. Frequently, even when a decision results in failure, there are valuable things that can be salvaged. Not just the learning, but perhaps artifacts, segments of code, market data, or simply the elimination of an option.

Fast-moving environment

No plan of operations extends with any certainty beyond the first contact with the main hostile force. Helmont von Moltke

In the fast-moving environment that is typical of technology and start-up endeavors, pushing authority downwards will result in more timely decision-making, simply because it eliminates delays in decision-making. More specifically, distributed decision-making helps to remove wait states: time during which nothing is happening and people are waiting.

A side-effect of pushing decisions downwards is to distribute decisions. Rather than one person making decisions for many others, each individual – or perhaps small groups of individuals – will make decisions independently. As a result decision-making is distributed. By bringing more minds to bear on decision-making the bandwidth for decision-making will also increase, further accelerating the process.

Pushing decision-making downwards will also accelerate the process of putting decisions into action, even if the actual decision-making takes longer and involves more people.

Arie de Geus[4] has described how a more inclusive, learning-oriented decision-making process used at Royal Dutch Shell resulted in more rapid action once a decision was made. It appears that while involving more people may mean that it takes longer to make a decision, once the decision is made it is enacted faster. When more people share an understanding and share responsibility for making the decision, they act on the decision that much sooner.

However distributed decision-making also results in greater variability: two decisions may not be consistent. Organizations often strive for consistent decision-making and commonality. Such an approach reduces experimentation and undercuts responsibility. Heterogeneous decisions, resulting in different actions, increases learning.

---

[4]*The Living Company*, Arie de Geus, 1997

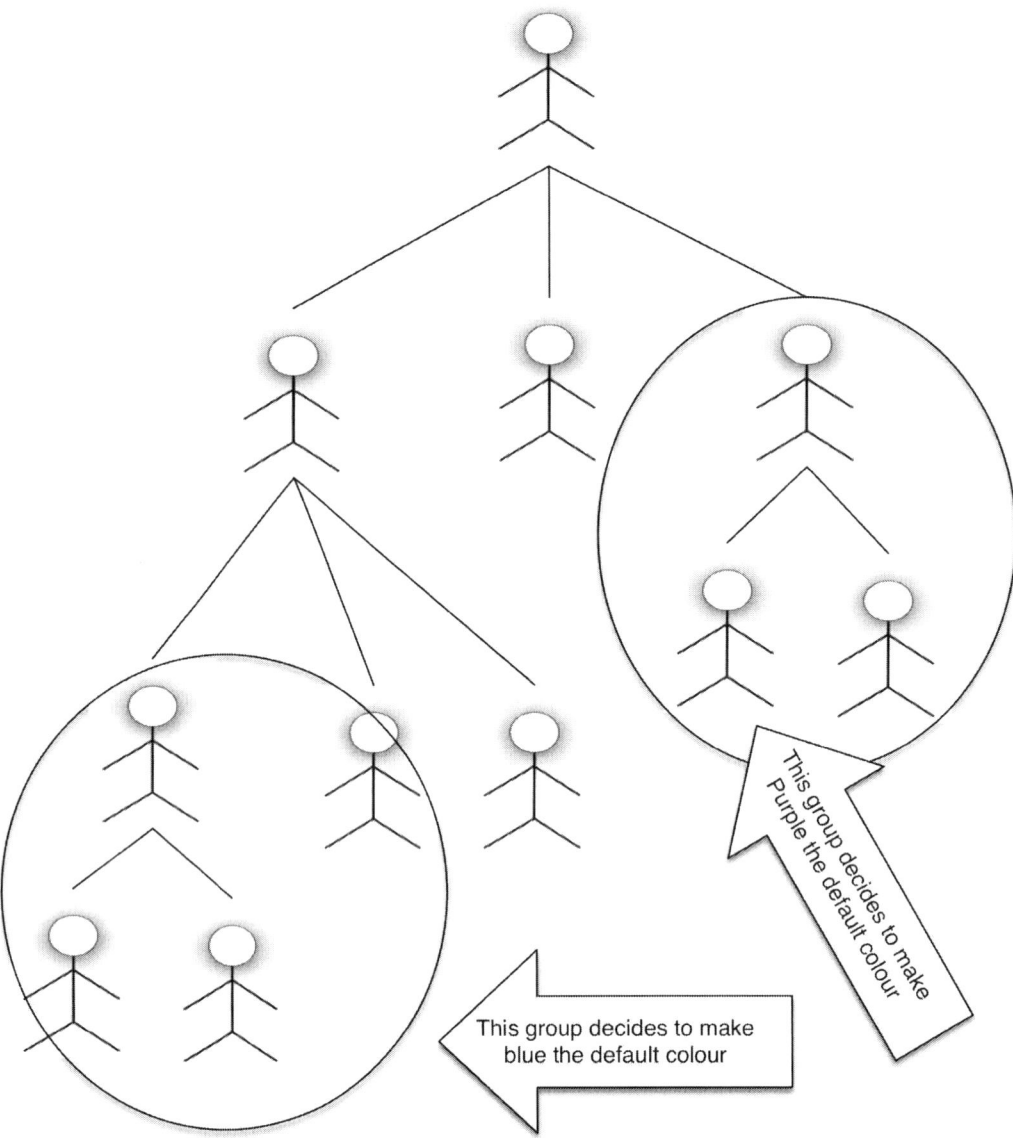

Conflicted decision-making can happen when decisions are distributed

Finally

Traditional organizations seek to avoid diverse decisions and designs, in part because of the cost of supporting multiple designs, in part to avoid duplicating work, and in part because of later costs in harmonizing the decisions. Much energy and thought therefore goes into the initial decisions, and consequently action is delayed and additional costs imposed.

This again is economies-of-scale thinking. While not denying that divergent decisions will impose costs, divergent decisions and designs have advantages:

- Decision-making is accelerated.
- Multiple decisions allows for more learning.
- Ongoing work is decoupled, so teams can continue to advance at their own speed.
- Individual groups have more motivation, because they are making their own decisions.

In short, while there are economies of scale from common centralized decisions, there are also costs. These costs constitute diseconomies of scale and are often overlooked. I suggest that in many cases the costs from the diseconomies of scale outweigh the benefits from the economies of scale. Further, as technology and tools advance, the diseconomies of scale are increasing, while the economies of scale are reducing.

18. Team strategy

Never tell people how to do things. Tell them what to do, and they will surprise you with their ingenuity. General George S. Patton

The team is the goose that lays the golden digital eggs. The team is the production unit: need goes in, valuable working software comes out.

The team is also responsible for deciding *what* work goes in: the team is *value-seeking*. It looks at the needs of customers or potential customers and decides both how it can add value and how it can maximize it.

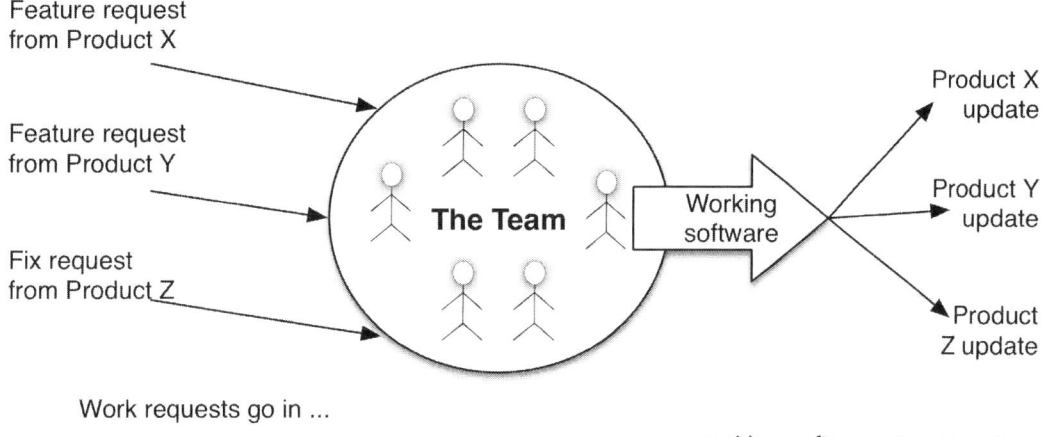

The team is the unit of production

By implication that means that some potential work will not be done, because while it is valuable in itself, it does not represent the greatest value. In other words, the need is out-competed by work of greater value.

Teams don't just accept requests, they go out and find them. If desirable the team can include analysts and other requirements specialists. Within their area of specialization they will seek out valuable opportunities. The team identifies and generates its own work to produce business benefit. The team is responsible for what it does and accountable for the value delivered.

Earlier chapters have already highlighted the importance of giving the team a higher purpose, maintaining team stability, giving the team control of its own destiny, and the amoeba model. This chapter and the those that follow expand on those themes.

Strategic sizing

Teams should be sized and staffed according to business priorities and strategy rather than the effort required to do any particular piece of work.

Companies need to allocate resources – people, capital and so on – between competing priorities based on expected returns and higher purpose, rather than costs. Some allocations will quickly return hard value – revenue – but some will take longer to return value. Other allocations may not return any revenue at all, but instead open options for future investment.

Strategy does not just inform choices between competing priorities. Choosing what to invest in and what not invest in *is strategy*.

Rather than ask "How long will this take? How many people do we need?" one needs to first ask "Which team will do this work?", and ask the team "How will you approach this piece of work? What else might you need?".

The team that receives the work can then examine the time-value profile together with the profiles of other potential work. This allows the team both to decide the priority order and determine how much time is available. Knowing the time-value profile and available time allows engineers to create appropriate solutions.

The team always has the option of going back and asking for more resources. Provided that the team can make a credible case for how more resources will unlock more value, it makes sense to allocate more.

People will still move between teams; teams will grow and shrink, but hopefully less often. Occasional personnel moves are normal and should be expected, but frequent team changes are disruptive and destroy capacity.

Given all this, how is an organization to decide how many people to put into each team? Two crucial questions emerge:

How are they to know when to expand teams?

How are they to know when to shrink or merge teams?

This is a set of questions where, instead of moving to the small, it makes more sense to move to the large. Rather than micro-managing resources, the approach should be to make broad decisions and allow teams to decide for themselves within that setting.

Traditionally much software management work centers on allocating individuals to projects. These conversations can seem almost constant and absorb much valuable management time.

It sometimes seems that software managers only have one lever with which to control work: team resources. One team is slow, so managers pull the lever and someone moves from another team to the slow one. In so doing they sow the seeds of the next crisis, when the same lever will be used again.

Having stable teams and allocating resources strategically removes many of these conversations and frees managers to do valuable work while simultaneously giving authority to teams. Strategic team sizing and devolved authority allow managers to move away from managing piecework.

Strategic staffing aligns with stability because strategy, like teams, should be stable over more than the short term. Good strategies should last for years; if they do not they are not really strategies – or at least not good ones.

Looking at the value to the business is not the whole story. Organizations should also examine the benefits delivered by a team and the potential benefit, insofar as it can be seen. Partly this is good governance: if a team repeatedly fails to deliver benefit, something needs to be fixed.

At a strategic level it is one thing to say that the organization should invest in an area, but another to actually perform well in that area. Simply deciding to invest in an area does not guarantee success.

Competitors, the market, customers and many other factors mean that realizing desired strategies can be hard work. On occasions it makes sense to reverse course or change strategy. Only by executing a strategy is it possible to determine such factors: on paper all plans look possible.

Amoeba teams

Lean manufacturing has long utilized the concept of 'cell manufacturing'. The idea is that one team – one cell – is responsible for creating a whole product or subsystem. At Kyocera this idea is carried further: each amoeba team[1] is seen as a mini-business unit.

Each amoeba team is one cell that makes up a bigger organization. Each has its own purpose and lifecycle. Amoebas grow and expand in size up to a point at which they split, cell-like, into two independent entities.

---

[1] *Amoeba Management*, Kazuo Inamori, 2013

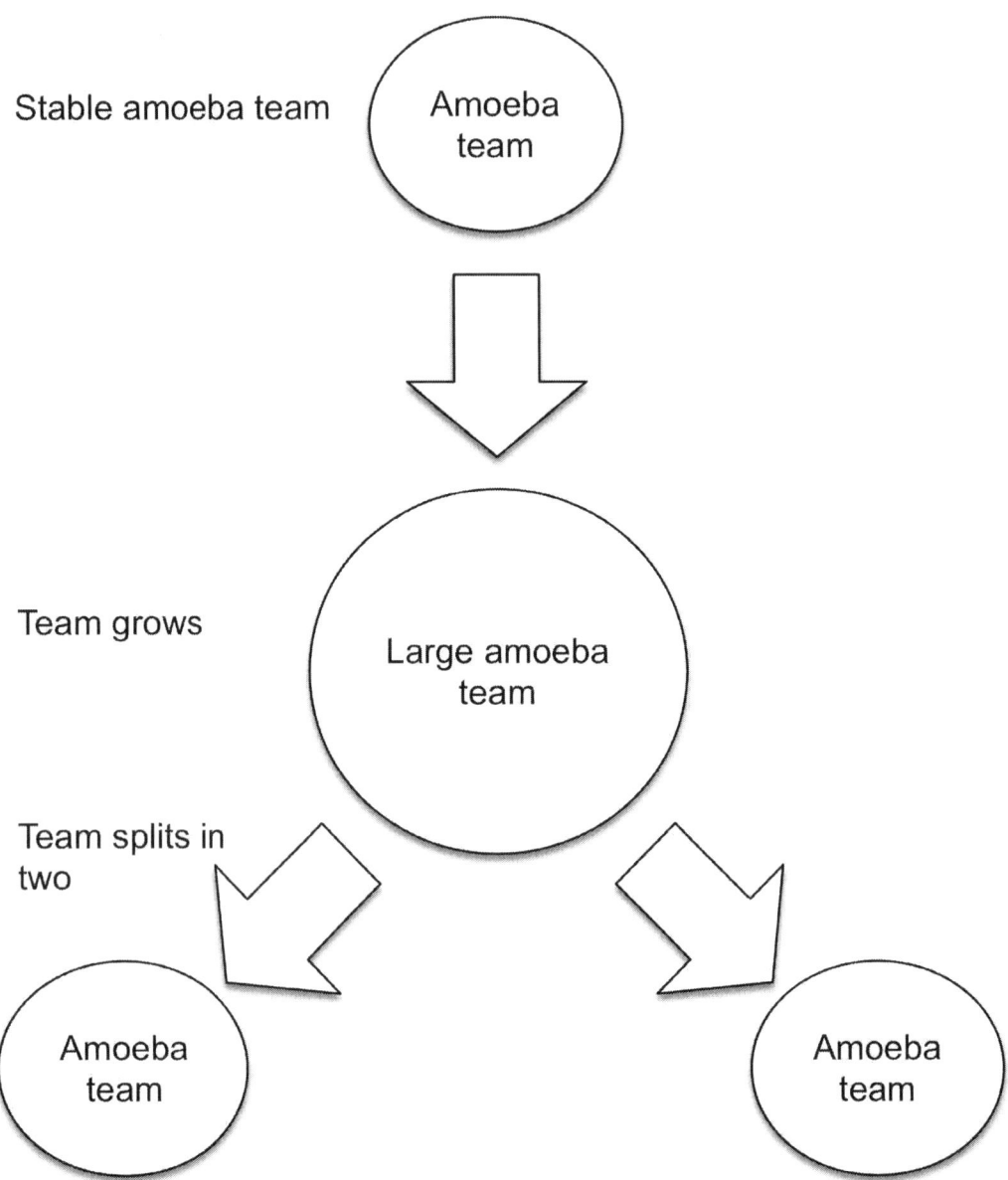

Teams grow and divide like amoeba cells

A successful team that is delivering business benefit should be able to justify growth. At first growth might actually deliver some economies of scale, as specialists can be added to the team, but quickly diseconomies accrue as communication costs increase. At some point it makes sense to split the team in two, amoeba-like.

After the split each amoeba is itself a self-contained unit. Each amoeba controls all the skills to do work; it has capability, together with authority and responsibility, for the delivery of business benefit.

A split might not be into equal halves: a team of ten might split into one team of three and another of seven. With success both can grow and in time split again. The opposite might also happen: a team working on a declining product could well shrink as the revenue from the old product falls. At some point it might make sense for a, say, five-strong team working on a declining product to merge with a four-strong team working on another declining product. The single team would then be responsible for two products and would need to balance their workload accordingly.

Team splits and mergers must respect architectural boundaries, constraints and technologies. It would not make sense to merge teams if one team worked in C++ and the other in Pascal. Nor would it make sense if one team worked on short lead times (for example days) and the other worked on long lead times (for example months).

There may be fewer considerations when a larger team divides, but it would still need to find a place in the architecture where the team could split without the new teams hindering each other. The architecture split would need to allow both teams to deliver business benefit independently.

For example, it would not make sense to split a large sales platform into a front-end team and a back-end team, because neither can deliver much value independently. It might however make sense to split the team into a catalog and checkout team and a second payment and refunds team.

Finding a good place to split a team is critical: both technology and commercial forces need to be considered and balanced. When one – technology or commerce – dominates the thinking, the split will be weak.

Flow the work to the team

Work is transient. Teams are stable and already exist. An organization may have several teams, so work needs to be directed to the team that will do the work. If a team is experiencing a surge in the amount of work it is asked to do, then expanding the team can be justified. Equally, if a team is not receiving very much work, it might be shrunk. Teams can merge and teams can split.

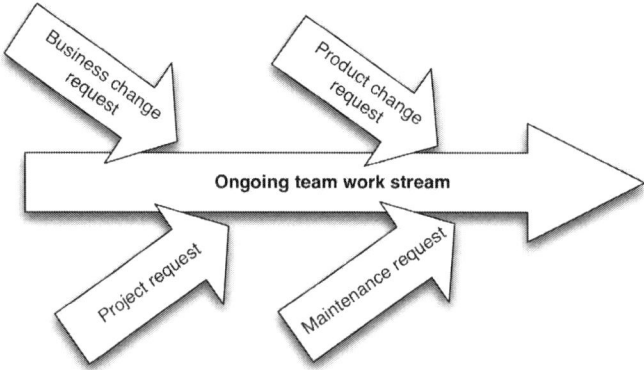

Flow the work to the team

As the team has an area or areas of speciality and responsibility, one hopes it will be obvious to where work should flow.

Imagine a team as a sausage machine: sausage meat goes in one end, sausages come out the other. Work requests go into a team, working software comes out. If pork meat goes in, pork sausages come out, if chicken meat goes in, chicken sausages come out. Software teams specialize in specific products, but the work they do at any one time depends on the requests put to the team. Such requests can take a team into unexpected territory.

When a suitable team does not exist it may be necessary to create one. New teams are created as minimally viable teams: more on this later.

Fail fast, fail cheap, learn and salvage

One of the repeating themes of Continuous Digital is creating lots of options and quickly culling those that are not promising. Options that prove valuable should receive more investment and growing teams.

This theme is repeated in the approach to teams. Existing teams should try many ideas, cull the ideas that do not work and build on what does, while all the time learning.

Similarly, when the need for completely new work or products appears, it makes sense to start a new, small, team, or perhaps even several. New ideas start with a new team: those that don't work are culled, the team disbanded or repurposed. Ideas that work are enlarged.

Teams begin life small and explore the problem and potential solutions. It is not enough to explore just one side, because problems are understood and defined by solutions. This is more than parallel working: it is co-evolution.

Teams are autonomous and can decide that an opportunity is not suitable for exploitation. Even if they decide that an opportunity is a valid area for further work, they may be overruled.

This isn't so far away from the traditional project model, but different in two important ways. Firstly, work on the technical solution begins at the same time as investigation of the opportunity. The two must co-evolve, because the 'problems' that technology 'solves' cannot always be defined in isolation from the solution. In other words, without some understanding of what a solution might be, the 'problem' cannot be defined. For example, how many readers knew they had a problem with Internet download speeds until they heard that faster speeds were possible?

Watts Humphrey is sometimes credited with stating this as 'Users do not know what they want until they see working software'.

Secondly, no commitments are given in the beginning as to the final, or intermediate, state of the work. Commitments cannot be given at the start because to do so would require information and understanding. These in turn imply that pre-work has already happened. Non-trivial commitments can only be given and accepted rationally with understanding.

Having that understanding implies pre-work. Pre-work would imply that work happened *before* 'the start' – the 'pre-project phase' found in some places. If work happened before the start, then 'the start' is not the start, because something has happened: 'the start' has already occurred. The start of the pre-work was the real start.

It is not wrong to do some initial work to gain information or understanding, but it needs to be recognized for what it is: work. Such work may have been performed by one of the existing teams, or in 'spare time'. When information is available it can – even should – be used. However, the moment such work is officially sanctioned in its own right, then work has begun.

The sooner such work is officially acknowledged the better. Once it is officially acknowledged, it can be organized like the work that it is. Unofficial 'under the radar' work is not free; it detracts from other work, and risks disrupting other work.

Teams are free to begin work with analysis – the typical activity in a 'pre-project phase' – if this is the best way of understanding the opportunity. Copious amounts of analysis without any technical work however creates two risks.

Risk one is that the analysis is not grounded in what is technically possible, or where the technical challenges lie. Risk two is that the embryonic team is not capable of delivering working products. Failure to demonstrate the ability to deliver technical artifacts – be they a complete solution, a minimally viable product, a prototype, mock-up or a proof of concept – raises the question of whether the team have the ability to deliver anything of value, let alone a final product.

The early stages of a new initiative seek to prove two things:

- The viability of creating a product to solve a particular problem and further the aims of the organization (for example building towards the higher purpose, or making profit).
- The ability of the team to create and deliver technical products.

Meeting these two criteria provides a platform for the team to build on and grow. When teams cannot meet these criteria it is better to accept the failure and learn from it, salvage what can be salvaged and move onto the next thing.

Team skills

Each team needs to be cross-functional and its members multi-skilled. If a team is expected to deliver business benefit and is to be held accountable for this, the team needs to be staffed with all the skills it needs to deliver that benefit.

Teams should contain all the skills required to do the work they are expected to do. Every time they have to 'call out' for work to be done, dependencies occur, delays arise, complexity rises and responsibility for doing the work becomes opaque. Each call out to another team or individual diminishes accountability.

Team members can have specialisms, but are encouraged to work outside of specialisms on high-priority items. The more team members are able to cross specialisms, the smoother and more effectively the work will flow. Yet when deep technical knowledge is needed, specialists are needed: this might be a reason to avoid technologies that demand deep specialization.

Specialists, in particular software testers and requirements experts (be they analysts, product managers or others), should be embedded in the team. These are first-class members, although no team member should be considered second-class – as unfortunately happens sometimes with software testers.

There are limits to the skills of individuals. While a business analyst may be able to help with testing, they are unlikely to know the finer points of C++. While teams can and should help individuals increase their skills, it is wise to avoid technologies that demand deep specialization.

Managers

A full discussion of the role of managers is beyond the scope of this book. That said, management needs to be recognized as a skill set in its own right. Management is not only about 'commanding and controlling workers'. In a agile and continuous environment very little command and control should be going on, but that does not mean there is no management work to do.

Some management work is administration. Some is that special type of administration that can only be done by those with authority. Some management work is actually specialist work, the special skills that lie under the nebulous name of 'management'.

More importantly, some management work concerns the design of the organization that support multiple amoeba teams. Managers play a major role in setting the rules and shaping the environment in which individuals and teams operate.

I am prepared to concede that the future of work – a Continuous future – may well require fewer specialist managers. While some managers will remain, more people will need to understand management work and have management skills. Paradoxically, having fewer managers in a company implies that more people need management skills and knowledge.

Devolving authority to the teams and team members will improve the flow of work through the system: decisions can be made in a timely fashion by those who are closest to the work and who know most about the details.

Managers are busy people, too busy to be involved in details about who's doing what. Team members will be more motivated if, instead of being assigned tasks, they have a part both in deciding what the tasks are and deciding which tasks they will work on. The days of managers allocating individuals to work and occasionally intervening to move individuals from Project X to Project Y should be history.

Instead, managers need to deal with bigger concepts. They form the teams; the teams agree a goal, and managers leave the teams to do what needs to be done. They certainly need to review work with a portfolio review or similar, but not every week. Managers review completed work, not small pieces, and not work in progress. Results-oriented managers should be less concerned about what is happening and how it is happening and more concerned with the end product. Once in a while they may become involved to rebalance teams as company priorities, objectives and strategies change, but only when necessary.

Finally

Teams are the unit of production. Organizations should allocate their people to teams according to strategic priorities, while aiming to keep both teams and priorities stable over the longer term.

Achieving quality, responsiveness and flexibility – what might be called 'agile' – comes, not from constant changes to teams, but from stable teams: teams that are stable and have the skills, authority and responsibility to do the work.

Setting strategy, establishing teams to match strategy and staying the course requires less, but deeper, management: less knee-jerk change, more strategic thinking.

19. Stable teams

You can't have great software without a great team, and most software teams behave like dysfunctional families. Jim McCarthy, *Dynamics of Software Development*

Teams should stay together; teams need to be stable and enduring. Teams stay together and roll from one piece of work to the next. Over time a team may grow or shrink. Once in a while a team may be dissolved and occasionally a new one created.

'Stable' does not mean static: team membership will change, new people will join and others will leave. Changes should be occasional; regular changes will not allow a team to be stable. Like successful sports teams, the nucleus of the team stays together and changes gradually.

At a mundane level team stability is needed to provide continuity in data. If a development organization is to be run in a rational manner then data on past performance and capacity will prove useful. If a team has not worked together before there will be no data, so it is not possible to assess what might be achieved. Only with stable teams can past performance provide the data required to produce accurate forecasts of future work.

Stable, not static

Just because a team is stable does not mean that it never changes. Indeed, there should be some change in team membership to promote alternative views and approaches, to avoid groupthink and to help the team to renew.

Team members will occasionally move to other teams, either temporarily or permanently. Some changes may be at individuals' own instigation, or because teams need to rebalance, to reflect strategic decisions to put more emphasis into one product and less into another.

Occasionally people leave teams for their own reasons – retirement, parenting, illness or even another employer. To maintain a steady size, therefore, teams need occasionally to hire new team members. In fact one can argue that teams should hire continuously, because hiring takes time but people can leave quickly.

Rather than changing team composition regularly to cope with changing demands, stable teams can look for other solutions. They seek mechanisms to reshape demand, perhaps by moving work from periods of high demand to periods of low demand, by shedding low-value work, or by finding creative synergies in requests.

Teams may agree to borrow and loan individuals over the short term. Such decisions should be made by the teams themselves and should reflect organizational priorities.

At times teams might need to expand to take on a lot of new work, or they might shrink when peak working is over. Such transitions need to be managed carefully.

A core team that stays together and services a number of products that can when necessary expand to cope with extra work is possible. Experience will show whether the team shrinks back to the same size when the work is completed. The core team is home to the shared knowledge of business and technology.

Optimization

Because the team continues to work together it can also optimize its thinking. This might be thinking around technology, application or processes. The team is the unit of production, and should seek to improve its productive capability – that is, optimize itself.

Because a team stays together it has reason to improve its technology and processes: because it stays together, it will see the benefits of its efforts. If a team is destined to be broken up at the end of a piece of work, why would it strive to improve its methods of working and productive capacity?

The closer a team gets to 'the end', the less attractive it will be to invest any time in team and productivity improvement. Indeed it might be more sensible for team members to impede their productive capacity so as to prolong the time they spent together.

When managers outside the team intervene to optimize a team by moving people around, the result is often counterproductive. Firstly it reduces the incentive for team members to improve their practices if they know managers will ride to the rescue with more resources. Secondly, by removing responsibility from the team for solving its own problems, it also removes the impetus and authority to actually solve the problems.

Adding people to the team may increase capacity – after a lag – but it will not improve efficiency. Since new people need to come from somewhere, other teams can suffer as people are moved.

Expanding a team through recruitment will reduce productivity long before any new employee starts work. Decision-makers need to be lobbied to agree recruitment, job specs need to be written, approved and issued, resumés (CVs) filtered, interviews conducted and so on. Doing this work removes productive capacity.

When a recruit starts work, they need help in learning their way around. It can be several weeks, if not months, before they become productive. It is not unusual to hear of recruitment taking three months, and that is often regarded as quick. Hiring new people is a time-consuming process and reduces productivity for many months.

Camaraderie

Teams that work together over time develop a camaraderie – a friendship, an empathy, for each other. They share successes, they share failures; a success for one is a success for all, and when one has difficulty others will rally round to help. Building such camaraderie is part of the 'storming, norming, forming and performing' process[1]. But no amount of team-building activities can substitute for years of shared experience, pain and joy.

When a team shares success, each member also shares responsibility for bringing that success about and the joy when success is achieved. In this way team members can see how their work and their relationships make a difference. Keeping teams together allows camaraderie to build and allows a team, and its wider organization, to benefit from these shared bonds.

Unfortunately teams that are too stable and lack diversity can suffer from the phenomenon of *groupthink*. When this happens team members' search for harmony leads them to stop raising objections. To some degree stable teams can offset this by looking for diversity in the recruitment process.

Area of speciality

Successful software exhibits longevity and continuity and underpins successful digital businesses. It makes sense therefore to match the longevity of the software and business with a long-lived team.

This approach allows the team to gain specialist knowledge of the technologies used, both in the software and the business the software supports. The longer the team and software coexist, the more specialist knowledge will be created and shared.

Since much of this knowledge is tacit knowledge, disbanding the team will destroy much of it. No other team will be able to support the software so well, and therefore no other team can support the business so well.

---

[1] *Developmental Sequence in Small Groups*, Tuckman, 1965, Psychological Bulletin vol.63 no.6

Business domain knowledge (the application or problem domain) and technical knowledge (the solution domain) go hand-in-hand. Individuals on a particular team will have both, and will support each other in their knowledge.

New team members are often recruited because of their knowledge and experience or some subset of this knowledge, usually the solution technologies. For example, a team working on an accounts payable system written in Java and Oracle SQL would hire a programmer with Java and Oracle SQL knowledge. While they may have some knowledge of accounts payable, they will not have knowledge of the actual application and the existing code, because this is unique.

Area of responsibility

Hand-in-hand with a speciality goes responsibility. When a team specializes in an area it is also responsible for it. Team members know – because of stability – that they will be responsible for it next month, next year and into the future. They therefore have a reason to look after the area, to improve it and to help the business benefit from it.

A team's area of responsibility is largely implied by the purpose of the team and the benefits it is entrusted to deliver. Together purpose and responsibility allow teams to have pride in their work and to derive pleasure and self-respect from it.

Teams may have more than one area of responsibility. The greater the similarities and specialist knowledge between the areas, the more effectively this will work. The greater the variance in technologies, differences in business domains and variety of users, the greater the difficulty of keeping multiple responsibilities in the same team. This is a particular consideration when teams need to shrink.

Finally

Constantly micromanaging teams to match resources to goals is counterproductive. Changing team members, forming new teams, disbanding existing teams and changing goals not only reduces productive capacity, but also reduces the continuity workers need to foster responsibility, their sense of purpose and their pride their in work.

Conversely, long-lived stable teams keep, share and propagate knowledge and skills. They have camaraderie and sense of purpose. When given authority and allowed to see how their decisions make a difference, they will do the right thing.

20. Team lifecycle

No organization which purposefully and systematically abandons the unproductive and obsolete ever wants for opportunities. Peter Drucker, *Age of Discontinuity*, 1992

By definition, innovative ideas look like bad ideas, and if they didn't, everyone would have them. Bill Gross, Investment Fund Manager

In Continuous Digital the team is central to everything. Rather than think in terms of the software development lifecycle (SDLC), it is better to think in terms of the *team lifecycle* (TLC). Other chapters have already described aspects of the amoeba model. Here I set out an example lifecycle and expand on the ideas so far.

In an ideal world a team would only work on one product and would have no external distractions, for example past work demanding time from team members. Since ideal world examples are few and far between, the TLC model acknowledges multiple products and external demands, while acknowledging one-team-one-product as a goal to keep in mind.

Running parallel to the TLC is the product lifecycle[1]. In the case of one-team-one-product this is particularly clear. When teams are dealing with multiple products, however, there will be multiple lifecycles in play.

Example scenario

Let's imagine a company that produces software for mobile telecoms operators such as Vodafone, AT&T, Deutsche Telekom, Telefonica and so on. The company has a number of products and a number of teams working on those products in one-team-one-product configurations.

Each team is value-seeking and is staffed with programmers and testers, plus industry technology experts and product managers as needed. Product managers are charged with

---

[1] The product lifecycle is discussed by many writers. *Crossing the Chasm* by Geoffrey Moore (1998) is one of the better-known discussions.

understanding customer needs for their products and communicating these to the team. Product managers must also work with the commercial account managers (sales).

The company holds a monthly governance and portfolio board (described in a later chapter). Each team sends a product manager and senior engineer to report to the board. Many of the board members will be peers on other teams. Indeed, the same manager and engineer who are reporting to the board may also be board members and take part in the review of other teams.

Most of the opportunities identified within the team, or by commercial managers, can be handled within the team as a product modification or extension. Sometimes these opportunities cross product boundaries; when this happens the teams coordinate and work out a solution.

From time to time an opportunity arises that does not fit into one of the existing teams. Perhaps it is a new product idea, or an investigation into a different sector. It might even be a opportunity that could be directed to an existing team but which the company wants to explore differently. Or maybe the opportunity does not fit clearly with one team, but spans several. Having several teams work on the idea would bring significant coordination costs and a loss of accountability.

Whatever the idea, from time to time there is something that cannot be handled by the current teams and products. When this happens the company creates a *new initiative* and a *minimally viable team*.

New initiatives and MVTs

Faced with a new opportunity that does not obviously match an existing team, the company creates a new team. The team is created to be as small as possible, a *minimally viable team*, or MVT.

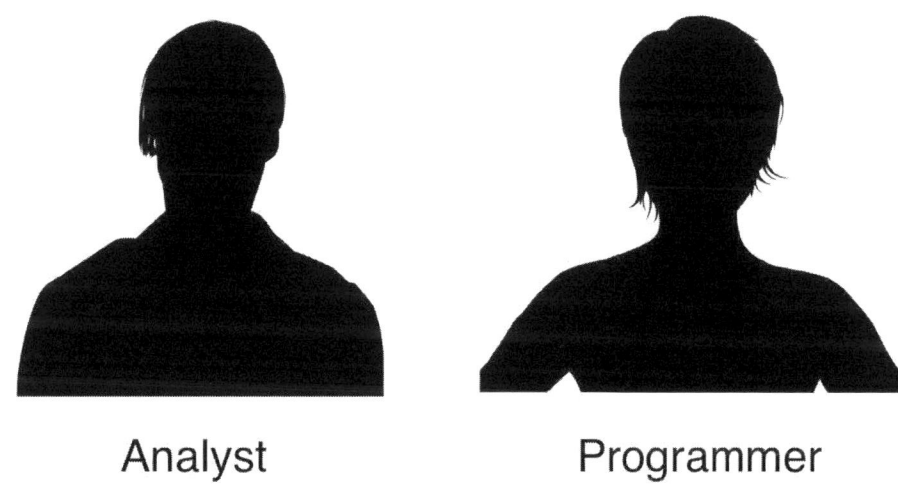

Analyst   Programmer

New minimally viable team

The team starts with two or occasionally three members, but rarely more. If the team is to be able to produce minimal product it needs to have minimal resources. Remember *Kelly's first law of project complexity*, described earlier: 'Project scope will always increase in proportion to resources'.

Momentum and sunk costs too often power endeavors long after they would be better off dead. Overstaffing a team immediately directs the architecture because of Conway's Law, and makes it more difficult to kill the initiative, because money and influence have been spent on the work.

(The term *team* really demands a minimum of three people – after all, there are no sports with teams of two. Doubles tennis, two-man bobsleigh, synchronized diving and various other sports are played in pairs, but these are not graced with the word *team*. So it is debatable if two people really form a team. Still, in this case I hope the reader will tolerate this slight abuse.)

A new team's members are probably drawn from existing teams, although they may be fresh hires or seconded from external partner organizations. Most likely one team member will have technical skills, a programmer perhaps, and the other will be from a more analytical and commercial background such as business analyst.

This may seem like a very small starting base, but it is designed to allow the team itself to determine the skills, resources and other capabilities that are needed. Adding more team members, in particular adding specialists, implicitly makes assumptions about both the problem and its ultimate solution.

In all likelihood the new initiative will fail. Failure to dismiss an opportunity that later proves to be a costly mistake, however, is worse than dismissing a few viable opportunities by mistake. If the team finds a viable opportunity, then this approach will also provide a solid foundation on which to grow.

The new team is handed the initiative challenge. Indeed, if possible those who originally identified the challenge will be included in the team.

How the challenge is communicated is open. It may be by way of a mission statement, a big-hairy-audacious-goal, a simple statement of an objective or some other means. What the challenge is *not* is a long list of 'It must do...' demands: the challenge should be short and sweet. Few words are often best for describing large challenges. Consider what is probably the best-known such challenge:

> "This nation should commit itself to achieving the goal, before this decade is out, of landing a man on the Moon and returning him safely to the Earth." President John F. Kennedy

The challenge also comes with expectations, namely that the team must be able to report progress and findings to the same governance and portfolio board to which other teams report. The challenge may also come with deadlines, important dates or other targets.

The team begins work. Its members are free to adopt whatever working stye they see fit. For the sake of explanation let's assume they adopt one-week iterations in the Scrum style.

The first thing the team needs to do is to work out what the challenge is. This might see its two team members visiting various stakeholders in the organization. Gradually an idea will take shape. At this point – and the sooner the better – the technical team member may well start coding, while the analyst continues to visit stakeholders and conduct research. Both team members will be in close contact, speaking at least daily, most likely many times a day.

Starting the technical work, the building of possible solutions, needs to start as soon as practical. It is frequently tempting to do more analysis and research before coding begins, but since problem understanding and solution creation co-evolve the normal mode of working needs to be in parallel. Learning about the problem occurs more rapidly when possible solutions are offered. The problem defines the solution and the solution defines the problem.

Teams may be started with more than two people or with a different skills combination. However to do so risks predetermining the solution, so caution is required. Team members themselves can request additional help. Indeed, the governance and portfolio board will probably expect this. On occasion it may make sense to start a team with two programmers and one analyst, or one software engineer, one hardware engineer and an analyst, or some other combination.

At the end of the first week the MVT actively reviews its work. Maybe it has something to show others, or maybe its members ask others to help them undertake their review. At this point they may have a refined challenge statement, they may have the beginning of a product backlog, and maybe also a mock-up to demonstrate.

Before the review is finished the team has determined what it aims to do in the next week, most likely more research and more prototyping. If necessary members can plan to travel to see potential customers elsewhere, or even lock themselves in a library to read technical specifications for days on end.

This process repeats until the first governance and portfolio board: review and plan, investigate, analyze, build... review and plan... and so on.

The board

The first formal checkpoint for the work is the governance and portfolio board. The team is expected to report back and describe what it has found and/or built. Of course, if the team has been able to test its products with real live users, or in the market, lean startup-style[2], their report will carry more weight.

The team will also recommend a course of action to the board. For example:

- Continue the work as is for another month: more research and development is required.
- Discontinue the work immediately: the idea has already been invalidated.
- Expand the team with specific people or skills: the work is promising.
- Merge the new initiative into an existing team: the work is understood sufficiently to combine it with something else.

Assuming that the second or third options are pursued, the cycle repeats: the team continues research and development and if necessary also recruits. Let's assume that the board sanctions the addition of two more software engineers to the team.

---

[2] *The Lean Startup*, Eric Ries, 2011

The team expands to four

At this point a tester has not been added to the team. The team could have requested a tester, or the board may have insisted on a professional software tester. While it normally makes sense to add testers to a team as early as possible, an exception may be made for early stages of a team while its viability is still being established. This does not mean that testing is not done; team members are expected to undertake any necessary testing themselves. So programmers must test their own work and each others'; the analyst attached to the team may conduct some testing too.

One reason for not adding a professional tester early is to force the small team to take quality seriously. Without a tester they will quickly trip up on their own mess. Experience shows that software testers, for all their worth, are not always essential for software teams.

More growth

The team continue with analysis and technical development. Team members revisit the board regularly, as do members of other teams, and make their recommendations. Their initiative could still be closed down, but the longer it continues the greater its chance of continuation.

The board continue to examine the potential the team can see for their product and their track record of delivery. Failure to deliver, or failure to live up to the potential the team outlined, are both reasons why the board may discontinue the work.

Success brings further growth: the fifth team member may well be a software tester, the sixth a UXD designer and the seventh another programmer.

It is the existing team that decides when to pull resources from the wider organization, whether these resources be money, machines or people. The team is allowed to requisition the most valuable resources as they see fit. The board sanctions or prohibits such requests depending on potential, track record, wider business strategy or other criteria.

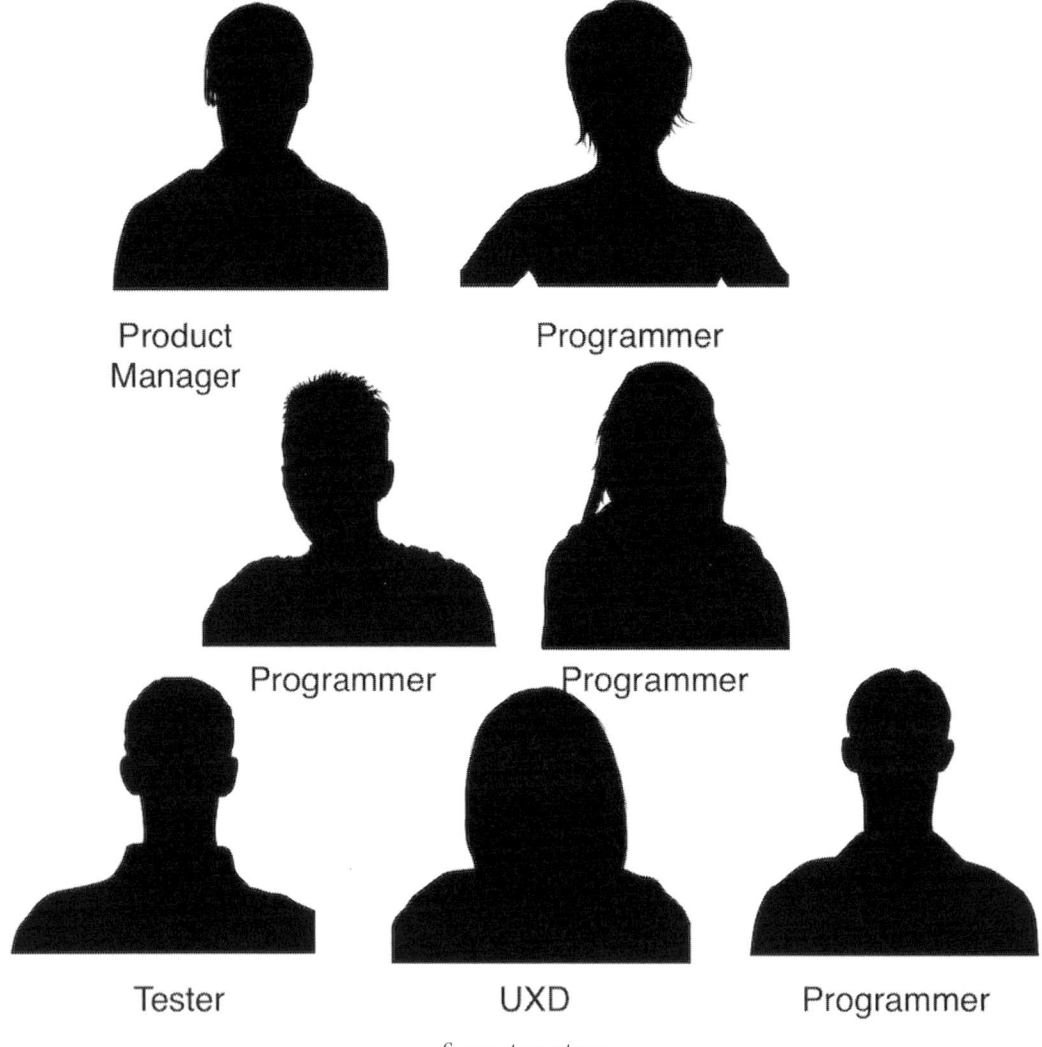

Seven-strong team

Steady state

At this point the team is most definitely not a minimal viable team; it is a full amoeba team and the initiative is no longer new. Significant resources are being spent on the team and results are expected. The board may be prepared to tolerate losses while the promise is bright, but with each month of loss that tolerance will be reduced.

A team of seven is not insubstantial, and the team should by now be producing good results. Indeed the team may not grow any further. Certainly there are many in the agile community who would regard seven as the optimal team size. One might expect the team to remain in this state for some time.

More growth

Provided that the team continues to show a successful track record and continues to turn potential into value for the organization, it may grow again. The team could grow to nine, although exactly which roles those nine fill is debatable.

Adding two more programmers would potentially maximize the tester's ability to keep up. It would also make it hard for the analyst – by now probably a full product manager, or at least recognized as a Scrum-style *product owner* – to keep the value of each work item uniformly high.

Assuming that the eighth team member was a second tester and the ninth another programmer, then the tenth, when they are needed, would most certainly be a second product manager/analyst.

Large team

My personal rules of thumb are:

- One professional product manager (or business analyst) for between three and seven other team members. If there are many customers, customers who are spread in distant locations, or there is active market competitors and sales support to do, then one product manager to three team members. If the market is quieter and customers more homogeneous, then one product manager to seven team members.

- One professional tester for between three and seven other team members. If the product is new, fast-moving and the team unfamiliar with the domain, then one tester to three team members. If the team knows the domain, is long-established and the product is stable, then one tester to seven team members.
- An upper limit of 14 people in one team.

Of course all teams are different and the exact mix of roles and what those roles are will vary. A UXD might be the wrong specialist for your team, but a database specialist might be right. I am prepared to tolerate larger teams while the cost of having a larger team is (expected to be) less than the cost of having multiple teams communicate and coordinate.

Optimal team size is not static. At some points in the team lifecycle it is justifiable to have bigger teams. A team that is preparing to split might well become oversized – say 14 or 15 people – in the run up to a split. Such oversizing allows each of the post-split teams to be adequately staffed.

Split

14 team members is about my personal cut-off. Once a team reaches this size it is time to split. Importantly the split must:

- Result in two viable stand-alone teams with a full complement of skills. A team therefore cannot split until there are multiple specialists (for example UXD, testers and product managers) who can join each new team.
- Each team must have a clear and commercial raison d'être. While one product might be split into two, both resulting teams need a clear understanding of how each adds value.
- Any split must be architecturally logical. Conway's Law demands that team and architecture are congruent.

Meeting and balancing these rules-of-thumb is probably going to be hard: they sometimes pull in different directions.

Team before the split

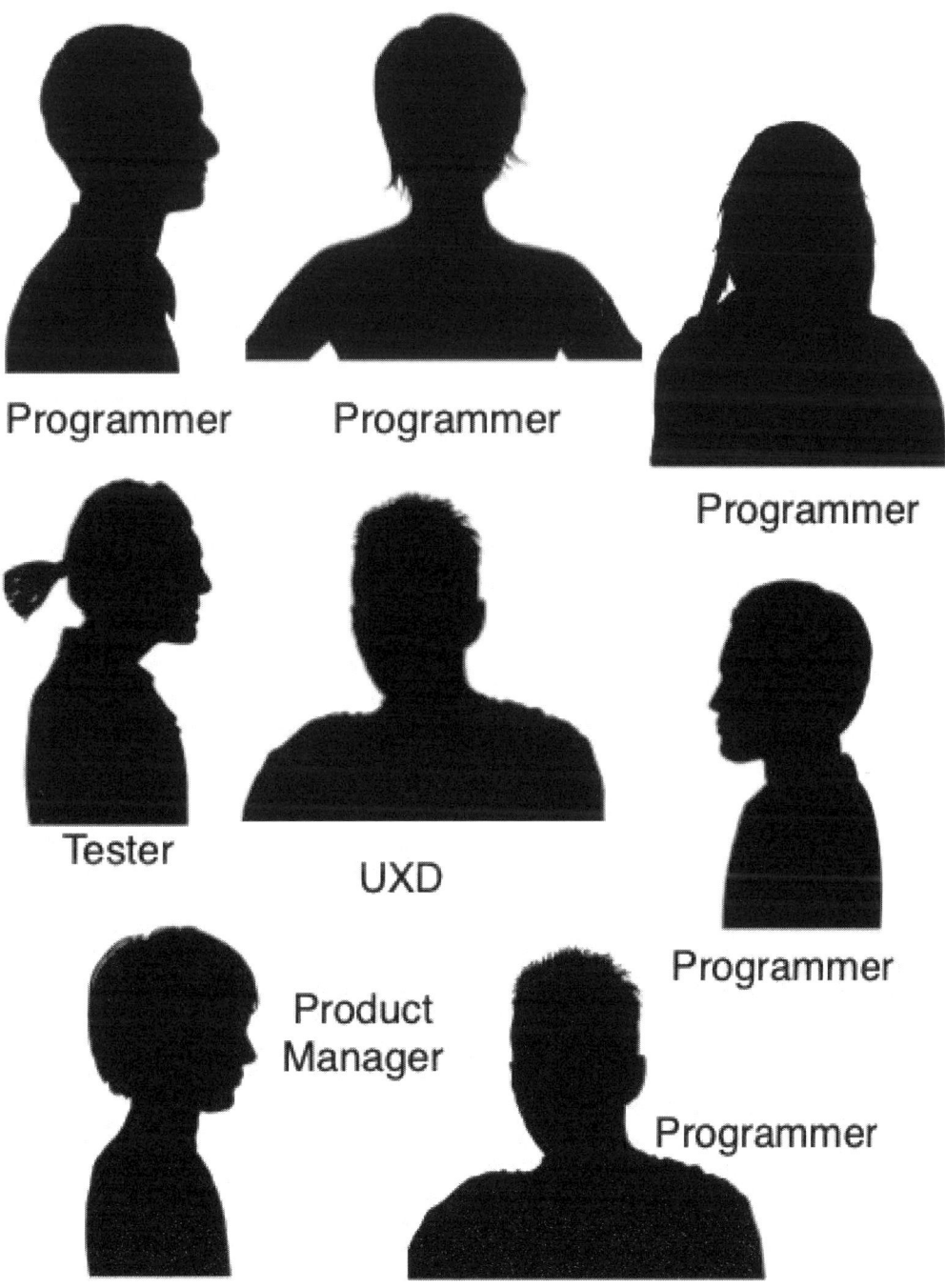

Programmer   Programmer

Programmer

Tester

UXD

Programmer

Product
Manager

Programmer

Team Blue after the split

Team Green after the split

When teams split the resulting new teams do not need to be of equal size. A team of 12 might split into a team of four and a team of eight, or it might split into two teams of six.

In this example one of the resulting teams is larger than the other. Similarly, while this example shows each of the three specialist roles present in both teams, that need not be the case. As long as each team contains the skills it needs to do its work there is no need to duplicate roles on each team. It would certainly be a strange team that had no product owner/manager, but in a team that worked on a system with minimal user interface the UXD role might be absent.

I tend to avoid using team names such as 'Team 1', 'Team 2' and 'A Team' and 'B Team'. Such names imply superiority and inferiority. I also avoid frivolous names such as 'Super Smurfs' because they lack credibility. When the company has a named product or service it makes sense to use the same name for the team. If no suitable names are obvious, then use neutral names such as colors. The US Navy used Blue and Gold crews on ballistic submarines for many years.

Continued growth

The amoeba split principle can continue. Each of these two teams may grow and each might split in time. New teams created this way initially share the same working practices as the pre-split team, but they can be expected to diverge over time.

Each team can be expected to diverge as each finds new and better ways of working. A little competition between teams is no bad thing, but while the teams work for the same company and work on closely related products or aspects of the same product, cooperation should be the order of the day.

This does not mean that all teams need to work in the same way. Indeed, each team can be considered an experiment in working practices. Each team should try new ideas and vary the way in which it works. Some of these experiments will fail and teams will return to the way they were working. Other experiments will succeed. Teams should learn from one another, so if one team experiments and finds an improved way of working it should share it with others.

Following a split the new teams will most likely follow the practices and processes from the earlier, larger team. Diverging practices are not a problem, though, as each team exists in a unique context with different demands and forces. Teams should be judged by results, not process. It makes sense for all teams reporting to a common portfolio board to use a standard reporting format, but that does not require common processes.

Reverse process

The team lifecycle parallels the product lifecycle. So far I have described a product in a growth phase, but what of a product toward the end of its life?

Unlike an amoeba, the team lifecycle model can be reversed. Teams can shrink over time as work dries up – or, more importantly, if the value returned from work falls, meaning a larger team is not justified. The teams shown before would continue to be viable with a few team members missing.

For a mature product it might be possible to drop some specialist roles. Where a strategic decision has been made to let a product die slowly, specialist roles may no longer be justifiable. Eventually, however, a team can cease to be viable. At that point teams may merge.

Consider the two teams shown at the end of the growth phase. Several years after the split the product may be mature, there might be no new customers, just recurring revenue from existing customers. One team might have lost a programmer and its UXD but still continues. The other team might have lost a tester and a programmer. The two could merge back into one team and potentially lose a product manager in the process.

Merging teams do not have to share a common origin. As long as the teams have complementary work and are agreeable, then it makes sense to merge the teams.

Multiple products

Teams are the means of production and team members control the team. As long as a team is capable of determining the priorities between different products, it may work on multiple products. Of course problems can ensue if the products use different technologies, for example a Windows C++ application and a PHP web application.

Similarly a team may find it easier to work on multiple products when the products share a customer base. When products serve diverse customer bases the workload on the product manager is doubled. When two products have different customer bases, more customer visit are needed. When customers are in different locations the time taken to visit customers increases further.

In such cases it may make sense to have two product managers in one team. When this happens the two must agree on priorities across the products. The product managers may agree on a fixed ratio of work, say a 40:60 split, or they may negotiate on a regular basis depending on immediate priorities. However they do it, the results should be tracked. A simple graph that shows, for each iteration, how much was delivered for each product will suffice.

Unplanned work and interruptions

Unplanned work happens. Interruptions happen. Whenever possible both should be deferred to the next planning meeting, but often such requests are also urgent.

In Xanpan[3] I discuss management of such work in detail. Basically: accept it, do it, track it

---

[3]*Xanpan: Team-Centric Agile Software Development*, Kelly, 2014, https://www.leanpub.com/xanpan

and then review the information – a simple graph will again suffice. Armed with the relevant information the team can reason about what to do.

For some unplanned work the answer might be to refuse it: give notice that the team will no longer accept such work and refuse to action it when it arrives. For some interruptions the answer might be to demonstrate to the interrupter the damage their 'just five minutes' requests cause. Sometimes process changes can help to deal with such work, for example the *Sacrifice One Person* pattern[4].

Sometimes, however, unplanned work and interruptions are valuable; they may even be more valuable than the planned work. When unplanned work is more valuable than the planned work it is irrational to turn it down. The question then becomes one of balancing planned work and predictability with capturing value from unplanned and therefore unpredictable work.

In the first instance, record unplanned work and graph it. In fact, graph all the different sources of work for the team. When the team can see how much work is coming from different sources – either as percentages or units of work – the team can reason about its work and decide what, if anything, to change.

It is the work actually done, rather than the work planned (that is, intended) that is important to see. Since this is a team view, there is no point in measuring units per person. Indeed, even calculating such a statistic detracts from the team-centric view.

---

[4]*Organizational Patterns of Agile Software Development*, Coplien and Harrison, 2005

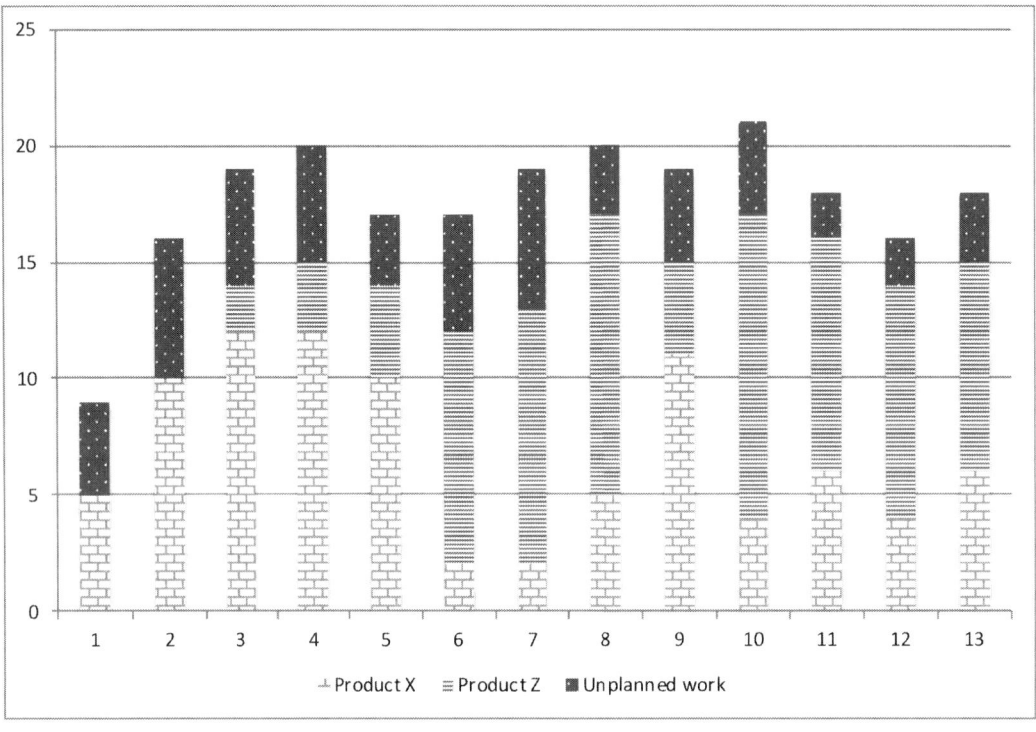

Units of work done for two products and unplanned

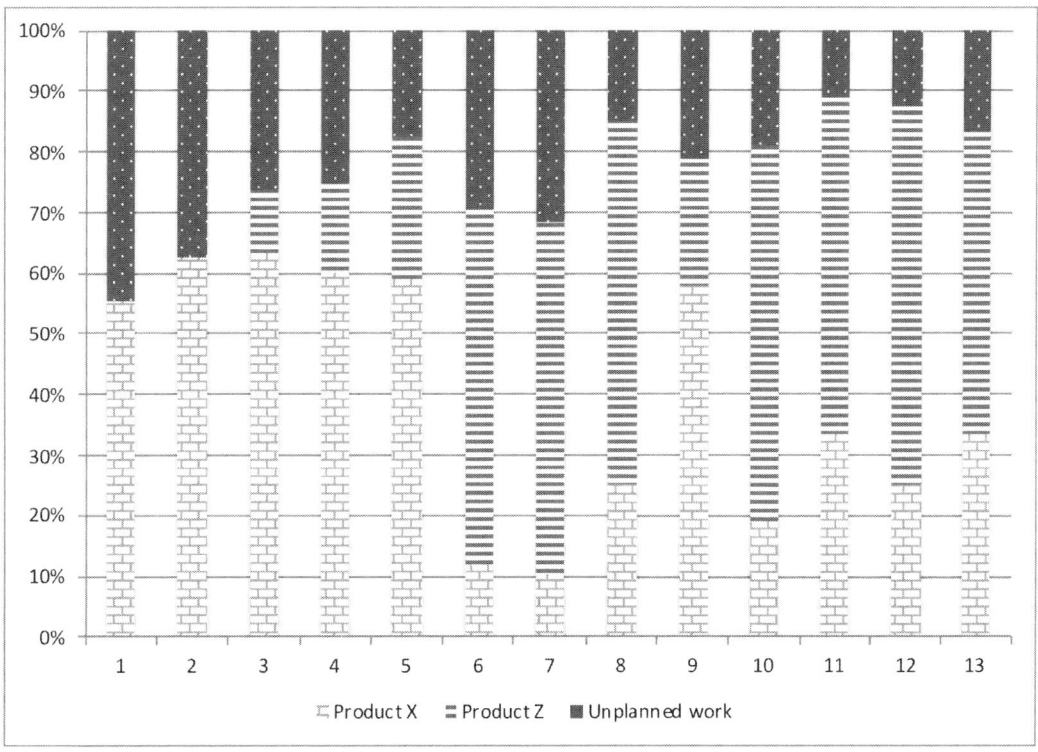

Percentage of work done for two products and unplanned work

21. Team lifecycle – another example

We began with this idea of Bob's [Robert Rauschenberg] that you work with what's available, and that way the restrictions aren't limitations, they're just what you happen to be working with. Steve Paxton, dancer

Let's take an another example of the team lifecycle and show how it works. To make this different, let's imagine a very un-agile organization – a legacy bank – and a very un-agile scenario: regulatory change.

The imaginary legacy bank is faced with a new set of regulations that require it to offer third-party access to its internal systems. These systems – there are several – run on legacy code dating back decades. As it is a regulatory demand, the bank has no choice but to comply – and comply by a drop-dead date. Needless to say, the new access mechanisms are decidedly twenty-first century technology.

Surely, you might say, *isn't this a case where a large team will be essential?*

A large team may well be needed in the end, but if the bank jumped in with a large team at the start, or even just the assumption of one, the option to take a smaller approach would be off the table. Large teams have greater communication overheads because there are more people with which to communicate. When learning is rapid, as it is at the start of a new piece of work, concentrating that knowledge in fewer heads is more efficient. In time more people will need to share the knowledge, but starting with a tight team will accelerate learning because the dissemination costs are lower.

Small teams also suffer less from the need to justify themselves. Once the budget for a large team is approved, let alone the team itself assembled, those who manage the work have little motivation to look for a smaller and simpler solution. If such an option did arise, anyone who recommended it would by implication be suggesting that the incumbent team had done something wrong.

Setting up and staffing a large team takes time. To start with, those funding the work would want to understand what the team was to do and how long it would take. While such demands are entirely reasonable, answering such questions would take time. When there is a hard deadline, that means that time is lost.

Budgeting

Even for a small team you might reasonably ask "What about a budget?".

Coming up with a diligent budget would also take valuable time. Fortunately there is a crude but reliable approach: 'burn rate'.

Once the size of the initial MVT is known, so is the monthly cost of the team. A small amount of money can be allocated to fund the initial MVT for a period of weeks. Since the work *must* be done, part of the challenge to the team is to understand how much money is needed over the longer term.

One of the team's tasks during the initial period would be to understand the cost of different options over time. However, even here the team would not devote as much time to budget forecast as a traditional pre-project phase. In the early stages of such work any budget is likely to be wrong, as initially there is little hard data available for forecasting, whatever the methodology used. Without actual data on team performance no forecast or budget is likely to be accurate.

Even today and even in strict project environments, managers frequently engage in (unofficial) *reverse budgeting*. Once they know approximately how much money is available, plans and estimates are revised to match the possible budget. I can vividly remember a project manager at one bank reworking his budget request figures to match the budget he thought he would be allocated.

Rather than engage in educated guesses, massaged estimates and large contingency reserves, the matter of money is deferred until more information is available. This is simply a recognition of the position that all 'projects' find themselves in at the beginning of work.

(A later chapter explores budgeting in more depth.)

What are you building?

Surely, you might ask, *if there is a hard deadline, then there is no time to work agile or explore options?*

Agile working is nothing if it is not about working to deadlines. Delivering something (almost anything!) in short cycles is the modus operandi. Every iteration should result in deliverable working software. Every iteration is potentially the last iteration. Every iteration should move the team towards its goal, as well as providing data for forecasts.

In this scenario each of the early iterations is adding to understanding of the problem. Initial iterations deliver very little software to solve the primary request; instead they deliver information about what needs to be done and what might be done. It is only through the exploration of options that the optimal solution can be found.

The solution defines the problem and the problem defines the solution: the two co-evolve. The existence of a regulatory document does not define the problem – the regulations only define the expected outcome. The problem, and how those regulations are satisfied, evolves with the solution.

Exploration won't end when delivery starts, but over time the amount of exploration of the problem and the solution spaces will decline and the volume of delivery will increase.

The aim is to shift the focus away from exploration and towards delivery over time. The process is accelerated by using the same team for both tasks. Further, the initial exploration iterations act as a proving ground for the new team to learn how best to work together. Since governance looks at the capability to deliver, any team that does not learn to work together effectively will fail.

Set-based engineering

If the bank wants to mitigate risk by having more people work on the problem, it might initiate several similar teams with the same brief in parallel. Each team would explore the problem and different solutions before one, or possibly more than one, would be tasked with implementing their solution.

This approach is known as *set-based engineering*[1]. The teams would be set broadly the same goals but with different expectations: one might be tasked with exploring minimalist solutions, another asked to examine a complete overhaul, and a third to look at COTS[2] options. The first represents a safe option that would meet the deadline, the second might be a better long-term solution but risks missing the deadline, the third a low-probability/high-reward option.

In the extreme all three might be funded to completion, but it is more likely that one or two options would be closed off and the teams redirected at some stage. Learning will be accelerated by having three teams explore the same or very similar problem and its solution.

---

[1]Set-based design, or set-based concurrent engineering, is described in several books about Toyota's 'lean' design practices, for example *Product Development for the Lean Enterprise*, Kennedy 2003, and *The Toyota Product Development System*, Morgan and Liker 2006.

[2]Common off-the-shelf software

Naturally the teams should share their findings, although they should not be dependent on one another. Teams might agree to regular cross-briefings, but they should not expect to share every detail of each others' work, and they certainly shouldn't divide the exploration between them.

Set-based engineering may sound – and even be – costly. But extensive research and analysis plus a subsequent large delivery team is also expensive. Starting with a 'large and expensive' mindset precludes smaller options. If a company can afford a team of 30 people for 12 months, it can also afford three teams of three for a month or two at the beginning. This may be especially true when external suppliers are used, as such suppliers have a vested interest in bidding up the amount and cost of the work to be done.

Scope

Look, you might say, *this is regulatory: the scope – that is, what must be done – is fixed.* But scope is never fixed. Scope is always variable dependent on interpretation, the time available and what is possible.

Formal regulations might have the appearance of being fixed, but they are both open to interpretation, as court judgments regularly prove. Regulations change, both as interpretation advances and the implications, and potential conflicts within, emerge.

Banks usually have the option – albeit not usually an attractive one – of ignoring regulation and paying a fine instead. Or they may comply with the regulations but over a longer period than initially envisaged, while paying fines until a full solution is in place.

Within any scope document there is more flexibility than is initially apparent. One recurring area of flexibility is that of *non-functional requirements*, specifically performance requirements, such as how quickly the system must respond or how many simultaneous users it should be able to handle.

It is entirely possible that a bank could meet a new regulatory requirement with a product that, while meeting the letter of the regulation, did not represent the final answer. Indeed, it may not even be possible to define what the 'final answer' is until initial versions of the product go live: those who attempt to answer this question can only do so by allowing copious amounts of spare capacity and gold-plating the supplied functionality.

An iterative approach, however, would be to implement a more basic solution and observe how it performs. When performance and usage patterns have been observed, the solution can be improved. Such an approach can allow the bank to meet the initial deadline at lower cost and risk, then continue work beyond the initial deadline. The overall duration of the initiative would be longer, as the team would not stop on the deadline.

Alternatively the bank could run the work at a faster pace and seek to deploy a solution early, before the regulatory deadline, then move into a 'measure and improve' phase. Having satisfied the regulatory deadline early, most of the additional work is discretionary. Continuing work would be governed using the value the team delivers, just like any other Continuous Digital team.

Not only is much regulation subject to interpretation, it can often be changed through political lobbying. Banks are no strangers to political lobbying. Inevitably, as regulations are examined by bank staff, difficulties will arise that demand interpretation or potential change. Early discovery of such issues is advantageous, and this provides us with a convenient place to talk about testing.

Test-driven regulation

Faced with new regulations, our imaginary bank needs to be able to show compliance with them. This is a perfect situation for a test-driven approach.

Reframing each regulatory requirement as a test will itself reveal differences in interpretation and therefore where clarification is needed. Once a regulation is cast as a test, the test will itself pass or fail. A failed test indicates work to do, a passed test demonstrates compliance. Tests effectively form the detailed specifications that are derived from requirements. As the tests are (programmatically) executable, any deviation between program code and specification is quickly revealed.

By specifying the regulations as tests, it becomes very clear when the regulation is met: the test passes. When a test passes, a piece of work is done.

Executable tests can be source-code controlled and referenced back to regulations, providing traceability. Unlike a traditional traceability matrix, because the tests are executable, any deviation of code (or test) is quickly highlighted.

Framing regulations as tests also has another benefit: it will highlight where regulations are inconsistent. If work to make one test pass causes an earlier test to fail, then there is a clear inconsistency.

When all the tests pass, all the regulations are met and all the work is done. The tests form the boundary conditions of the work.

The minimally viable team

It is unsurprising then that in this example a professional tester is an essential element of the MVT from day one. Interpreting the regulations and engaging with stakeholders will require an analyst. These two roles form the core of the team, but as technology solutions will also need to be investigated, an experienced programmer will also be needed.

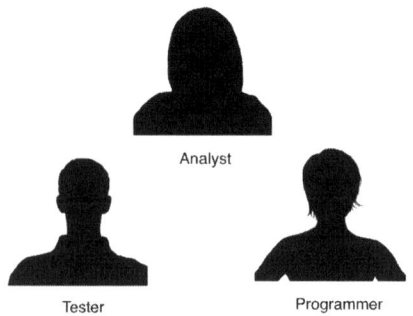

Minimally viable team for bank regulation

With apparently fixed requirements and a hard deadline there will probably be pressure to have an even larger team: perhaps a second tester or analyst, perhaps a test automation expert and perhaps a manager to run the team. However, each additional team member implies more assumptions about the problem and its solution. It is better to let the initial team expand rapidly than to impose assumptions.

When faced with lots of work and an unmovable deadline there is a danger that people make assumptions that are left unquestioned. Once the assumption is made that lots of people are needed, it follows that lots of money is needed. When lots of money is needed it is reasonable to ask for upfront analysis. Such analysis itself costs money and delays the start of work. Once money is allocated and people are in place there is an incentive to 'make work', even if other options might be available.

In this case the first problem the team faces is to define what needs to be done: hence the analyst and tester come to the fore. It is even possible that the bank might already be in compliance with the regulations but doesn't know it.

Initially the tests might be entirely manual, or even rhetorical. Suppose that the tests start to show up ambiguities and omissions in the regulations. The analyst or tester might need to raise this with others in the bank or directly with the regulators. Indeed it is possible that the MVT quickly finds that it needs extra non-technical staff – lawyers, maybe – to aid with interpretation of the regulations and liaison with the regulators.

Tracer bullets

While the analyst and tester work on turning the regulations into tests, the technical team member starts to fire 'tracer bullets'[3]. A 'tracer bullet' is a thin production-quality end-to-end slice of functionality. In creating such limited slices the team explores what is needed and the problems it faces. Like the better-known 'spikes'[4], tracer bullets are intended to increase knowledge and enhance understanding of the potential solution.

The idea of a tracer bullet is to explore what might happen in a potential solution. Many tracer bullets may be needed before the best solution is identified, but in each case knowledge is gained: knowledge about what the technical challenges are, what is technically possible and how teams and processes perform.

In the bank scenario it is probable that teams already exist to maintain legacy applications; even if these teams labour on 'projects', the membership of the teams may well be stable. Typically each project is followed by a similar project on the same code base with largely the same people.

Firing a tracer bullet may therefore require the technical team member to work with one or more of these teams. They may need to go to the team and persuade the team to allocate some time away from their current work to help with exploration. If the standing teams exist in a project-based organization this will be more difficult, because allocating time to regulatory work and tracer bullets will hinder the current legacy project. As tracer bullets are investigative and aim to increase knowledge rather than deliver products, it can be hard to show value or return on investment.

As tracer bullets are fired it is likely that the need for more tracer bullets will be identified. In time it is likely that the team will need to add more technical staff to keep up with the tracer bullets. However, teams should not fire tracer bullets forever – that would be akin to 'paralysis by analysis'. There comes a point at which firing more tracer bullets may well increase knowledge, but a decision needs to be made, a solution selected and the focus shifted to delivering the chosen solution.

At some point the knowledge gained from going deep into one solution will be greater than continuing to look at wider options. One of the tracer bullet may well form the initial *walking skeleton* upon which the solution is built.

The team needs to deliver to the deadline. Delivering a 'perfect' solution is not the goal, but delivering *a* solution within the timeframe and other constraints is. At some point the team

---

[3] *The Pragmatic Programmer*, Hunt and Thomas 2000
[4] *Extreme Programming Installed*, Jeffries, Anderson and Hendrickson 2001

needs to commit to options even if more investigation could result in a 'better' solution.

The bank may even impose a budget limit on the team. If so this is merely one of the constraints it must work within: part of doing the work is crafting a solution within such constraints. So...

> The team does not build the 'best' software solution possible – it builds the best solution it can within its constraints.

Expanding the technical side

As the exploratory work turns into actual delivered work, decisions will need to be made about which teams deliver the work. Completely new work, such as writing an API, can easily be taken on by the regulatory team, or perhaps a sub-team spun out of the initial team.

Where legacy applications require work there are several options:

Option 1: Take the work directly. It is possible that the main team could take on the legacy system work. This makes sense because the legacy teams have plenty of existing work to do, while the regulation team has capacity.

However, this approach would mean that the regulatory team will not have the knowledge to undertake the changes, so the two teams would need to coordinate the work on the legacy system. To do this technical practices would need to be very strong, and the work would eventually need to be folded back into the legacy team when the regulatory work is complete. Both of these represent particular challenges with a legacy code base.

Option 2: Inject the work. The second solution would be for the regulatory team to inject work into the existing team. Such work injections would comprise requirements with tests – specifications – to be satisfied.

As the existing team has the knowledge to do the work, this option should be more efficient than the first. However, if the legacy team is still working under the project model then conflicts will arise. Conversely, if the legacy team is working under the Continuous model the requested work will need to demonstrate value. The regulatory team should be able to assist here, although a strategic view might need to be taken as how much value the different teams each add independently.

Option 3: Second staff. Current legacy team members could be seconded to the regulatory team to undertake the work. Like the first option, this option creates problems with multiple teams working on the same system, but there should be fewer problems folding the work back in.

Alternatively, regulatory staff could be seconded to the legacy team. This would both increase capacity in the legacy team and bring knowledge of the legacy system and regulatory changes together. This would reduce the set-up time for work, as the legacy team would have existing development environments, release pipelines and so on. However, the existing processes and practices of the legacy team could present challenges.

Non-IT work

New regulations are likely to require changes to bank processes, terms and conditions and other non-technology aspects. The process of writing tests against the regulations will highlight what changes are needed. As the technical solution starts to become clear, other changes may emerge.

The team probably started without any specialist in this area, so it should pull in the necessary people as the need emerges. However, specialists assigned to a team before the outline of a solution is known might make assumptions about the work to be done: while specialists would bring useful knowledge, their assumptions may be premature.

Growth

Before the team is expanded too far it is important that the MVT demonstrates that it is capable of performing and delivering. Prematurely expanding the team before it has demonstrated working practices capable of delivery risks making delivery more difficult. It is easier to get a small team to deliver and then expand the team than it is to fix a large team that cannot deliver.

A track record of actually delivering work is also important for governance. The governance process examines a team's delivery record, so a team that has not delivered or has experienced problems with delivery will probably fail the governance and portfolio board.

As the MVT adds testers, lawyers, analysts, technical staff, non-IT staff and others it will become necessary to split the team, amoeba-style, into smaller sub-teams. These teams have not been identified in advance, because to do so would require identifying what work was yet to be done – that is, pre-work. Such pre-work is itself just an earlier start date, and pre-work without implementation effort does not allow solution and problem to co-evolve.

As work packages are identified sub-teams would be spun out of the main team. Each team would be capable of operating independently. Technical teams would be staffed with their own programmers, testers, analysts and others. Non-technical teams wouldn't need such skills, but only when the work has been understood will the required skills be identified.

The test-driven approach makes it easier to demonstrate progress, because the number of tests and the number of tests passed should increase. Of course it is not possible to know how many tests will ultimately be written, so the trend is more important than the actual number.

Peak and beyond

At some point there will be a peak in the work undertaken by the team. This will probably only be identifiable in retrospect. Once the peak has passed the team configuration will start to change again and staffing reduce.

MVT grows into a larger team with sub-teams, then shrinks

Some sub-teams may disappear completely. They may start by shrinking, shedding staff as work finishes and eventually closing. Remaining work and ongoing support can be handed to other teams.

Even if a sub-team does not disappear completely it may well shrink. As the regulatory demands are satisfied and deadlines met it is probable that there will still be ongoing work to be done, for example to ensure continued regulatory compliance. A shrunken team may continue indefinitely provided that it can demonstrate that it is delivering ongoing value.

As sub-teams shrink they will disband or merge as the overall team takes on a new form. Shrunken teams may merge with other regulatory sub-teams, or even with teams that were never part of the regulatory work.

There may well be a continuing need to ensure compliance. Where new technology has been created this will need ongoing maintenance and enhancement, as with any other piece of software. In the longer term some sort of residual team that supports the regulations and technology required to meet them will be needed.

In cases in which staff have been seconded from other teams they will naturally return to their original teams. Quite possibly such staff will take with them ongoing support of the new software they have created.

A project in hindsight

Hang on, you say, *this sounds like a classic project!*

In a way you are right. Teams following this lifecycle may in retrospect appear to comply with the definition of a project.

If all the staff are released and the initiative marked as 'done', then the initiative can be considered a project: it had a start when the MVT was created, and it has an end when the last team member is stood down. It fulfilled a need: to meet the regulatory requirements, and it was unique – the same people didn't work on any similar piece of work. But all this is only seen in hindsight: the work was never compromised to fit a predefined template.

In the digital world it is more likely that some work will continue. Our imaginary bank is dependent on software technology systems. Since these systems are used, and since the world around them changes, the systems themselves require ongoing change.

With the benefit of hindsight one might consider this initiative a project, but there are two key differences to a traditional project.

Firstly, the end state is not determined at the beginning: the bank needs to comply with the new regulations, but how it does that is itself part of the work. It is in doing the work that the work is understood, and what else needs to be done becomes clear and can be decided on.

The problem and solution are allowed to co-evolve and define one another. Deciding what needs to be done and how work gets done happen in parallel: the two activities feed off one another. The resources required are acquired as they are needed; different decisions result in different resource requirements. Such an approach defies the definition of a project and the usual approach to project work.

Secondly, closure at the end is not predetermined. The work may never end: there may always be ongoing support and maintenance. Indeed the relevant regulations themselves may continue to evolve over time, requiring ongoing development work. It is also likely that as third parties connect to the bank's systems, new requirements that were never considered by the bank or regulator will arise.

Pre-project?

Foreseeing the demise of a team before it even starts work would have required pre-work done by people outside of the team. Such pre-work would have been imperfect, because without actually doing the work all understanding would have been theoretical.

When the delivery team came into being – as a result of the pre-work – then the work of the pre-work team would need to be handed over. Yet pre-work handover is costly in terms of time, money and lost knowledge. The simplistic approach – passing documentation from one team to another – results in significant knowledge loss. A more sensible approach, with team members discussing the findings of the pre-work team, would be costly in terms of time and money and would still leak knowledge.

Alternatively, the pre-work team could metamorphose into the actual team. This would retain knowledge and reduce costs. Conceptually this is the MVT approach. In project model terms the project start date is backdated to the start of the pre-work, but again this is only possible with hindsight.

The Project Model

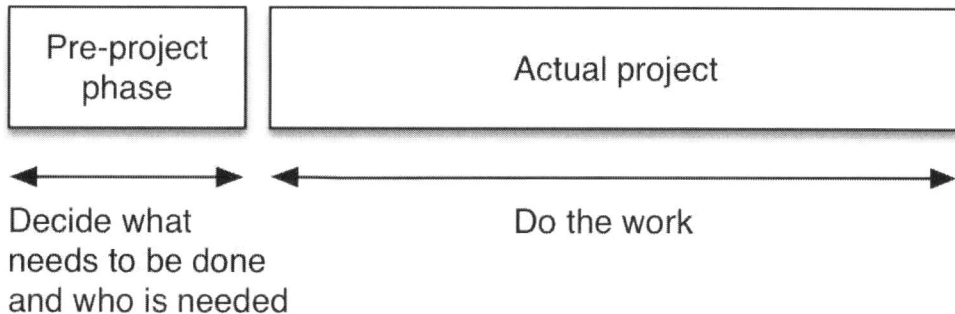

The Continuous Model

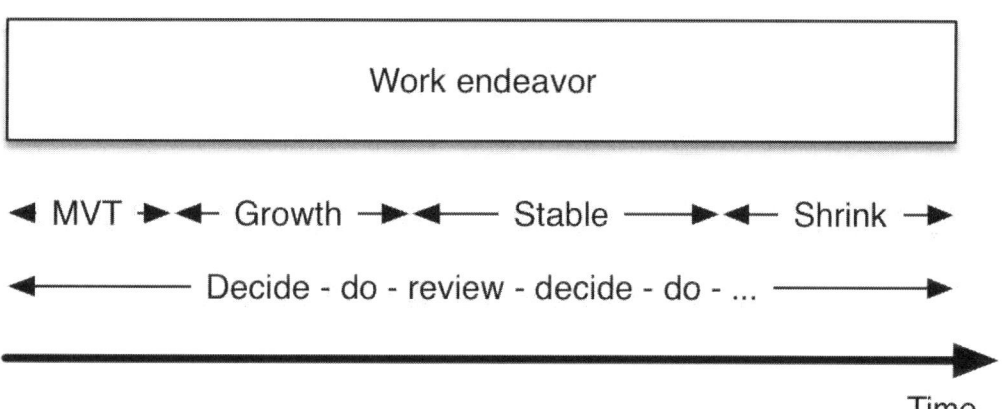

Project model requires a pre-project phase; stream model starts with an MVT and constantly reviews what else is needed

To end or not to end

Closing and therefore disassembling the team is but one possible outcome: the possibility of never-ending work is always there – an ongoing stream of work. As a result the team is able to make decisions for the long term rather than to meet some arbitrary date.

Provided that the team can continue to demonstrate ongoing value, perhaps by avoiding regulatory issues or by adding new value, it can continue indefinitely. Delivering sufficient value above and beyond costs is the key criterion for continued existence.

Finally

> *Man is not a rational animal; he is a rationalizing animal.* Robert A. Heinlein, science fiction author

I hope – I expect – that many readers will find that the team lifecycle approximately describes what they see happening in the real world. I believe this model is legitimate, acceptable and deserving of acknowledgement.

The software industry has a history of creating development process models by looking at what has happened and rationalizing from it. Such models benefit from a knowledge of hindsight. When such a model is used in a forward-looking and prescriptive fashion, however, there is no such knowledge.

A model that accurately describes the past might be inaccurate when used to describe the future, because the level of knowledge is vastly different. One can have vast knowledge about the past and everything can be rationalized: the same is not true of the future.

Parnas and Clements' classic *A Rational Design Process: How and Why to Fake It*[5] describes the same phenomenon. The same message is also found in Royce's 1970 *Managing the Development of Large Software Systems* – often called 'the waterfall paper[6]', and Conway's 1968 *How do Committees Invent?*[7].

This author hopes that he has himself not used the advantages of a knowledge of hindsight to make the same mistake.

---

[5] *A Rational Design Process: How and Why to Fake It*, Parnas & Clements, 1986 *IEEE Transactions on Software Engineering* (volume 12, issue 2) and 2001 *Software Fundamentals: Collected Papers of David L. Parnas*.

[6] *Managing the Development of Large Software Systems: Concepts and Techniques*, Proceedings of IEEE WESCON 26, 1970

[7] *How do Committees Invent?*, Conway, Datamation, April 1968

IV Money

By relieving the brain of all unnecessary work, a good notation sets it free to concentrate on more advanced problems, and in effect increases the mental power of the race. Alfred North Whitehead, Mathematician and philosopher

22. Real options and venture capital

If you want to have good ideas you must have many ideas. Most of them will be wrong, and what you have to learn is which ones to throw away. Linus Pauling

Hopefully much of what has been said in this book should sound familiar. Like agile software development before it, the Continuous Digital model draws on much that has gone before.

When Agile Software Development appeared in 2001, it wasn't the product of some brilliant minds coming up with a new model of software development. Rather it was the emergent wisdom of those who looked at *what actually worked* in software development teams. Consequently much of what constitutes 'agile' looks familiar to those who have experienced different software development environments prior to the formulation of agile.

Similarly, there are two established models for Continuous Digital to build on: venture capital and real options.

Venture capital funding model

Starting and governing work within the Continuous Digital framework broadly follows the model used by entrepreneurs and venture capitalists when starting and funding companies; start-ups in particular, but spin-outs and takeovers too.

In the beginning entrepreneurs have minimally viable teams because they lack the money to have anything more. Anything more than a minimal viable team represents excess, anything less results in failure, and plenty of initiatives fail simply because they lack resources. The constraints imposed by limited resources force entrepreneurs and their teams to be innovative. If the entrepreneurs' efforts are successful, then sooner or later they will start to seek external investment.

(A small number of start-ups are so innovative and good at working with constrained resources that they are able to bootstrap themselves without further financing. However most look for outside investment sooner or later.)

Venture capitalists (VCs) and angel investors – particularly in Silicon Valley – will invest small amounts of money in promising companies. Periodically the company leaders will be asked to demonstrate what they have achieved with the money and outline their future plans.

When companies are successful VCs will invest more money and will invite other VCs to invest. Adding additional investors increases the funding available but, more importantly, spreads the risk. Some companies aim to reach profitability quickly and free themselves from the need for more capital injections; others aim for growth and revisit VCs for successive rounds of funding.

VCs don't expect all their investments to pay off. Some investments will: most won't. Most will go bankrupt, possibly without ever making a sale, but those that become profitable will more than offset the losses incurred by those who do not.

Fail fast, fail cheap. Filter out the ideas that don't work. Learn and salvage what can be salvaged.

Because each company is a self-contained entity they pose little risk to one another. Indeed one VC might invest in multiple direct competitors.

VCs don't care about reuse of software or reuse of much else. When one company fails, another might be able to salvage something from the remains, for which they will pay by buying up the failed company or acquiring its assets.

Nor do VCs hand out vast sums of money easily. They have their own due diligence processes: there is no reason why a portfolio panel cannot do likewise. Even when VCs agree to invest, the money will be delivered in a series of tranches that may be conditional on performance.

For example, if Company X makes a successful pitch and VCs agree to invest $50m, the money may be delivered in five tranches of $10m each. The first $10m is paid immediately, the second is conditional on the entrepreneurs showing they have spent the first $10m wisely: good hires, enhanced business plan and so on. The third $10m may only be unlocked after the first sales start coming through.

Investing in very early stage endeavors is high-risk, but also produces the greatest rewards. Investing later, when the business plan has been written, has less risk but less reward. Waiting until an initial product is in the market and the market is proven is even less risky, but produces even lower financial returns.

Profit is the return on risk: the greater an investor's appetite for risk, the greater the returns they can expect, but also the more failures they will experience. Different investors will have different risk appetites and different expectations about return.

Although VCs might have a time horizon of four to ten years to see payback on their investment – or the company to fail – they expect the company to continue far beyond that horizon. If the company is not built with some longevity then the VC will not be able to sell the company or float it on the stock exchange.

While there has been much criticism of venture capitalists over the years, this does not mean that the entire model is rotten. While some have bemoaned the 'short-term' view of venture capital, a five-year view actually represents a long-term view compared to the common project model. One does not need to adopt every practice of a venture capital firm to utilize the model.

Real options

> **option** n. 1. the power or liberty to choose; 2. something that is or maybe chosen; 3. exclusive right, usually for a limited period... *Collins Paperback English Dictionary*

Many readers will be familiar with the idea of financial options. Many more readers will be a little intimidated by talk of financial instruments. Yet at the core, stripping away all the talk of finance, instruments, valuations and so on, *options* are just options – things that may be chosen:

- The option to have a beer tonight, probably not a big deal if you live close to a pub or bar.
- The option to buy a new car, which is only an option if you have the money to buy it.
- The option to buy $1m for £700,000 in six months' time: more complicated – you need to find someone who will want £700,000 in six months' time.

The last of these examples is a financial option, but all three are options. *Real options* is the name generically applied to non-financial options in business.

Options only exist if one has prepared for them. If you only prepare for one eventuality then there is only one option. With one option there is not really an option: there is no decision and no choice – only one path is possible.

Options also expire: they time out. Options often expire before one gets to the point of making a decision to take the option. When options expire they are not available at the decision point. Failure to invest in an option may well mean that the option ceases to be available.

For example, if I am camping in the wild and did not pack beer then there is no option to have a beer tonight. Alternatively, packing beer with the tent means I can have beer, but there is no obligation to drink beer just because I packed beer. I have the option.

However, that option only exists because I chose to spend money on buying the beer in the first place. The option also costs me, because I had to carry the beer as well as the tent. Indeed the beer may also have cost because something else – say water – was left behind to make space for the beer. All those decisions needed to be made before I left civilization. Failure to spend money and pack beer before leaving town closed the option long before I wanted to drink beer.

The Continuous Digital model creates options.

Most obviously, the Continuous Digital governance board faces options when reviewing a team: continue, expand, shrink or close. But options proliferate in the Continuous model.

Creating a minimally viable team to explore an idea creates a future option. If one does not explore an idea then there will not be an option in future. Creating a team and letting it work on the idea for three months might only produce learning without anything of immediate commercial value. At the end of the three months, however, there is an option that would never have existed had the team not been formed.

If the team had not been formed their learning would not exist, so the option to do more would not exist. In some cases the original option to create the team may still exist and the option has simply been postponed for three months, but in other cases the opportunity will have past and the option is gone.

The Continuous Digital model is full of options:

- In choosing a team goal.
- In choosing what the team will work on next.
- In choosing how long to work on something, how much of something to build and when to release it.
- In choosing to expand or shrink a team.

Each feedback loop represents a point at which an option can be exercised, the feedback evaluated and the next decision made.

Continuous Digital aims to create many options and to discard them efficiently at the right time.

Cones of uncertainty

The option-rich Continuous Digital model contrasts with the traditional project model, which attempts to close down options early and often. The project model seeks to generate value by building something that has been identified as valuable. The Continuous Digital model, in contrast, seeks to generate value both by delivering early and often and by opening up options to find and build valuable things.

A traditional project model approach assumes a *cone of uncertainty* in which the present – "What are we going to do? What problems will we encounter?" – is initially very wide. The aim of a traditional project is to close down options over time until the desired thing is produced at the end, at which point there is no uncertainty and no options.

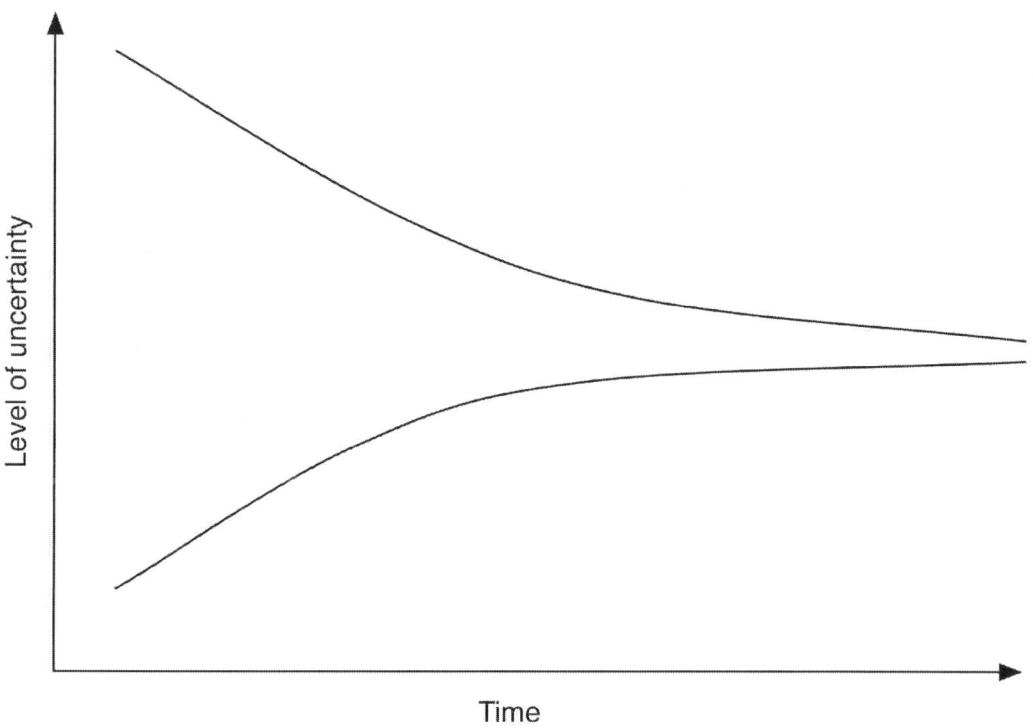

Traditional view of the code of uncertainty

The Continuous model assume the exact opposite. Today one has specific knowledge: Google is the dominant search engine, Uber is displacing local taxi companies, WPP is the world's biggest advertising agency and Donald Trump is President of the USA. But the future is very uncertain.

Therefore the Continuous model seeks to deliver value – and therefore information – in the short term, where things are reasonably certain. Simultaneously, by creating learning and knowledge, Continuous Digital opens options in an uncertain future.

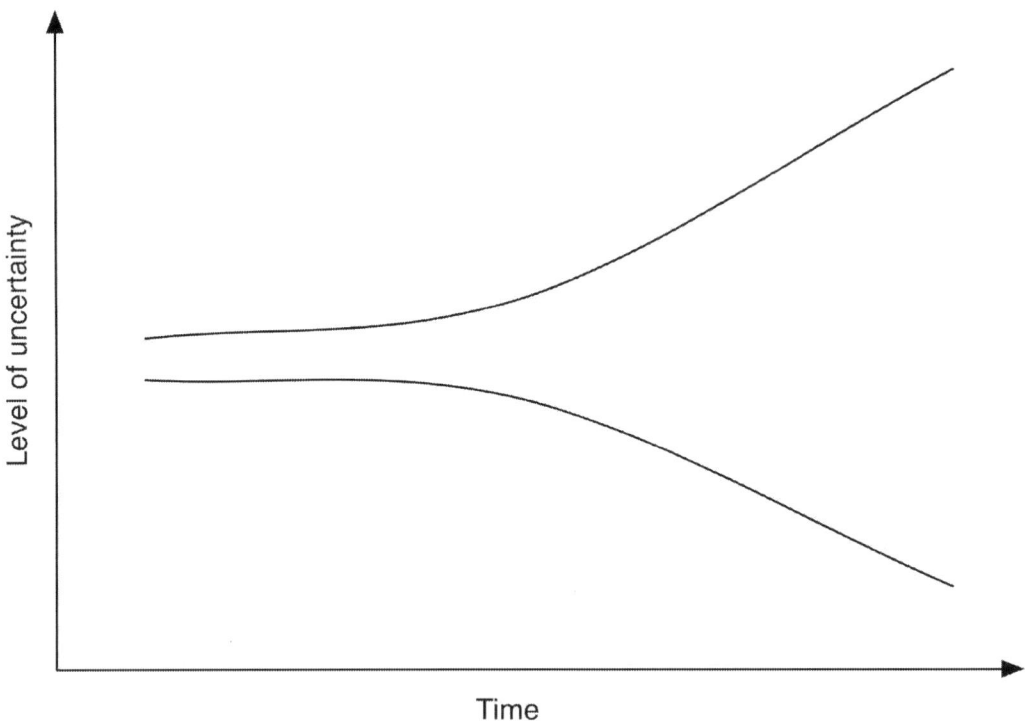

The Continuous Digital view of the code of uncertainty

Options only exist within the cone. Narrowing the cone narrows uncertainty but reduces the possible options, and since options are valuable, having fewer options reduces value.

Finally

The strategies pursued by entrepreneurs and venture capital investors create real options. Most of these options fail, but those that work create enough value to cancel out the failures: Google, Amazon, Facebook, Apple and Intel, to name a few – all are the result of venture capital investments.

The history of technology and of Silicon Valley is littered with the names of companies that venture capital helped to grow, even if some of their stars later faded. AOL, Compaq, Netscape, Sun Microsystems, Intuit and Lotus Development are some of the venture capital investments made by just one firm, Kleiner Perkins.

Investing in a company creates an option – an option to succeed – but not a guarantee. Firms only invest money that they are willing to lose.

This doesn't mean that entrepreneurs and VCs want to fail, nor does it mean that they don't work hard at making their *projects* work. Indeed, entrepreneurs and employees may work even harder simply because they can fail. Because failure is an option, they have responsibility.

By bringing the VC funding model inside the corporation, the Continuous Digital model aims to enhance innovation and value. This doesn't mean however that one should expect employees working in an MVT to start behaving as if they have joined a start-up. They might, but since most employees have opted to join a company that is not a start-up they are, presumably, not seeking 80-hour working weeks and insecure employment.

23. Continuous governance

All organizations need a discipline that makes them face up to reality. They need to recognize that the probability that any activity or program will fail is always greater than the probability that it will turn out successful, let alone that it will accomplish what it was designed to do. Peter Drucker, *Age of Discontinuity*, 1968

Even in a Continuous environment there is sometimes a need to stop. The higher authority offered by governance has a vital role to play, and the governance model needs to match the way the organization works. Applying an inappropriate governance model is itself a failure of governance.

In a Continuous environment stopping is perhaps more difficult, but is simultaneously more important. One plans for success and continuation, but failure is often ambiguous: only by taking a step back can failures be recognized and resources redeployed. Sometimes changes need to be made even to successful endeavors; sometimes external events prompt the need for change.

In order to compare different teams, governance needs to apply a common structure for comparison and a common reporting framework for all teams. While teams are free to organize themselves as they wish, are free to decide their own processes and standards, and even to define value themselves, all teams need to report in a similar fashion. Common reporting is necessary if those who read the reports aren't to face a multitude of different reports and reporting standards. Common reporting allows the wider organization to compare teams and understand what is happening in total.

When a team is created it is licensed to work. The governance process exists to revalidate this license and allow work to continue. Sometimes however the license needs to be revoked.

What is governance?

In a commercial setting ultimate governance is provided by the market, by the customers. If they buy the product then things are good; if they don't then something is wrong. However, history is littered with corporations that managed to sell products and make money while doing bad things. So it is wise, especially in larger organizations, to add additional checks.

Traditionally the governance of information technology has been separated from more general corporate governance: the discipline of ensuring that the management, processes and actions of the organization are effective, efficient, legal and so on. Obviously as digital businesses dissolve the division between business and technology, so the division between corporate and IT-specific governance is also going to dissolve.

In either case teams need to explain themselves. Are they delivering value? Are they improving? Are teams working well together? Are they within the law? Just being asked to answer such questions benefits the teams by triggering reflection and providing opportunities for improvement.

Why do governance?

If a team is truly self-organizing, then surely there should be no higher authority? After all, surely any higher authority exercising power or control over the team reduces the element of self-organization?

In a small company in which team members are only a few steps removed from customers, governance is probably not going to be a major issue. There will still be some governance, perhaps by way of the board, which represents the investors' interests, but the combination of self-organization and the market should be the primary drivers.

Of course many digital endeavors take place in a non-commercial setting: the public sector, third sector or deep inside a corporation. Without the ultimate sanction of the market, governance becomes more important.

There are several reasons why even a self-organizing team can expect to be held to account under a governance system:

- Not all teams are close to the customers. A team may well be buried several layers away from real external customers.
- Larger organizations will have overarching goals and strategies and will want to ensure that teams are progressing in a coherent direction.
- Organizations will want to ensure that capital allocations, investments and the use of resources are wise, effective and build towards those overarching goals and strategies.
- Companies will want to balance risks, between some high-risk/high-reward initiatives and some low-risk/low-reward ones.
- Larger organizations will want to ensure that disparate teams are not working against each other: while some internal competition is healthy, too much is unhealthy.

- New opportunities and new initiatives need to be balanced against ongoing work; periodically resources and priorities need to be rebalanced.
- Governance can provide an additional feedback loop, perhaps even a faster one.

Despite some inevitable loss of self-organization, teams too will benefit from being properly governed. The governance process will help to ensure that teams are honestly delivering value and are not deluding themselves.

Pragmatically there is another reason why the Continuous model needs to include a governance component: organizations expect there to be governance. If governance is not included in the Continuous model, the model will lack credibility with larger organizations. Those organization that do adopt a Continuous model will retrofit a governance model of some description, most probably one similar to the project-based governance model found in most organizations.

Flip control

Some elements of Continuous Digital fit poorly into a traditional governance framework. For example, the team-centric pursuit of value with experiments would not fit well in a framework that requires a team to state unambiguously what it is going to do at the start of a governance period.

Similarly, devolving authority to the team and front-line engineers would not fit well in a traditional governance model. At best, traditionalists would see such devolved authority as a loss of control: at worst it could be seen as a recipe for chaos.

Modifying the governance model for Continuous requires three changes:

- *Authorizing the team* to do what is right in the team's judgement, rather than authorizing the team to do a thing that is judged to be right by others.
- *An acceptance that learning and innovation require some 'failures'*: if a team is not failing, it is not pushing forward or taking risks.
- *Resequencing the traditional governance model*: a greater emphasis on what has been achieved rather than what is promised.

These changes follow the same logic found in the *Beyond Budgeting* movement. Rather than measure progress against a plan or budget, employees are trusted to do the right thing and know they will be judged by the result, not by some proxy yardstick.

For a working software team the *primary measure of progress should be working software and the resulting business benefit.* Better still, teams should be able to identify business benefits delivered by their working software. For non-software teams the primary measure should be advances in the product or service offering.

Governance and portfolio management processes need to trail the work and operate retrospectively. Rather than looking forward to what is predicted to happen (which has a poor track record), governance looks at what *did* happen, and specifically at how much value was actually delivered.

This may sound counterintuitive, and so it is when work packages are large, but when work is small then how much damage can be done? Wasting two weeks might not be good, but how much time is lost waiting for decisions? Evaluating proposals? Gaining work authorizations? How much money is lost by late delivery?

When development work was slow (think Cobol) and expensive (think mainframes) then it made sense to ensure that nothing wrong was done. But in a world in which development is fast (think Ruby) and cheap (think cloud) the cost of doing analysis and the time lost in governance and hence delay is far greater.

In such a world it is preferable to spend a little bit of money and later discover that the money was wasted, rather than spending more money and time to ensure that no money at all is spent on activities that might turn out to be wasteful. The cost of determining what expenditure is waste and what is beneficial can itself be greater than the potential waste.

Project management tools of analysis and authorization take time. Today's technology allows solutions to be built and tried out in less time than it takes to agree formal sign-off for work. It takes too long and is too costly to set up temporary teams and then tear them down. That's all before even considering the value of what might be learned as a by-product of doing something wasteful!

What governance is not

Governance should not be management by the back door. Governance should not be a mechanism to manage the team by another name. Hence governance should not be concerned with details or minor decisions.

Governance should not be a box-ticking exercise, or a standard report that is filed each month that air-brushes the failings of the team.

In a commercial setting governance should not be a substitute for the market and customers. Governors may have a view, informed or uninformed, of what customers and the market as a whole wants, but governance should not attempt to second-guess the market or the team. Governors may assist, but it is the team's job to understand the market.

In a non-commercial setting the governance model needs to be particularly clear about the objectives of governance and how these relate to team goals. There is a vast range of non-commercial organizations – Governments, charities, social enterprises – and the aims of these organizations differ massively. Since the aims of such organizations are so different, the governors must be clear on expectations. Given this range, further discussion is beyond the scope of this book.

Project-centric governance

In many organizations the governance model is inherently tied to the project model. Governance processes expect to measure teams against some predetermined plan and deliverables. Even in organizations that have embraced digital, agile and continuous delivery, governance systems are often still tied to the project model.

This creates tension, as the higher operating functions of the company are expecting project-style working, while the day-to-day operations have moved beyond the project model. Governance processes become burdensome and, more importantly, using a governance model that does not reflect the way the company actually operates is itself a failure of governance.

Consider a team that is delivering daily, listening to customer needs and providing technical solutions. A team that is, consequently, delivering real value to the company, but in project terms is 'making it up as they go along'. If such a team is asked to show progress against plan, or to demonstrate efficient working, it will probably come up with a way of meeting those requests too. But in so doing it is telling the governors what they want to hear: governance is not working.

Framework

The Continuous Governance framework set out here draws on established agile approaches and on the thinking of Chris Matts. His blog posts[1] discuss many of the issues raised here. The key elements are:

---

[1]https://theitriskmanager.wordpress.com/

- Regular (iterative) governance reviews based on the *portfolio management* model. Continuous governance is a lot like portfolio management.
- Balance scorecard-style reporting[2]: no one measure is enough; even the focus on benefit delivery that runs though the Continuous model is not enough. Quality, risk, ongoing improvement and higher purpose also need to be considered.
- Interactive face-to-face governance: a faceless board reviewing a silent report will not provide the rich feedback that Continuous teams require. Individuals from the team should proactively present the team's reports and discuss them with governors face-to-face.

Fixed governance iterations

Governance needs to operate in the same iterative way in which agile teams work. The length of governance iterations is likely to be longer – perhaps monthly or quarterly. Importantly, they occur on fixed dates, with a regular rhythm.

Work streams are not allowed to postpone a governance event because they are 'not ready' or 'now is not the right time'. Such excuses allow teams to prevaricate and avoid real governance. If a team is not ready on the date of a governance review, then a) it should explain why not, and b) team members should ask themselves why they allowed themselves to get into that position.

Repeated calls to delay governance reviews and stage-gates because a team is 'not ready' are themselves a sign of problems.

Fixed-length governance iterations mean that each team knows far in advance that it needs to explain itself and when it will be expected to demonstrate effective working. Every team should have something to show at any point in time; to have nothing to show is clearly a problem that needs to be highlighted to higher authority.

Such reviews probably occur quarterly; sometimes shorter periods may be appropriate and sometimes longer. Indeed, there is no reason why different teams can't be reviewed on different schedules. Mature teams in stable business lines might be reviewed annually, while an MVT in a high-risk area might be reviewed monthly.

---

[2] *The Balanced Scorecard: Translating Strategy into Action*, Kaplan and Norton, 1996

Portfolio

The governance process operates much like the portfolio management model – indeed in some organizations these are already the same activity, while in others they are separate. At each review the governance board has four basic options:

- *Continue* as is: renew the license to work without change. The team can continue to work as it is, with the same resources and aims.
- *Increase*: renew and expand the license. The team is granted extra resources, perhaps extra funding and extra staffing or another resource. This may well mean that another team has to surrender resources.
- *Reduce*: renew license with constraints. A team might have resourcing reduced, meaning that staff need to be let go or transferred to another team. Resources might be reduced because the team is not performing as well as expected, or because the value delivered (or expected to be delivered) from the team is less than expected.
- *Closure*: revoke the license. From time to time teams may be repurposed or wound up entirely. This might be because the team is not delivering on expectations, because the business the team supports is not delivering as expected or for many other reasons.

It is also possible that a team might be reduced or even closed not because of any failure on the part of the team, but because the organization has decided to deploy resources elsewhere. This might be a strategic decision to exit a business line, or simply a shifting of resources to streams that deliver higher returns.

None of these reasons contradict the concept of a stable team. From time to time teams may well be disbanded, and organizations may choose to put more resources into one area and thus less into another. As I have said before, stable teams are not necessarily static: they will change occasionally, but stable teams are not in a constant flux.

Similarly, forced closure should not be seen to detract from self-organization. Sometime even the best of us needs an outsider to intervene and point out what we don't or perhaps cannot see. Left to their own devices individuals and teams may well find justifications for recurring failures to deliver expected value month after month. One should not expect a team to voluntarily offer to disband – it goes against human nature. But from time to time teams do need to disband, and sometimes an outsider needs to step in and point out the unpleasant truth.

Scorecard

The Continuous approach puts great emphasis on the delivery of business benefit, specifically value and money. While this may be the primary means of measuring progress and success, it cannot be the only one.

Chris Matts[3] has suggested a scorecard for agile teams that uses four criteria:

- *Value delivered*: is the team delivering business value?
- *Sustainable quality*: can the team demonstrate sustainable quality?
- *Risk management*: is the team managing risk?
- *Lead time*: how long does it take a team to move a piece of work from idea to delivery?

Matts argues that these four criteria are necessary because they act to balance one another and prevent teams from gaming the system, or pursuing one criteria to the detriment of others.

- *Example 1.* A team might be able to deliver a valuable piece of work very quickly by disregarding quality, working large amounts of overtime and consequently incurring very high risks.
- *Example 2.* A methodical team might take its time planning, assessing risk and building in quality without any overtime. Such an approach would have a long lead time, a slow payback (hence lower value) and incur the risk of a late delivery that was too late to unlock potential value.

Matts' scorecard should be the starting point for any team. In the Continuous model it would be appropriate to add progress towards a team's higher purpose, and possibly progress towards the organization's higher purpose. However, the more criteria are added to a scorecard, the less efficacious the scorecard tends to be. Having too many criteria has downsides too.

Measuring the scorecard

Having identified a few elements a scorecard might contain, it is logical to look to quantify these measures. For some of the criteria measurement is relatively easy:

---

[3] *Agile Risk Management Framework* blog entry https://theitriskmanager.wordpress.com/2016/05/30/an-agile-risk-management-framework/

- Value can be measured in revenue, some proxy 'business points' currency or some other measure that the company values.
- Lead time can be measured in days, or perhaps hours.

Sustainable quality and risk management present greater challenges. Measuring quality requires one to take a view of what constitutes quality. Several proxy metrics are available, such as automated test coverage, cyclomatic complexity or defect counts, but all tend to present problems.

Risk management is perhaps the most difficult to measure, although in this case it may be more important to see evidence that active risk management is being practiced rather than measuring it quantitatively. Because people can be very inventive in gaming a quantitive measurement, it may be desirable to retain some qualitative element in the scorecard.

The fact that measurement presents problems is not a reason to reject it: difficulty in measuring something can indicate that the measurements are themselves valuable. Tom Gilb's work presents something of a tour de force in measuring aspects of software[4].

Change over target

> *When a measure becomes a target, it ceases to be a good measure.* Goodhart's Law

Rather than set targets for any of the measurements in Matts' scorecard, a better approach is to observe the direction of travel. Is lead time reducing? Is value increasing?

Observing the direction of change indicates whether a team is improving and getting closer to its goals. Measuring them against a target not only invites game-play, but robs the measurements of information content.

Measurements can also be used for benchmarking. Benchmarking a team against its own past performance can be useful, if only as a source of enquiry. It may also be useful to benchmark against other teams in the same organization. However, care needs to be taken here: while some competition between teams can be healthy, too much competition can be counterproductive and fail to appreciate differences in team environments.

Teams need to see peer teams as a resource for learning. While teams in one organization can be in friendly competition, they should also be sharing their learning and their experiments.

---

[4]*Competitive Engineering*, Tom Gilb, 2005

Face to face

Our job is to make project status reports look good. Anonymous PMO Manager at FTSE100 company

When a team or individual writes a report there is a tendency to try to show that things are good. Sometimes project reports take on an excessively positive tone. Even when reports contain bad news, the executives reading the report may not assimilate the news, or may not want to in take the news. (Keil et al describes a number of problems with project status reporting[5].)

Part of this is because when a report is written it loses its voice. One cannot ask a question of a piece of paper or PDF document, and a written report cannot contain every piece of information the reader may want to know. If it does then it becomes too long to read.

Therefore the most important part of Continuous Governance is face-to-face reporting. One or more team members need to deliver the team report physically to the review panel or board that is carrying out governance. No longer should governance be a paper-based administrative exercise. Paper documents might supplement a verbal report, but should not replace face-to-face reporting.

In my mind I see a jury of governors (such as senior stakeholders, resource controllers, representatives from other teams) forming a panel on one side of the table, while on the other side several team members state their case verbally. The courtroom model may be adversarial and maybe not to everyone's taste, but within every team there should be someone who can fill the role. Ensuring that the portfolio review is an active trial aims to move away from whitewashed reports that use euphemism and metaphor to disguise problems.

Printed reports, PowerPoint presentations or other supporting artifacts are not prohibited, but they should be confined to a supporting role. The team should be able to justify its work, demonstrate business benefit and – importantly – answer questions about its delivered and planned work.

The aim is to let each team operate as an independent business unit. Thus the portfolio process needs to identify failure quickly and cheaply, so that it can be corrected within the team or outside it.

There may be times when teams appear before the panel with no actual deliverables to show and no business benefit realized. There are times when teams are working on long-term

---

[5] *The Pitfalls of Project Status Reporting*, Keil, Smith, Iacovou and Thompson, MIT Sloan Management Review Spring 2014

initiatives that will not show benefit for a while. Each time a team appears before a panel with nothing to show for its work one can expect the questioning to get harder and the squirming greater. Teams should feel bad when they have nothing to show for weeks of work, and panels should close down work that goes on too long with no tangible results.

As with traditional portfolio review processes, the panel may consider evidence outside of that given by one team. In a large organization teams will be competing for resources; giving one team more resources can mean reducing the allocation to a second team even if that team is performing well.

Portfolio panels may also be privy to company information not known to teams, such as takeovers and mergers, changes in strategy, financial constraints and so on. Of course it would be good for the team to know about all these things, but sometimes they cannot.

The future

Much of this discussion has centered on looking at how a team has been working and what benefits it has delivered. While measures such as lead time, risk management, sustainable quality and higher purpose look to the future, these too are seen in a historical context – that is, how has the team performed to date.

Governance needs to go further and ensure that teams have a view of the future that will continue to deliver benefit. In addition to showing what has been achieved recently, teams should be able to outline what they see coming up in the next review period. For this they may use plans, backlogs, roadmaps or other artifacts that help explain their thinking.

Teams are not expected to show a detailed plan, although some teams might be able to give more detail than others. Teams are trusted to deliver value, but that trust is built on past performance.

Some teams have predictable workflows while others have very unpredictable flows. The important thing is that a team can describe what it sees itself using its extended license for and how it will benefit the business. It is especially important that teams describe their future ideas when requesting an increase in resources.

Finally

Making teams answer to a higher body forces them to be honest, both with themselves and with the higher body.

Continuous governance occurs *on the metal* – actual achievements, deliveries and business benefits realized by the work streams and by the teams themselves – rather than indirectly through project management and proxy measurements such as plans, milestones or budgets.

Reviewing actual business benefit delivered combines the questions of "Are we delivering the right thing?" and "Is the team delivering it right?". Teams that are not delivering business benefit are inevitably failing on one or both of these criteria and deserve to be called to account.

Responsibility for delivering business benefit – and therefore delivering both the right thing and in the right way – is the responsibility of a team and any team leaders. The team is therefore also responsible for fixing things if it is not delivering benefit. Whether a team decides to fix its failure by changing what it is building or how it is building it is up to the team itself.

24. Budgeting

A target is what we want to happen. A forecast is what we think will happen. Never combine the two in one number, like a budget does. Bjarte Bogsnes[1]

Cost budgets tend to be spent, even when the initial budget assumptions change (which they almost always do). Managers do not behave like this to cheat; they do it because the system encourages them to do so. Managers see budgets as entitlements, as bags of money handed out at the beginning of the year. Nobody gets fired for spending their budget. Spending too much is, of course, bad, but spending too little is not good either. Bjarte Bogsnes[2]

I often get asked, "*How do you budget without a project?*"

The answer is actually very simple: just look at what a team costs and project that forwards. If your team costs £100,000 per month and you want to know how much money you need for the next year, £100,000 x 12 = £1.2million. This is what venture capitalists and entrepreneurs call *burn rate*. It measures what it costs to retain the capability.

Of course it helps to have an existing team, and a stable team best of all. But there are ways around that, such as looking at other existing teams or sketching an MVT.

Since any team will be governed on the basis of value delivered, the quid pro quo is a promise to deliver more than £1.2million in return for that funding. If part way through the year it becomes apparent that the team cannot deliver such value, then it makes sense to reduce the size of the team and reduce the costs.

Similarly, if the team sees greater opportunities and can justify an increase in spending to the review board so that it can deliver more value, then the team should expand. This can happen at budget time or at any other time if need be.

In a Beyond Budgeting environment such decisions would be revisited on a regular basis, perhaps quarterly. In a more traditional budget environment funding the annual review may be more significant, but that is by choice.

---

[1] Bjarte Bogsnes, on Twitter@bbogsnes, Feb 2013
[2] *Implementing Beyond Budgeting*, Bjarte Bogsnes, 2009

Of course, while one can tell accurately how much the team will cost for the coming year, it is impossible to promise what they will deliver. The team may have some ideas, but in an uncertain world making promises would be rash, keeping promises potentially value-destroying. Instead of arguing over what might be, one should look at the team's delivery record: if a team has a history of delivering more value than cost it should be funded. If it doesn't, then it probably shouldn't be.

Unlike financial investments, past performance is a pretty good indicator of future performance, even if there is no guarantee.

Budgeting for a 'project'

Teams exist and continue to exist. They undertake work in a particular area – an application, a business unit, a service or whatever. By demonstrating that the value it delivers exceeds its costs a team justifies its continued existence.

So what happens when a 'project' comes along?

Or, to refine the question, *what happens when a large chunk of work comes along?* A piece of work that requires a lot of changes that builds towards some objective.

At one level the question is redundant: the team identifies valuable work to do and chooses what to do. If the work items contained in the project are justified – that is, they are of a higher value then other items – then the team undertakes items from the 'project'.

Stable value-seeking teams already have ideas of what to work on, often referred to as a *backlog*. When a project arrives that contains some additional ideas for work, there is simply more work to do.

Whether from a project or elsewhere, it is all *work to do*. Work items contained in the project are not special: they are evaluated in the same way as any other work item. If the value is not justified, then the work is not undertaken.

When capability is constrained (that is, the team size and therefore its capacity is constant), taking on new work forces displacement. If work items suggested by a project offer greater value than other work, then the project items displace other work. If the project work items do not demonstrate sufficient value, then they are not done.

A project should not be seen as a single indivisible entity. A project should be seen as an objective, and possibly as a collection of work items. The teams have authority to decide how to pursue their objectives (and thereby define their own work items) and to accept or not accept any suggested work items.

Alternatively a team might increase capacity specifically to take on extra work. When a team is presented with opportunities to deliver more value, perhaps packaged as a project, then there is an opportunity to increase capacity. This might happen because, at a portfolio level, it was clear that Team A was not doing items that would be done were they undertaken by Team B.

Two teams, two backlogs

Consider the two backlogs shown in this diagram. Team A is undertaking items in the $80,000 to $120,000 value range, while Team B is working on items typically half that value. In such a scenario it might make sense to shift people from Team B to Team A. Alternatively it might make sense for Team A to expand while Team B remains unchanged. Again, the team needs to justify its expansion in terms of value against cost.

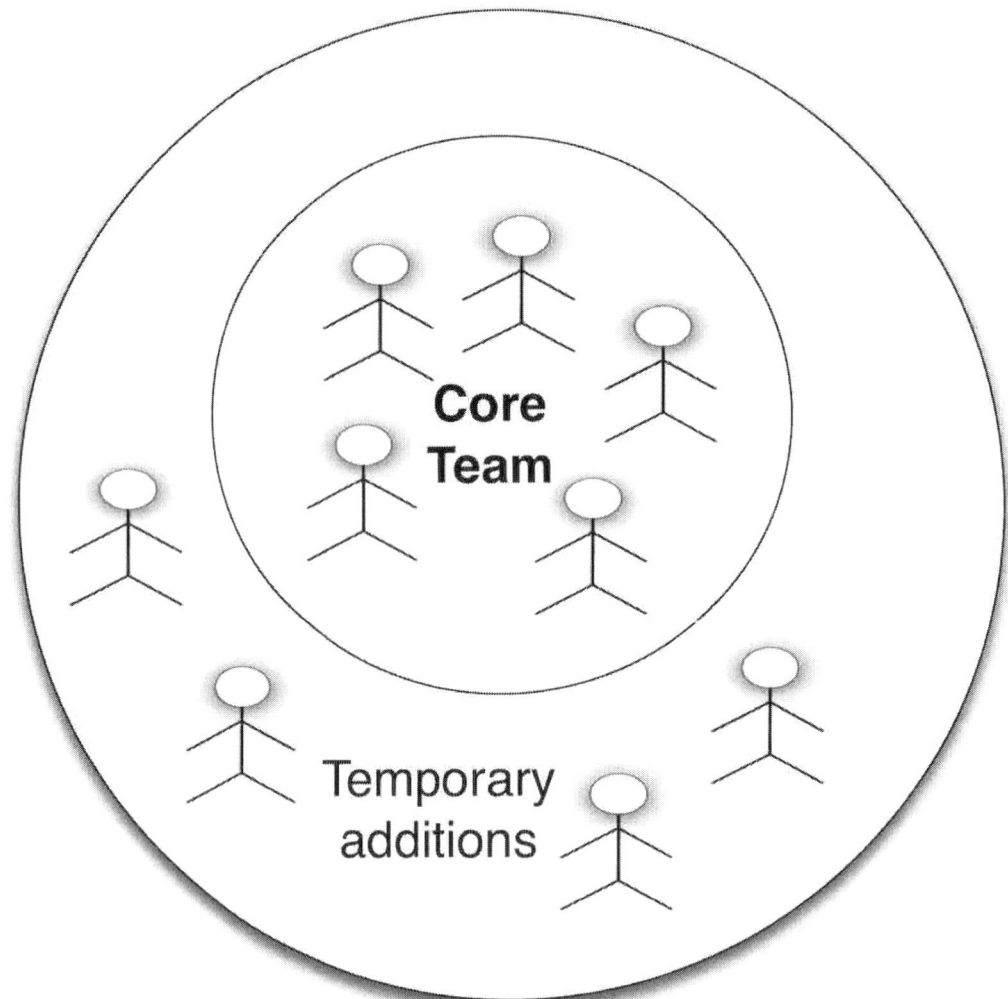

The core team may be supplemented during a surge

Quite possibly in this scenario Team A has been passed a chunk of high-value 'project' work. Hence it might make sense for Team A to expand – *surge* – by means of temporary secondments and contract staff to deal with the peak, then later contract.

The existing Team A may well form the core of a temporarily enlarged Team A. Since the core team has historic performance data, the team may engage in some modeling to calculate how big it should grow and how long the surge will last. When the extra people arrive, the core team will be able to share knowledge and working practices with the temporary staff.

Others have likened a project to a wave passing through an existing product team. The team exists and does broadly the same work on the same product again and again. Periodically a project wave increases the work to be done and maybe the team size increases. As the work is completed the wave passes and the team returns to normal, at least until the next wave.

If a project is seen as a collection of work items then conflicts can arise when, as the project proceeds, the team finds the value of work items from the project is less than other opportunities. A value-maximizing team would leave the project items undone, but if the team is expected to deliver a defined project to satisfy project success criteria (on budget, on schedule, on features), then there is a conflict.

Alternatively, if a project is defined as an objective – and the team is able to define the work – then it has more flexibility in what it does. This might not eliminate all conflict, and the team may still question the objective, but it is able to find constrained mechanisms for reaching the objective.

Budgeting for something new

Another scenario in which budgets are commonly expected concerns new endeavors. If an organization wishes to embark on a new initiative, perhaps to meet some goal, then it might want to set a budget for the initiative. A new MVT might also be required for an initiative, or an existing team might need additional funding. Either way the same principles apply.

In this scenario the organization has little idea of the total size and complexity of the endeavor. While it could initiate a pre-project investigation, such an investigation would itself cost time and money. Further, unless the pre-project team was allowed to start doing the work, the understanding gained would be less than it could be.

Using an MVT allows the work to be 'understood by doing'. Traditional paper-based analysis makes sense when attempting the actual work is expensive, as it was in the 1970s. Today, with powerful tools and seemingly limitless cheap processor cycles, learning by doing is a more effective and cheaper analysis technique.

The organization therefore needs to launch an initiative to start investigating the 'new thing'. The organization can think of this as taking an option on this goal – or to put it more crudely, make a bet.

The organization should devote enough money to the initiative – and perhaps a new MVT – but should not devote so much money that the initiative cannot be allowed to fail. In betting terms, the organization should only allocate money it can afford to lose. After all, it may turn out that the suggested work is more complex than initially envisaged, or represent less value.

When money is spent without any apparent benefit and failure is not allowed, then organizations are locked into past decisions. The need to not fail leads organizations to spend more money in an effort to justify the money already spent. The more money that is spent, the harder it is to recognize failure and move on. This is known as the *sunk cost fallacy*. The first rule of investment is to ignore past costs: the money has gone, and future investments need to be judged against future expenditures and potential benefits.

When failure is acceptable a small amount of seed money can be spent on an initiative, to the point at which the common governance-portfolio mechanism can take over. After the initial period the initiative should be able to demonstrate value and justify continued expenditure. In the early exploratory period *value* might not be financial revenue: it could be increased knowledge, perhaps technical research or market research.

This approach parallels the way in which venture capitalists fund start-up businesses. VCs and 'angel' investors can provide funding to a fledgling business with little more than a half-baked business plan. The more promising the idea, the less detail they may demand.

John Battelle tells how in 1998 Larry Page and Sergey Brin had no idea how to make money from search. After being rejected by the incumbent search providers, they eventually gave a demo to Andy Bechtolsheim. Immediately recognizing the potential, Bechtolsheim wrote a cheque for $100,000 and Google was born. Bechtolsheim did not ask to see a business plan, revenue forecasts or any of the other usual business artifacts, which did not exist[3].

Few entrepreneurs or business executives have ideas as overwhelming as Google, that stand on their own and do not require detailed justification. When a business idea is not as overwhelming as Google – and indeed, few *are* as overwhelming as Google – they usually have to prove their ideas with additional analysis.

Managing risk

>   *Profit is the return for risk.* Origin unknown

Venture capitalists expect that many, if not most, of their investments will fail. VCs limit their exposure to losses by forcing companies to go through a series of funding rounds, a process akin to the governance and portfolio board. Even when a funding round has been

---

[3] *The Search*, John Battelle, 2005

agreed, covenants may be required and funding only released in tranches. VCs seldom fund loss-making ventures indefinitely.

Within a company portfolio risk can be be managed. For example, a VC might invest in several start-ups in a similar arena; they expect one to succeed and the others fail. They do not know which will succeed. They do not know which start-up has the best strategy, best personnel or will execute best. By investing in several they hedge their investment. This is akin to Toyota's set-based engineering model.

The portfolio will seek to balance risk with some high-risk and some low-risk bets, some long-term options and some short-term ones. The portfolio might balance new technologies against tried and tested ones, or new markets against existing ones.

In the traditional project model risk is managed by attempting to reduce the risk that any one project will fail. In the portfolio model risk is managed by accepting that many initiatives will fail, but:

a) Risk is balanced through a portfolio approach.

b) Those that succeed will cover the losses of those that fail.

c) Failing quickly and cheaply will reduce costs overall.

Failure contains knowledge and learning. Sometimes there are artifacts that can be salvaged from failed work, but almost always knowledge is generated. Again the mantra needs to be:

Fail fast, fail cheap, salvage, learn.

Although one may talk about a particular initiative failing, each one will expand knowledge and experience. Unfortunately it is difficult to put a value on knowledge and experience, and it is hard to tell when enhanced knowledge will pay back.

Knowledge gained on a 'failed' initiative might immediately contribute to the success of another, or it might lie dormant for years before it proves useful.

Beyond budgeting

Those familiar with the Beyond Budgeting framework – and in particular the work of Bjarte Bogsnes – will see parallels with the budgeting approaches outlined here and the Beyond Budgeting framework:

- Both approaches embrace goals and objectives, but both approaches shun early commitment.
- Both approaches allow for forecasts and targets, but both approaches separate the two.

Ultimately a Continuous approach is going to work better in a Beyond Budgeting environment than in a traditional budgeting environment. This does not mean that Beyond Budgeting is a prerequisite for Continuous.

For example, while the wider organization might be budget-centric, a small enclave might be carved out for Continuous endeavors. A traditional budget could allow for a sum of money to be used to run a Continuous governance-portfolio model – a 'budget within a budget', if you like.

However, there is an inevitable tension between the traditional hard budget and a Continuous approach. The more use an organization makes of Continuous, the greater and more obvious the tensions will become. In the long term the two approaches may well be incompatible.

Indeed, traditional budget-centric organizations that have embraced agile software development already experience this tension. Continuous can be thought of as the next step up. A traditional organization that sees the tension between agile and hard budgets will find that a Continuous approach relieves many of the tensions, but the organization will shortly find that a new set of tensions have been created.

Finally

Traditional budgets and the budgeting process are a management control mechanism. If authority is to be devolved downwards then budgets – or at least some financial control – must also be devolved to teams.

Traditional budgets are often 'gamed' – knowing the expectations of the budget setters, those requesting budgets present requests they expect to be passed and build in their own safety margins. What looks like a rational process is more often than not a simple extrapolation of the past dressed up to look rational.

The Continuous model, taking after the Beyond Budgeting model, instead works on two principles:

- Build on actual data: *what does a team costs to run?*, rather than *what do we think a team would cost?* It is eminently sensible to extrapolate from the past and to be open about doing so.

- Make strategic decisions: if an organization wants to grow a business line, then invest more money in it, and if it wants to exit a line, reduce funding.

When data is lacking or strategy is unclear then be prepared to spend a little money to gather more information: gather some data and probe strategic options.

25. Assets and accounting

Do not be alarmed by simplification, complexity is often a device for claiming sophistication, or for evading simple truths. J. K. Galbraith

Software is an asset to the business that owns it but it cannot be a static asset. This book

Any mention of the term *asset* is inevitably going to trigger financial questions, so it is worth considering the way in which companies account for their software. The accountancy profession has long recognized software as an asset. Unfortunately the accountancy profession still thinks in terms of projects rather than continues working.

Capital or expense?

If a company has $1m dollars in the bank it has an asset. It will be shown on the company balance sheet and everyone will be happy.

If the company takes that million dollars and pays for a software system to be built, accountants will recognize the system as an asset. They will also reason that if it cost $1m to build it must be worth $1m – after all, if the source code was lost tomorrow and the company needed to rebuild it, it would cost $1m[1].

So the company spent $1m, but now has an asset worth $1m that it can show on its balance sheet. This is called *capitalization*: $1m has been turned into a capital asset. Everyone is happy. Spending $1m to build or buy and asset is known as *capital expenditure*, or CapEx.

This sleight of hand doesn't make the asset free. Assets are generally depreciated or amortized over a period of years. This allows the company to pay for the asset over a longer period.

If the company likes the software and spends another $100,000 to enhance it, then this too is capital expenditure and another $100,000 gets added to the balance sheet, which again gets paid for over time. But if the company spends $100,000 fixing *defects* in the software, that

---

[1] I am sure many readers will point out that having built it once a second build would be cheaper and faster. I encourage such readers to discuss this with their company accountants.

is not capital expenditure. Defect fixes won't increase the value of the asset, so this can't be capitalized and can't go on the balance sheet. The $100,000 is an *operational expense*, otherwise known as OpEx.

The 'bug versus feature' debate – sometimes philosophical, sometimes jocular – becomes serious when it has financial consequences. Unfortunately accounting rules sometimes encourage people to make bad decisions.

One day the accountancy profession might rethink its rules over expending and capitalizing expenditure, but this is going to take a long time. In the meantime the distinction can appear subjective: there are accounting rules, but even these rules are open to interpretation, as WorldCom proved.

WorldCom

The case of WorldCom demonstrates how subjective the classification of CapEx and OpEx can be, how what qualifies as one or the other can be redefined or even abused to the point of fraud.

During the turn of the millennium dot.com boom the telecoms company WorldCom was very successful. Then it went bust almost literally overnight.

When WorldCom's accounts were examined it turned out that the company had capitalized $3.9bn of 'maintenance expenditure' – fixing wear and tear – inflating the balance sheet and its net worth[a].

For example, if WorldCom spent $100m installing a new fibre-optic cable between New York and Boston it would be a clear capital expenditure: $100m would come out of the bank assets and then appear as $100m of network assets. So far, so good.

But if WorldCom then spent $10m fixing defects in the same cable, should that be an operational expense or a capital expenditure? Most accountants would call it an expense, but WorldCom booked it as a capital expenditure and added another $10million to the balance sheet. Executives could argue that without maintenance fixes the asset was worthless, so fixing wear and tear was necessary to maintain value.

The management team at WorldCom were found guilty of fraud, and CEO Bernie Ebbers was sentenced to 25 years in prison. Consequently it is natural that managers and accountants become nervous when people start questioning expenditure classification.

[a]*The Economist*, 2 August 2002, http://www.economist.com/node/1268618

CapEx, OpEx and projects

Companies tend to prefer CapEx to OpEx, because capital spending reappears on the balance sheet and shows that the company is worth more.

There are certainly occasions when companies prefer OpEx spending to CapEx – companies might want to suppress profits, or take advantage of other provisions that favor OpEx. On the whole financiers prefer CapEx, and projects are often seen as CapEx. Projects are presented as efforts to enhance existing (software) platforms, so spending on a project is typically considered CapEx.

Conversely *business as usual* (BAU) tends to be seen as patching up platforms to keep them running and is therefore OpEx. When operational expenses are incurred the money doesn't reappear anywhere. Consequently many business people dislike 'business as usual' and associated expenses.

Not all projects are seen as CapEx, however: some may be classified as OpEx, but often that is as far as the accountants go. A project may be seen as an atomic accounting unit, either entirely CapEx or entirely OpEx.

Some projects are recognized as a mix of CapEx and OpEx, but this can lead to the 'tail wagging the dog': teams may be given targets of both CapEx (new features) and OpEx (bug fixes). Meeting or missing such targets is immediately obvious within the organization, but the longer-term consequences for the product are less so.

Sometimes short-term consequences have damaging effects on products. For example, I once worked with an airline on a web project. Most of the money spent on the project was CapEx, but some was seen as OpEx. The accountants handed down the CapEx and OpEx targets and the project team was asked to make their expenditure fit.

New development work was CapEx, so that could race ahead. Fixing defects, even defects in recently completed new work, was OpEx. In effect the accountants dictated how many bugs could be fixed.

This airline might be an extreme case, and it might show the ignorance of accountants who fail to recognize that all the CapEx money in the world doesn't create a usable product. But this example does demonstrate some of the traps development managers find themselves in.

Test first is CapEx

Ironically, the CapEx/OpEx split supports a 'test first' approach. Consider this:

Scenario 1. Urgent story X is given to a programmer who rapidly codes something (CapEx), and after a quick test (CapEx) it is pushed to release.

Shortly afterwards users start raising defect reports (OpEx). Eventually a tester examines the issues (OpEx) and concludes that there is a defect. The programmer is asked to fix the defect (OpEx). In doing so he creates a test harness (OpEx) and eventually a fix, which passes retest (OpEx) and is released to users.

Scenario 2. Urgent story Y is given to a programmer, who diligently meets with the product manager and tester to determine the acceptance criteria (CapEx). She then writes some automated unit tests (CapEx) before writing the production code (CapEx). Along the way the tester and programmer work together to create an automated acceptance test (CapEx). When the code passes all the tests it can be released.

Scenario #2 does not guarantee a defect-free release (although I certainly believe it will exhibit far fewer defects), but far more of the work is CapEx and therefore contributes to the balance sheet. Writing the tests first allows the tests to be classed as capital expenditure.

It is possible that a defect can slip through scenario #2 and still require some OpEx spend, but by moving spending into development mode rather than fix mode, spending is moved from OpEx to CapEx even if the total spend is the same.

Refactoring – CapEx or OpEx?

Refactoring is a great example of investing in a software asset to offset decay and keep a product flexible. However I'm not sure whether many accountants would take that view.

For an accountant, refactoring undertaken when developing a new feature may well be considered CapEx. But refactoring undertaken for the sake of refactoring, or in pursuit of a defect, is OpEx.

Here again the rules of accounting should favor the software as an asset model, but the issue is not clear-cut.

Refactoring

'Code refactoring is the process of restructuring existing computer code – changing the factoring – without changing its external behavior. Refactoring improves nonfunctional attributes of the software. Advantages include improved code readability and reduced complexity; these can improve source-code maintainability and create a more expressive internal architecture or object model to improve extensibility.' Wikipedia[a]

[a]https://en.wikipedia.org/wiki/Code_refactoring

Defect-free

Much of the CapEx–OpEx tension should be relieved by maintaining a defect-free policy. Consider this...

> *Company A* has a large five-year-old piece of software. It has a long list of potential features for the software and an equally long list of defects to fix. Since the company mandates that 75% of spend must be CapEx and at most 25% OpEx, classifying a 'defect fix' as a valuable 'feature' instantly improves its chances of being done. As a result managers spend a lot of time arguing over issue classification.

> *Company B* also has a large five-year-old piece of software, but maintains a no-defect policy. Test-first development, pair programming, static analysis tools and code reviews help drive the number of defects far lower, and are considered CapEx. Any defect reports are acted on quickly; if the product manager considers a defect worth fixing then it is fixed immediately, to comply with the no-defect policy. 'Defects' that the product manager does not schedule for an immediate fix are considered worthless and closed immediately.

In this scenario it might be possible to persuade an accountant that the fixes are CapEx rather than OpEx, as they maintain a policy designed to maintain value. However, as long as there are few fixes to be done the net effect will be small.

As a result company B only has a list of new features, and managers will not spend so much time arguing over what is a feature request and what is a defect.

Fundamental problem

So far I have shown that considering software as an asset is completely compatible with accounting practice. I have also shown that investing in quality is also compatible with accounting practices and can help boost a company's balance sheet.

But there is still a fundamental problem.

When a company builds a software asset it creates an asset that is listed on the company balance sheet. The asset immediately starts to depreciate in two ways.

In the technical and business context software starts to decay because it is static in a changing world. Without continued spending the asset declines in return.

In the financial context accountants start to depreciate the asset year-on-year based on the assumption that the asset ages, thus allowing payments to be spread over years[2].

These two concepts parallel one another but are different. One might argue that accountants should depreciate software until it is worthless, at which point the company should embark on a rebuild programme to recreate the asset. While this has a certain appeal it cannot be the answer, if only because it ignores the risks associated with product replacement.

Many software products increase in value as more people use the software. Network effects make products like Microsoft Word more valuable over time as they become recognized standards. At some point usage may peak, then decline, but depreciating a product when it is gaining in value seems absurd.

What is needed is a systematic way of recognizing the value of apparent OpEx expenditure that helps to fight decay in the software and therefore maintains the book value of the software as an asset. Not being an expert in accountancy, the details of such a solution are beyond me. However, if accounts are to recognize investment in software assets accurately without determining which work should be done and which left undone, then a solution is needed.

Coming up with a comprehensive solution for this problem is going to require help from forward-thinking accountants, and perhaps the accountancy standards boards too.

---

[2]Of course those building the software get paid at the time they do the work, so the company has less cash that day. In company accounting things are not so tidy, however, and these payments can be spread over time.

Finally

The value of an asset on a company balance sheet, and its change in value over time – either due to depreciation or appreciation – are frequent areas of debate even at board level. From a development point of view the book value of software is less important than a basic recognition that software is an asset and requires continual funding. Companies need to ensure that software assets are funded for their lifetime in order to preserve and enhance the value of the asset.

In a world of continuous development accountants still need to categorize work as CapEx or OpEx. This is going to require a more fine-grained examination of each piece of work, say at the development story level. Each story will need to be declared CapEx or OpEx.

Deciding at the story level which is CapEx and which OpEx is entirely compatible with the small-batch diseconomies-of-scale model outlined in this book. Authority for deciding which change is CapEx and which OpEx, however, may need devolving to the team, the team leaders or a team accountant.

Nevertheless there is clearly potential for tension between what the software needs technically and any mandated targets for CapEx and OpEx. Such tension needs to be recognized and actively managed.

Software products need to be considered as company assets – that is, investments that generate a return and require ongoing investment. Taken to its logical conclusion this view has financial implications. Hopefully you and your financial team can have a good conversation about these topics.

26. Money trouble

The twin policies of managing for profit and maximizing shareholder value, at the expense of all other goals, are vestigial management traditions. They no longer reflect the imperatives of the world we live in today. They are suboptimal, even destructive – not just to the rest of society, but to the companies which adopt them.
Arie de Geus[1]

Written over 20 years ago, at the start of the dot.com boom and long before today's digital age, Arie de Geus' words have greater meaning today than in 1997. The crash of 2007–2008 demonstrated once again the naivety of chasing shareholder value.

While the stated aim of many companies might be to generate profit, the real aim of many is simply to survive. Like animals, companies exist and desire to continue existing; making profit may be part of the survival process, but it is not the whole processes.

Economists define profit as *the reward for taking risk*. But taking risks may threaten survival. If the risk is too great then it might be better to forego the risk.

Longevity in companies can be at odds with making a quick buck. If the company values longevity then there is value in delivering products, processes and services that promote that goal.

Indeed, simply chasing money in the short term is myopic. There needs to be balance. Companies need 'jam today', but they also need jam tomorrow and jam every day. Again and again companies sacrifice tomorrow's jam so that they can binge today.

As this book draws to a close I therefore return to the question – indeed the quest – for value. Defining value is hard enough, but the need to balance different factors and timescales complicates things further.

Having spent much of this book arguing that value – or business benefit, to be more correct – should guide teams, this final chapter serves as something of a warning. Naive short-term definitions of value can be as dangerous as inappropriate success criteria in guiding work.

---

[1] *The Living Company*, Arie de Geus, 1997

The trouble with profit

Profit is not a good measure of value or benefit delivered because profit is subjective. To most engineers profit seems rather simple:

$$Profit = Revenue - Costs$$

At a high level this is undoubtedly true, but companies don't recognize profit like this. In any but the simplest of companies profit is the creation of accountants, the conventions they follow and the allowances they make at any point. A company can report several different measures of profit in one year. The profit reported for tax purposes (following government-stipulated rules) might be lower than the profit highlighted in the company accounts.

Debt in particular complicates issues: is a company's profit measured before or after debt and interest payments? If profit is measured without debt payments then it is not an accurate reflection of how much spare cash (*free cash-flow*, to use the terminology) the company has available.

But since the amount of debt a company holds at any one time is at the discretion of executives, measuring profit after debt payments is not accurate either. For example, Apple incurs debt to make dividend payments that it could easily make out of cash reserves in order to reduce its tax bill.

Similarly, venture capitalists often encourage companies to take on debt as an alternative source of finance. In most countries interest payments are tax-deductible, so carrying debt can actually increase post-tax profits.

Some years ago I attended an all-hands meeting at a company with which I was consulting. The CEO was delighted to tell staff that were it not for the debt the company would now be in profit. So they must work hard to pay off the debt.

To my mind this was an almost criminal statement. The company was loaded with debt because the venture capitalists who had bought it had decided to load it with debt. The debt was probably owed to another arm of the VC firm. Were the debt to be repaid, the same investors would probably take out more loans to pay themselves dividends.

In the world of financial engineering debt is good and profit is a meaningless term.

Time lag

It takes an average five to seven years before full productivity benefits of computers are visible in the productivity of the firms making the investment.
Brynjolfsson & McAfee, 2014[2]

In agile circles, particularly lean start-up circles, fast feedback is not just an objective – it is essential to make many techniques truly effective. Unfortunately sometimes fast feedback is difficult to come by.

Without fast feedback it becomes hard to direct a value-seeking team. When feedback cycles are measured not just in weeks or months, but potentially years, then how is a team to make decisions? Probing the market and testing products Lean startup-style becomes impossible when the results won't be seen for years.

For some this is reason enough to dismiss value-seeking teams and adaptive emergent approaches to planning and return to tried and tested methods. For this author such problems are the opposite: the fact that it might take years to get feedback simply reinforces the need to get better at value delivery, measuring value and improving – that is, accelerating – the process.

Consider this: if it takes three years for a team to know if its experiments have succeeded in increasing company productivity, it also takes three years for the firm to see the benefit of any productivity improvements. Add in the time it takes a team to create and deliver those potential improvements and it might be four years from start to finish.

What if such cycles could be accelerated? What if productivity improvements could be seen in two years? Not only would the team have faster feedback, but the company could benefit that much sooner. What if the improvements could be seen in one year? Or six months? Or one month?

Researchers Brynjolfsson and McAfee are far from alone in finding that technology improvements can take years to repay their investment. However, such research works with averages, thus some companies will see payback in months while others take decades. Even if your company currently takes years to see benefits there are opportunities to see benefits sooner.

Consider too that most research will largely be using data and case studies that predate the digital age. Most of the companies in these studies will even predate agile and lean start-up approaches. Even when studies include digital, agile and lean start-up examples they will be in the minority; their statistics will be lost in the averages.

---

[2] *The Second Machine Age*, Brynjolfsson & McAfee, 2014

Perhaps high-performing companies, applying such new approaches, can accelerate benefits. If agile practitioners are correct one can expect to see changes in future research: one should pay particular attention to the outliers. Why are they outliers? Why are some teams far better than others? What is their industry sector? What is their technology base? What are their methods of working?

Tightening benefit-feedback cycles demands that the technology team is embedded as part of the business. Which brings another inconvenient truth for technologists.

It isn't just software

> *For every dollar of investment in computer hardware, companies need to invest another nine dollars in software, training, and business process redesign.* Brynjolfsson & McAfee, 2014

There is more to recognizing value from technology changes than just creating and delivering new technology. Rather than developing new features, technology teams may be able to deliver more value, and more quickly, by spending time with end users in helping them use the technology they already have.

Extracting the maximum value from technology involves more than just creating new technology. It is well known that training users can help, but so can changing the culture, pushing authority down to front-line workers, changing performance incentives and recruitment criteria. These changes can take time.

Project managers have for a long time rightly highlighted the need for 'more than just software' – the training, process changes and such that need to follow delivery. In a traditional project environment such activities are planned, usually at the beginning, on the basis of a number of assumptions, and different people are used to 'deliver' these changes.

A 'change management' team might be used to prepare end users for the technology the technical team will deliver. This creates a costly hand-off and assumes certain tradeoffs. If a technical team can create an interface for its product as intuitive as typifies Apple products, the need for training might be less, the 'change resistance' might be less and the benefit–feedback cycle faster.

Rather than 'do change' to people, a better approach is to involve people in the change, bring them along, listen to their views – they are stakeholders and stand to benefit (or suffer) from changes. Those who will be on the receiving end of technology change can and should be involved with the change and contribute to it themselves.

Strategy

Value is also related to the business model and strategy of the organization. For a business attempting to grab market share, the 'value' of more eyeballs visiting a website, or more sales to new customers, can have greater value than repeat business from existing customers. Yet for a company targeting higher profit margins the opposite may be true.

Company strategy will have a bearing on what is considered valuable and what is measured. But value measurements should also have a bearing on strategy: there is another feedback loop to consider.

When talking about 'value' it is easy to fall into the trap of thinking value is a number and that higher is better. It is easy to think that higher revenue and profit, or lower costs, represent more value, but this is not true. Strategy will influence what is considered valuable. Because strategy is intimately connected with value, companies and teams need to have a strategy. They need to give some though to what their overarching approach is.

Assuming a strategy is in place, it needs to be shared with the teams. Similarly the teams need to be able to feed back to the strategy and understand what it means to them. Organizations need to spend more time clarifying and sharing their strategy, but they also need to be more open to feedback from teams about the strategy.

The attribution problem

Consider for a moment the company that might represent the digital age more than any other: Google.

Search is core to Google. Millions of searches are conducted on Google every day. What is the value of a search?

In traditional terms each search request adds nothing to the bottom line. Even combined, all the millions of Google searches each day fail to register on the official statistics of any country because Google does not charge for search. Google gives away its core product for free.

How can one measure the value of improvements when your company offers services for free?

Consider Google: *are more searches valuable?* Probably not, as searches do ultimately cost Google something. More clicks on adverts are valuable to Google, but clicks on adwords are generated from users using search. How is the value of improved search to be measured?

Removing the divisions, making the technology team part of the business and making it the business responsibility for changing processes and exploiting technology can reduce the attribution problem. Rather than technology and the business being different and arguing over who created the benefit, they need to be the same entity[3].

Faced with these difficulties it is easy to see the attraction of the project success troika that allows problems of value to become *somebody else's problem*. The first step in considering 'what is value' is simply to start having the conversation. Ask the question in the team, ask the question of those around the team, start making suggestions and taking feedback.

Understanding value and benefit requires a feedback loop. As changes and improvements are made they need to be evaluated to see what benefit was delivered. Could more benefit be unlocked by supportive changes? How can benefits be accelerated? Should more similar work be undertaken if benefits cannot be realized?

There is more to maximizing the benefits delivered from digital than simply delivering the technology. Rather than throw the definition of benefit delivery over the wall to another group, teams need to be aware of the issues and integrate value thinking into their processes.

Value can be simple, but simplistic thinking about measuring value and benefits creates its own problems. The danger is that the pursuit of simplistic value itself displaces the real goal of creating real value.

The value of null

In the digital age sometimes doing nothing can have big value. Not only can there be value in giving something away for free, like Google, but there can be value in throwing something away, such as excess lines of source code.

The value of Google searches is zero because Google does not charge for them. They do not appear in national accounts or in Google's accounts. There are other examples of digital business where nothing has value:

- The value of not doing a doomed project.
- The value of discovering early that customers will not buy your product.
- The value of replacing 50 lines of program code with five.
- The value of not writing 50 lines of program code in the first place.
- The value of employing a tight team of seven developers over a large team of 70.

---

[3]For a longer discussion of some of these issues, see *Wired for Innovation*, Brynjolfsson & Saunders, 2010

In the digital world less really can be more!

Think of all the corporate IT projects that if cancelled early would have saved corporations millions. Or think of all the start-up companies that have failed when their product entered the market after months of development.

How does one value the features Apple did *not* put into the iPod, Mac or iPhone? By offering a reduced feature set compared with competitors, Apple made products more usable and less prone to problems.

Finally

Earlier chapters have already highlighted the fact that defining what represents value is difficult. However the same chapters suggested that *money can be a shortcut for value*, and is often the default answer to the question "How do we measure value?".

This chapter shows that money itself has a number of problems, be it how you measure profit, the time lag in recognizing benefits, how you attribute benefits or how you measure the value of not doing something.

This doesn't mean that digital teams shouldn't be value-driven; if anything it redoubles the need for teams to question what is value, to seek value and to deliver value. The value digital teams deliver can be multidimensional: revenue earned, service quality improvements, learning (by the team, by customers, by others), risk reduction and even the creation of new technology.

Still, money should never be far from our thoughts. Indeed, money has two great advantages.

Firstly, generating and delivering money finances the team and allows it to continue working. Even in the best-funded organization there is a limit to how long costs will be incurred without a return before questions are asked. In a start-up environment money is essential to continued existence.

Secondly, and perhaps more importantly, money is itself an information flow. The fact that someone will part with money in order to use or own your product is itself information. Understanding what that information is and acting on it is *learning*.

Money is valuable not just for what it is, but it is valuable as information and as a source of learning.

About the author

Allan inspires digital teams to effectively deliver better products through Agile technologies. These approaches shorten lead times, improve predictability, increase value, improve quality and reduce risk. He believes that improving development requires broad view of interconnected activities. Most of his work is with innovative teams, smaller companies - including scale-ups; he specialises in product development and engineering. He uses a mix of experiential training and ongoing consulting. When he is not with clients he writes far too much.

He is the originator of Retrospective Dialogue Sheets[4], the author of several books including: "Xanpan - team centric Agile Software Development" and "Business Patterns for Software Developers", and a regular conference speaker.

Contact: allan@allankelly.net

Twitter: @allankellynet[5]

Web: http://www.allankelly.net/[6] and http://www.allankellyassociates.co.uk/[7]

Blog: https://www.allankellyassociates.co.uk/blog/[8]

Also by Allan Kelly

Project Myopia: Why projects damage software #NoProjects

Little Book of Requirements and User Stories

Available from your local Amazon[9]

---

[4]http://www.dialoguesheets.com/
[5]https://twitter.com/allankellynet
[6]http://www.allankelly.net/
[7]http://www.allankellyassociates.co.uk/
[8]https://www.allankellyassociates.co.uk/blog/
[9]https://www.amazon.com/Little-Book-about-Requirements-Stories-ebook/dp/B06XZZ6BQD

Xanpan: Team Centric Agile Software Development

Ebook: https://leanpub.com/xanpan[10]

Print on demand: Lulu.com[11]

And your local Amazon[12]

Business Patterns for Software Developers

Published by John Wiley & Sons

Available in all good bookshops and at Amazon[13]

Changing Software Development: Learning to Be Agile

Published by John Wiley & Sons

Available in all good bookshops and at Amazon[14]

---

[10]https://leanpub.com/xanpan
[11]http://www.lulu.com/shop/allan-kelly/xanpan-team-centric-agile-software-development/paperback/product-22271338.html
[12]https://www.amazon.com/s/ref=nb_sb_noss?url=search-alias%3Daps&field-keywords=Xanpan
[13]https://www.amazon.com/Business-Patterns-Software-Developers-Allan-ebook/dp/B007U2ZT7K
[14]https://www.amazon.com/Changing-Software-Development-Learning-Become/dp/047051504X

Major influences

While I might like to claim credit for all the ideas in this book, I can't. The acknowledgements section lists some of the many people who have contributed to my thinking. Steve Smith, Joshua Arnold and Even Leybourn deserve a second mention.

There are also a number of books, all already referenced in the text, that deserve to be highlighted. Those who wish to follow my thinking would benefit from reading further.

More importantly, those who wish to critique my argument would do well to read these books and critique the arguments of their authors, all of whom are far more eminent than I am.

The work of Professor Henry Mintzberg has profoundly influenced my thinking about business, strategy and management. His classic work *The Rise and Fall of Strategic Planning* should be compulsory reading for anyone who dares utter the word 'strategy'.

Mintzberg's work on managers, *Managing*, and the abridged version *Simply Managing*, are equally thought-provoking. In all three books Mintzberg demonstrates that the commonly accepted view of business is not what actually happens. Managers don't spend their whole time doing strategy.

Arie de Geus' *The Living Company* is a fantastic complement to Mintzberg's work. Companies exist to exist, not to make profit, and planning is not about plans.

Less well-known but highly deserving of being equally so is Kazuo Inamori's *Amoeba Management*. Quite possibly Inamori has created the blueprint for the corporation of the future.

Although #NoProjects was already established and much of this text written by the time I read John Kay's *Obliquity*, I have been a long-time reader of his work and have read many of the arguments in *Obliquity* before. In a world of *goals* and *outcomes* where *KPIs* are never far away, Kay dares to say the unsayable: embrace vagueness.

Finally, I will always be a disappointment to Tom Gilb. *Competitive Engineering* and his countless talks have helped to shape my view of software engineering. While I think everyone can benefit from a greater understanding of Tom's work, I do not share his conclusions. Now that I think about it, *Obliquity* and *Competitive Engineering* make ideal counterpoints.

Readers should note that of the seven books named here, only one is about software development. The more business becomes Digital the more it has to learn from software, and the more software engineers have to learn from business.

Henry Mintzberg

The Rise and Fall of Strategic Planning, 1994

Managing, 2009

Simply Managing: What Managers Do - and Can Do Better, 2013

Arie de Geus

The Living Company: Growth, Learning and Longevity in Business, 1997

Kazuo Inamori

Amoeba Management, 1994

John Kay

Obliquity: Why Our Goals are Best Achieved Indirectly, 2011

Tom Gilb

Competitive Engineering, 2005

Acknowledgements

Continuous Digital grew from the #NoProjects hypothesis which is detailed in Project Myopia[15]. As a result the acknowledgements here parallel those in Project Myopia...

First thanks to the programme committee of the 2013 Project and Analysis 'PAM Summit' conference in Krakow, Poland, whose request for a talk to business analysts and project managers challenged me to think long and hard about project managers, and therefore projects. BCS PROMS-G (Project Management Special Interest Group) then asked me to repeat the talk speak to their members, thanks PROMS-G. It was in creating these presentations that the nucleus of #NoProjects was formed.

Many thanks to 'Agile' Steve Smith and Joshua Arnold here in London for an ongoing Twitter dialogue which became the #NoProjects hypothesis. My original thinking focused on projects as a redundant management model; Steve and Josh put more emphasis on risk management and cost of delay. The three threads fused into one and I can no longer tell which of us added which ideas, or who first used the #NoProjects hashtag.

Thanks too to Evan Leybourn, who about the same time was having the same thoughts on the other side of the planet. Evan's book "#noprojects - A Culture of Continuous Value" - with Shane Hastie - was written in parallel with Continuous Digital and we had sight of each others work.

A word of caution: #NoProjects is not #NoEstimates. There is a strong synergy between the two but they are different ideas and have different solutions. Still, thanks must go to the fathers of #NoEstimates, Duarte Vasco and Woody Zuill, who spotted the synergies and adopted #NoProjects. Special thanks to Duarte for asking me to write about #NoProjects for the #NoEstimates community; that 'short' essay eventually peaked at 25 pages and forms a good deal of the first part of this book.

(The #NoProjects name itself keeps trying to evolve too, but for better or worse the name has stuck. For a while I tried using *Beyond Projects*, and at one point this book was called *Stream-Based Development*. Joshua Arnold prefers to use #ProjectLess but none of these titles gets the same attention as #NoProjects.)

I need to thank too Gwendal Tanguy, Dmitry Ledentsov, Klaus Marquardt, Kevlin Henney and Sunish Chabba for encouragement and feedback. Special thanks to Andy Longshaw,

---

[15]https://amzn.to/2wZW9JM

John Clapham and Matthew Skelton, who shared the implementation of stream teams on an undertaking that will remain nameless.

As noted in the book my thinking on governance has been strongly influenced by Chris Matts. Through conversations and his blog posts Chris has provided many of the missing pieces, both on governance and more broadly.

As always, thanks to my family – Tasya, Grisha and Anton – for allowing Daddy to indulge himself.

Printed in Great Britain
by Amazon